Lecture Notes in Computer Science   7848

Commenced Publication in 1973
Founding and Former Series Editors:
Gerhard Goos, Juris Hartmanis, and Jan van Leeuwen

Marina L. Gavrilova   C.J. Kenneth Tan
Arjan Kuijper (Eds.)

Transactions on Computational Science XVIII

Special Issue on Cyberworlds

Springer

Editors-in-Chief

Marina L. Gavrilova
University of Calgary, Department of Computer Science
2500 University Drive N.W., Calgary, AB, T2N 1N4, Canada
E-mail: marina@ucalgary.ca

C.J. Kenneth Tan
Exascala Ltd.
Unit 9, 97 Rickman Drive, Birmingham B15 2AL, UK
E-mail: cjtan@exascala.com

Guest Editor

Arjan Kuijper
Fraunhofer Institute for Computer Graphics Research
Fraunhoferstraße 5, 64283 Darmstadt, Germany
E-mail: arjan.kuijper@igd.fraunhofer.de

ISSN 0302-9743 (LNCS)   e-ISSN 1611-3349 (LNCS)
ISSN 1866-4733 (TCOMPSCIE)   e-ISSN 1866-4741 (TCOMPSCIE)
ISBN 978-3-642-38802-6   e-ISBN 978-3-642-38803-3
DOI 10.1007/978-3-642-38803-3
Springer Heidelberg Dordrecht London New York

Library of Congress Control Number: 2013939441

CR Subject Classification (1998): H.5, I.2, K.3, H.3, H.4, I.3, I.4

Typesetting: Camera-ready by author, data conversion by Scientific Publishing Services, Chennai, India

Printed on acid-free paper

Springer is part of Springer Science+Business Media (www.springer.com)

LNCS Transactions on Computational Science

Computational science, an emerging and increasingly vital field, is now widely recognized as an integral part of scientific and technical investigations, affecting researchers and practitioners in areas ranging from aerospace and automotive research to biochemistry, electronics, geosciences, mathematics, and physics. Computer systems research and the exploitation of applied research naturally complement each other. The increased complexity of many challenges in computational science demands the use of supercomputing, parallel processing, sophisticated algorithms, and advanced system software and architecture. It is therefore invaluable to have input by systems research experts in applied computational science research.

Transactions on Computational Science focuses on original high-quality research in the realm of computational science in parallel and distributed environments, also encompassing the underlying theoretical foundations and the applications of large-scale computation. The journal offers practitioners and researchers the opportunity to share computational techniques and solutions in this area, to identify new issues, and to shape future directions for research, and it enables industrial users to apply leading-edge, large-scale, high-performance computational methods.

In addition to addressing various research and application issues, the journal aims to present material that is validated – crucial to the application and advancement of the research conducted in academic and industrial settings. In this spirit, the journal focuses on publications that present results and computational techniques that are verifiable.

Scope

The scope of the journal includes, but is not limited to, the following computational methods and applications:

- Aeronautics and Aerospace
- Astrophysics
- Bioinformatics
- Climate and Weather Modeling
- Communication and Data Networks
- Compilers and Operating Systems
- Computer Graphics
- Computational Biology
- Computational Chemistry
- Computational Finance and Econometrics
- Computational Fluid Dynamics
- Computational Geometry

- Computational Number Theory
- Computational Physics
- Data Storage
- Data Mining and Data Warehousing
- Geology and Geophysics
- Grid Computing
- Hardware/Software Co-design
- High-Energy Physics
- High-Performance Computing
- Information Retrieval
- Modeling and Simulations
- Numerical and Scientific Computing
- Parallel and Distributed Computing
- Reconfigurable Hardware
- Supercomputing
- System-on-Chip Design and Engineering
- Virtual Reality
- Visualization

Editorial

The Transactions on Computational Science journal is part of the Springer series *Lecture Notes in Computer Science*, and is devoted to the gamut of computational science issues, from theoretical aspects to application-dependent studies and the validation of emerging technologies.

The journal focuses on original high-quality research in the realm of computational science in parallel and distributed environments, encompassing the facilitating theoretical foundations and the applications of large-scale computations and massive data processing. Practitioners and researchers share computational techniques and solutions in the area, identify new issues, and shape future directions for research, as well as enable industrial users to apply the techniques presented.

The current volume is devoted to the topic of security in virtual worlds and is edited by Arjan Kuijper. It is comprised of 14 excellent papers selected from 75 submissions to The International Conference on Cyberworlds 2012, held in Darmstadt, Germany, September 25–27, 2012.

We would like to extend our sincere appreciation to the special issue guest editor Arjan Kuijper for his diligent work in preparing this special issue. We would also like to thank all of the authors for submitting their papers to the special issue, and the associate editors and referees for their valuable work. We would like to express our gratitude to the LNCS editorial staff of Springer, in particular Alfred Hofmann, Ursula Barth and Anna Kramer, who supported us at every stage of the project.

It is our hope that the fine collection of papers presented in this special issue will be a valuable resource for Transactions on Computational Science readers and will stimulate further research into the vibrant area of computer security.

March 2013

Marina L. Gavrilova
C.J. Kenneth Tan

Guest Editor's Preface
Special Issue on Cyberworlds

Created intentionally or spontaneously, cyberworlds are information spaces and communities that immensely augment the way we interact, participate in business, and receive information throughout the world. Cyberworlds seriously impact our lives and the evolution of the world economy by taking such forms as social networking services, 3D shared virtual communities, and massively multiplayer online role-playing games.

The International Conference on Cyberworlds 2012 addressed a wide range of research and development topics. Out of the 75 registered papers a final selection of 30 full, 13 invited, and 6 short papers comprised the CW 2012 program. Full papers were sent to 4 reviewers; short and invited papers were evaluated by 3 reviewers. The 14 articles appearing in this special issue are revised and extended versions of a selection of papers presented at CW 2012. The papers were selected based on reviewers' comments, on the quality of the oral presentations, and the conference delegates' feedback.

Nowadays game consoles are very powerful and specialized for interactive graphics applications; therefore they are very suitable to be applied for rendering purposes. The first paper, *"Distributed Rendering for Interactive Multiscreen Visualization Environments"* proposes a framework developed on Microsoft's XNA Game Studio. It supports interactive distributed rendering on multiple Xbox 360 and PC setups.

In *"Training Interpreters Using Virtual Worlds"*, the design and development of the IVY Virtual Environment and the asset management system is presented. In IVY, users can make a selection from over 30 interpreter training scenarios situated in the 3D virtual world. Users then interpret the oral interaction of two avatar actors.

"Mathematical Foundations for Designing a 3-Dimensional Sketch Book" helps a non-professional user draw a mountain from a rough image to an image using filtration. The interactive procedure is repeated until a satisfactory result is obtained by giving the most important points and curves at the first stage and adding less important points and curves later on.

In *"Image-Based Virtual Palpation"*, 2D images rather than 3D polygonal models are used. A number of patients of different age and gender can be generated just by replacing the images. Internal organs are represented by implicit functions, so one doesn't need to construct every model independently. Instead, different scaling parameters of the respective defining functions can be adjusted to represent various conditions, i.e., normal or inflammatory, for a particular organ.

vAcademia is a 3D virtual world designed for collaborative learning. It enables a new approach to educational activities in virtual worlds, which is based on a new vision of content and learning processes.

"*Asynchronous Immersive Classes in a 3D Virtual World: Extended Description of vAcademia*" presents the functionality, scenarios of use, and the initial evaluation results of the vAcademia virtual world.

Emotions are important in human-computer interaction. Emotions can be classified based on a 3-dimensional Valence-Arousal-Dominance model, which permits the definition of any number of emotions even without discrete emotion labels. The paper "*Real-Time Fractal-Based Valence Level Recognition from EEG*" presents a real-time fractal dimension (FD) based valence level recognition algorithm from Electroencephalographic (EEG) signals. The proposed algorithm can be implemented in different real-time applications such as emotional avatar and e-learning systems.

The continual increase in losses from natural and man-made disasters in recent decades dictates a necessity both to develop new technologies for disaster prevention and response and also to reconsider the cornerstone concepts for disaster analysis, management, and engineering. This is discussed in "*Towards Multi-hazard Resilience as a New Engineering Paradigm for Safety and Security Provision of Built Environments*".

Face recognition is not limited only to recognizing human faces but can also be applied to non-biological entities such as avatars from virtual worlds. In "*Recognizing Avatar Faces Using Wavelet-Based Adaptive Local Binary Patterns with Directional Statistical Features*" a novel face recognition technique outperforms current methods on two virtual world avatar face image datasets.

"*Real-Time Reactive Biped Characters – Staying Upright and Balanced*" presents a real-time technique for generating reactive balancing biped character motions for use in time critical systems, such as games. It demonstrates the straightforwardness and robustness of the technique by means of simulation examples.

Modern interactive environments like virtual reality simulators or augmented reality systems often require reliable information about a user's future intention in order to increase their immersion and usefulness. For many of these systems, where human locomotion is an essential way of interaction, knowing a user's future walking direction provides relevant information. "*Using Head Tracking Data for Robust Short Term Path Prediction of Human Locomotion*" explains how head tracking data can be used to retrieve a person's intended direction of walking.

"*A Computational Model of Emotional Attention for Autonomous Agents*" proposes a biologically inspired computational model of emotional attention. This model is designed to provide AAs with adequate mechanisms to attend and react to emotionally salient elements in the environment.

In "*Haptic Rendering of Volume Data with Collision Detection Guarantee Using Path Finding*" a novel haptic rendering method for exploration of volumetric data is presented. It addresses a recurring flaw in almost all related approaches, where the manipulated object, when moved too quickly, can go through or inside an obstacle.

Recent studies have shown that people with mild cognitive impairment (MCI) may convert to Alzheimer's disease (AD) over time although not all MCI cases progress to dementia. *"Towards Early Diagnosis of Dementia Using a Virtual Environment"* presents a virtual environment that can be utilized as a quick, easy, and friendly tool for early diagnosis of dementia. This tool was developed with the aim of investigating cognitive functioning in a group of healthy elderly and those with MCI. It focuses on the task of following a route, since topographical disorientation is common in AD.

When realizing gestural interaction in a typical living environment there often is an offset between user-perceived and machine-perceived direction of pointing, which can hinder reliable selection of elements in the surroundings. The last paper, *"Providing Visual Support for Selecting Reactive Elements in Intelligent Environments"*, presents a support system that provides visual feedback to a freely gesturing user, thus enabling reliable selection of and interaction with reactive elements in intelligent environments

Thanks and appreciation go to the authors, the reviewers, and the staff working on the Transactions of Computational Science.

March 2013   Arjan Kuijper

LNCS Transactions on Computational Science – Editorial Board

Table of Contents

Distributed Rendering for Interactive Multi-screen Visualization Environments Based on XNA Game Studio

Evangelos Zotos[1] and Rainer Herpers[1,2,3]

[1] Bonn-Rhine-Sieg University of Applied Sciences, Department of Computer Science,
53757 Sankt Augustin, Germany
[2] University of New Brunswick, Faculty of Computer Science, Fredericton, E3B 5A3, Canada
[3] York University, Dept. of Computer Science and Engineering, Toronto, M3J 1P3, Canada
{evangelos.zotos,rainer.herpers}@h-brs.de

Abstract. In interactive multi-screen visualization environments, every output device has to be constantly supplied with video information. Such visualization environments often use large projection screens, which require high resolution visualization data. An efficient approach to master this challenge is to distribute the workload to multiple low-cost computer systems. Nowadays' game consoles are very powerful and specialized for interactive graphics applications; therefore they are well suited to be applied for computational expensive rendering purposes in real-time applications. The proposed solution (dXNA) has been developed on Microsoft's XNA Game Studio. It supports interactive distributed rendering on multiple Xbox 360 and PC setups. Application logic synchronization and network session management are completely handled by dXNA. The interface of dXNA is similar to XNA Game Studio's interface, which allows for efficient porting of existing projects. It has been proven that dXNA is an efficient and lightweight solution for distributed rendering for interactive multi-screen visualization environments.

Keywords: virtual environments, multi-screen visualization environments, interactive distributed rendering, multiple Xbox 360, XNA Game Studio, multiple computer systems.

1   Introduction

Three-dimensional scenes in computer graphics constantly gain complexity; objects which are to be rendered consist of large amounts of polygons. The performance of CPUs and Graphics Process Units (GPUs) increases frequently, enabling computer systems to master the challenge of computing and rendering the highly complex data in real-time. When large multi-screen visualization environments are used, it is common that high resolutions are applied. Special and expensive high-end graphics computing equipment might be required to supply those constantly with visualization data. Computer graphics components in the consumer market, like graphics boards, are still expensive in the high-end segment. If a visualization environment has to supply more display devices than a board has output ports, multiple graphics boards

M.L. Gavrilova et al. (Eds.): Trans. on Comput. Sci. XVIII, LNCS 7848, pp. 1–20, 2013.

in one computer, or multiple computers, or both are needed. As a result the overall hardware costs increase.

Nowadays, game consoles are equipped with powerful graphics and general purpose hardware (GPU, CPU), also they are network-enabled. Microsoft introduced the product XNA Game Studio which allows for application development for the Xbox 360 system. Software developed in XNA Game Studio can be executed on the Xbox 360 system, PCs and Windows Phone devices. The Xbox 360 system is a comparatively low-cost, powerful, and state of the art game console which meets the requirements of modern rendering-intensive computer games. The Xbox 360 system combined with XNA Game Studio qualifies for the development of graphics intensive and other applications.

2   Distributed Rendering

Techniques like low-polygon modeling, normal mapping, and approaches to reduce the number of polygons in 3D-models in an automated way [1] are applied to decrease the rendering time while still maintaining respectable graphics output. Moreover, the applied rendering method also influences the computation time; e.g. there is a general difference between rendering a 3D scene by ray-tracing or by rasterization. However, if the complexity of a scene and/or rendering method is too high to be efficiently computed by a single computer system, one option is to distribute the workload over multiple systems. One way to distribute the rendering load within a single computer system is to install multiple graphics boards which are enabled for workload distribution technologies, such as NVIDIA SLI [2] and AMD Crossfire [3]. The amount of supported graphics boards per computer system is limited by its mainboard's graphics board slots.

Another approach of distributed rendering is to use multiple systems which render simultaneously and synchronized. This way the computation power can be increased by adding more systems/nodes to the cluster. However, the distribution of the rendering workload on individual systems involves additional overhead and requires a general organization and control of the overall rendering process and synchronization. Therefore, computer systems inside the rendering cluster need to communicate with each other to ensure that all individually rendered frames or frame parts will fit together before they are displayed.

Many companies provide commercial or non-commercial software products addressing related tasks, for example OpenSimulator which uses a distributed scene graph approach [4] [5]. V-Ray also supports distributed rendering to accelerate its rendering jobs [6]. The following subsection summarizes general concepts of distributed rendering and the importance of synchronization.

2.1   General Concepts of Interactive Distributed Rendering

There are two general concepts of interactive distributed rendering, and available products and software solutions often support both of them. Multiple processing units might be used for:

1. Rendering of one frame for the same output device [2, 3, 6].
2. Rendering of different frames for separate output devices [2, 3, 6].

The first approach is used to decrease the required rendering time of one frame. It is used when there is only one output device [7]. The second approach is more common in multi-screen setups where it is important to supply multiple output devices with synchronized video data. In this case each computer system is assigned to a particular output device, but it still needs to know which part and perspective of the scene it has to render to display the correct image for its associated screen. Since every computer system has to render its part of the scene independently of the others. Overloaded systems could be a bottleneck which slow down the overall computation because a system which is finished with rendering might wait for the others to finish so that all systems can display their frames synchronously at the same time [7]. Therefore the application developers and content creators should keep computational complexity in mind.

3   Synchronization in Interactive Distributed Rendering

Independent of the chosen approach, one important topic to take care of is synchronization of the computer systems enabling them to render and display smooth and seamless looking synchronized video data. The systems may communicate using a local network with one server system and multiple client systems. In the first approach, if some systems are faster or slower than others, then the finally merged frame will most likely be inconsistent if the frame merging process does not use synchronized frame pairs. In Fig. 1 such a scenario is depicted.

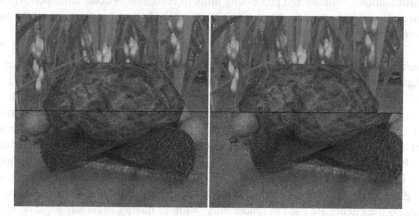

Fig. 1. Synchronized computer systems (left) vs. inappropriate temporal synchronization (right). 3D view of a rock while panning the virtual camera to the left (server frame is lower).

In the second approach an unsynchronized execution would result in inconsistent screen transitions. This means that frame parts would be rendered delayed, resulting in screen transitions which do not fit to each other [7] similar to the right part of Fig. 1.

4   Related Work

Many systems which apply the general techniques described above have been developed in the last years. There is jReality which is a Java library that uses a synchronized scene graph approach to perform synchronization of scenes in a cluster. The host machine is the one which executes the application logic and distributes changes to the clients so that they can reproduce them. In jReality clients are also called viewers [8]. The approach presented in this contribution follows a different way of synchronization. Every computer system in the cluster computes its own internal application state instead of being a passive viewer. That way it is possible to keep the network load constantly low. Synchronizing scene graphs can result in high network traffic, if every transformation/operation has to be shared over the network with all connected clients. Also, it would force the developer to use a specialized scene graph data structure.

Another approach which is also based on scene graph synchronization is described in "A Client-Server Scenegraph for the Visualization of Large and Dynamic 3D Scenes" [9]. This approach is applicable if large game worlds are to be rendered on a variety of platforms, like mobile phones or PCs. It ensures that every client will be able to render the scene by respecting its capabilities. For example, the powerful server, will stream only a small part of the game world to a handheld client, due to its limited RAM and update it when required. This approach is designed for large dynamic game worlds where multiple users (clients) can view and interact with the world while only the server holds the complete scene representation. Moreover, this approach is designed to supply content to a variety of different systems with quite different hardware configurations. The approach in this contribution involves less synchronization overhead and processing units of comparable computing performance because all systems execute the same application and must hold a representation of the whole scene.

A different approach, which is scene graph independent is presented in [10]. The product (WireGL) is implemented as a low-level OpenGL driver, which replaces the standard OpenGL driver. The WireGL driver is responsible for distributing the OpenGL rendering commands, which are performed in the main application to the clients, to which it is connected, so that they can execute the OpenGL commands remotely. There is no need to modify an existing application which is written in OpenGL. Depending on the number of renderers (clients) which are in a cluster, it might be a good choice to use a high-speed network connection because the geometry which is to be rendered gets sent over the network as well. The developers are suggesting Myrinet. In conclusion the WireGL distributes OpenGL commands to the clients, so the clients are used to render only, without having to do any logic computations. The downside of this approach is that it requires high network bandwidth because every single OpenGL command has to be shared as well as the geometry which is to be rendered, in contrast to the proposed approach in this contribution, which requires that the same application and its resources are located and installed on all rendering and processing units.

5   XNA Game Studio Fundamentals

An application developed in XNA Game Studio is a .NET Framework application. The developer has to create a class which inherits from the Game class (provided by XNA) instantiate an object of it and call its Run method to start its execution. The application logic, rendering and loading of resources has to be implemented in there. One very important part of an XNA Game Studio's application lifecycle is the update-draw cycle. In the update-draw cycle (also called game loop), XNA Game Studio invokes the Update and the Draw method of the instantiated object in an alternating fashion. Update is where all the application logic is to be computed. The Draw method is responsible for drawing the application state. It is possible to configure the way of how these two methods are invoked. There are two options:

1. Fixed time step
2. Variable time step

In the first mode XNA Game Studio tries to invoke Update a specified number of times per second. The XNA Game Studio standard value is 60 Hz, because this is the most common refresh rate for televisions and monitors [11]. It might occur that the Draw method invocation will be skipped, if the computation of Update and/or Draw take too much time. This mechanism of skipping Draw tries to ensure that Update is being invoked the preconfigured amount of times per second [12]. Fig. 2 depicts a scenario where a Draw method invocation is skipped because the previous Draw method invocation lasted too long.

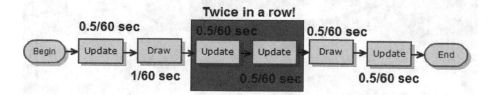

Fig. 2. Example of a Draw skipping problem

If the variable time step mode is chosen no special time treatment occurs while calling Update and Draw. The first mode is the standard mode of XNA Game Studio.

Another important aspect which is required by the approach proposed in this contribution is networking which is quite restricted on Xbox 360 when using XNA Game Studio. The NetworkSession class [13] provides methods for creating, finding and joining a network session and is the only possibility for the Xbox 360 system to connect to other devices in a network. It is intuitive and straightforward, enabling to transmit byte streams to all and to specific systems in the active session. XNA Game Studio networking has its own network layer on top of UDP. Even though UDP is not considered a reliable protocol to transmit data packets [14], XNA Game Studio provides a ReliableInOrder mode, which guarantees that the sent packets will reach their destination and in the order they were sent. Therefore the proposed approach does not solve networking problems, since the XNA Game Studio networking facilities handle that part satisfyingly.

6   Interactive Distributed Rendering Based on XNA G. Studio

This section describes the architecture, the applied synchronization technique, and further functionalities of the interactive distributed rendering approach which is realized as an extension of XNA Game Studio.

6.1   Introduction to Distributed XNA Game Studio

The proposed approach for interactive distributed rendering based on XNA Game Studio has been implemented and named distributed **XNA Game Studio** (also dXNA). dXNA is applied in multi-screen visualization environments to allow for interactive distributed rendering. Stereoscopic rendering of an application has been realized using two Xbox 360 systems and a back projection system with two projectors with polarization filters and polarized glasses. One Xbox 360 system was used to supply one projector with information for one eye. A multi-screen setup with three projection screens is depicted in Fig. 3, each projector was supplied with data by one Xbox 360 system.

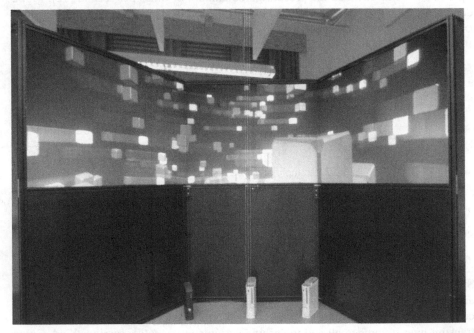

Fig. 3. The three-screen visualization environment FIVISquare [15] supplied with video data by three Xbox 360 systems executing an application developed on dXNA. While capturing the photo the virtual camera of the application panned slightly to the left.

6.2   Architecture of Distributed XNA Game Studio

A distributed application that applies the distributed rendering approach implemented in dXNA consists of two components. One is active and one is passive. The active component is responsible for establishing the network session, guaranteeing synchronization, and for executing the passive component. The active component is associated with the passive one controlling and performing its method calls. An actual application that uses dXNA is implemented as the passive component. The active component, also called launcher, is represented by the `DistributedGame-Launcher` class. The implementation of the `DistributedGameLauncher` is provided entirely by dXNA and cannot be modified by the actual distributed game. The passive component has to be implemented by the application developer. Since the implementation of the launcher cannot be changed by the application developer, it is not aware of the names and functionalities of the passive component's methods in order to allow invoking them appropriately. The concept of polymorphism is applied to solve this particular problem. dXNA provides an abstract base class called `DistributedGameBase` which the actual distributed application has to inherit from. The `DistributedGameBase` declares important virtual[1] methods of the same name as the XNA `Game` class preserving the standard XNA application architecture, which allows for efficient porting of existing XNA Game Studio projects to dXNA Game Studio. Additional methods provide common and additional functionality and to a certain degree access to the `DistributedGameLauncher` of a running application. The actual distributed application might override and/or use them to implement its own functionality. Considering the interface of `DistributedGameBase` the `DistributedGameLauncher` does not need to know more specific details about the distributed application's actual type to be launched/executed [16].

In Fig. 4 the relationships between the `Game` class provided by XNA Game Studio, the `DistributedGameLauncher`, the `DistributedGameBase`, and the `ActualDistributedGame` provided by dXNA are illustrated (simplified).

The `DistributedGameLauncher` is realized as an XNA Game Studio application as it inherits from the `Game` class. It owns a reference of the `ActualDistributedGame`'s base class represented in dXNA through the `Distributed-GameBase` class, empowering it to reference every instance of a class which inherits from that base class. The `ActualDistributedGame` represents the implementation of an actual distributed application, the name of the actual class is not important but chosen like this in this example to express the relationships. In Fig. 4 the actual distributed application overrides all five virtual methods of its base type. The `DistributedGameLauncher` can access only those methods which are defined in the actual distributed game's base class implementation defined by dXNA. In fact every defined method is designed for a special purpose and will be called by the `DistributedGameLauncher` at the appropriate time, which is in the most cases when its own method with the same name will be called by the XNA Game Studio. Other methods defined by the `ActualDistributedGame` might be invoked within the

---

[1] A virtual method of a base class may be overridden in an inheriting class to extend/replace the existing functionality [16].

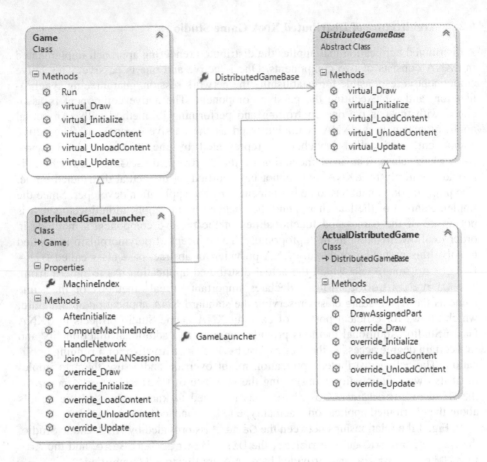

Fig. 4. The relationships between the `Game` class the `DistributedGameLauncher`, the `DistributedGameBase`, and the `ActualDistributedGame`

overridden methods; otherwise they would never be called. For example, `DoSomeUpdates` may be called within the overridden `Update` method, in order to be called on every update step, since the overridden `Update` will be called directly by the `DistributedGameLauncher`'s `Update` method. This concept is chosen to empower dXNA to control the actual application during its execution entirely. It even allows distinguishing between launcher update steps and `ActualDistibuted-Game` update steps. Every method invocation of the `ActualDistributedGame` is controlled by the `DistributedGameLauncher`. The launcher has the ability to skip update and draw steps of the actual distributed application if necessary.

In conclusion, the bidirectional association of the `DistributedGameLaunch-er` with the `ActualDistributedGame` enables the actual distributed application to access properties and methods of the launcher.

6.3   The Lifecycle of a Distributed XNA Game Studio Based Application

In all systems of the cluster the distributed application installed and running is exactly the same; every system executes the same `DistributedGameLauncher` and `ActualDistibutedGame` implementation.

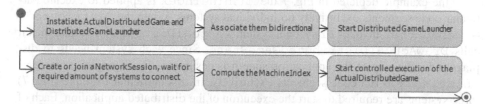

Fig. 5. Sequential workflow of the start of a sample distributed application based on dXNA

In Fig. 5 a sequential workflow is presented showing the main tasks which have to be performed before the execution of the actual distributed application can be started. To enable distinguishing the individual systems the `MachineIndex` needs to be computed by the `DistributedGameLauncher`. The result of the computation is a number which is unique on each system. However, the computation is based on the currently signed-in profiles and their associated gamertags and is deterministic. Each system will compute the same number for itself on every application startup, for the same signed-in profiles and gamertags. A gamertag is a worldwide unique Xbox Live specific account string of characters, therefore on each system a different gamertag is available.

```
static void Main(string[] args)
{
    DistributedGameLauncher.Launch<ActualDistributedGame>();
}
```

Fig. 6. The `Launch` method of the `DistributedGameLauncher` class starts a distributed application. All overhead is computed internally and hidden for distributed application.

```
public override void Draw() {
    DrawActualDistributedGameState();
}

private void DrawActualDistributedGameState() {
    switch (MachineIndex) {
        case MachineIndex.One:      RenderCenterScreen();   break;
        case MachineIndex.Two:      RenderLeftScreen();     break;
        case MachineIndex.Three:    RenderRightScreen();    break;
    }
}
```

Fig. 7. Example of an application of the `MachineIndex` to control the execution of specific code segments on individual computer systems

The code segment depicted in Fig. 6 demonstrates how a distributed application is started in dXNA. The method Launch accepts any type which inherits from DistributedGameBase. dXNA specific overhead like the instantiation of the DistributedGameLauncher and of the ActualDistributedGame, their association etc. is realized internally.

In the example depicted in Fig. 7 the MachineIndex is applied to execute particular code segments exclusively on individual systems. When the DistributedGameLauncher invokes Draw on a system's ActualDistributedGame then it calls DrawActualDistributedGameState. Since each system needs to display/render the part of the application state it is designated for, it might use its MachineIndex to run code segments exclusively. In this particular example (Fig. 7) three systems are required to start the execution of the distributed application. Each of them will only invoke one of the three methods RenderCenterScreen, RenderLeftScreen, and RenderRightScreen because the MachineIndex is computed at application startup and usually (depending in the signed-in profiles) the same unique MachineIndex is computed every time for one system. The machine with the smallest MachineIndex will be chosen as the server by the standard server determination algorithm, although the serving system can be changed to any other system during runtime.

6.4   Synchronization of the Application Logic Execution

All computer systems need to compute consistent and synchronized results, which means that the systems in the cluster are supposed to run synchronously. This is achieved binding a user input packet[2] to an update step. This guarantees that all computer systems will apply (or consume) the same user input packet for the same actual application update step. When XNA Game Studio invokes the Update method of the DistributedGameLauncher of the serving system, it requests the current GamePadState instance of the connected gamepad and distributes it over the network to all connected computer systems in the cluster and to itself. Each system performs an ActualDistributedGame update step only in combination with a received GamePadState instance. After the ActualDistributedGame's update step, the GamePadState instance is consumed and a new one is required to perform its next update step. All systems use a copy of the same GamePadState instance for an update step. As long as all application state changing calculations and initialization values of the application are the same on all machines, all will compute consistent and synchronized results. The only difference between the server and the clients is that the server serializes GamePadState instances and distributes them over the network to the clients and to itself. This way the server receives distributed user input packets over the network exactly as the clients do. Consequently, all systems receive and

---

[2] A user input packet is a packed GamePadState instance. GamePadState is a data structure that represents a state (which buttons are pressed, the direction of the analog sticks, etc.) of a gamepad which is connected to a system.

process the same data so that the implementation of an application is realized the same in all systems. The sending code is invoked in consideration of the MachineIndex of the systems, ensuring that one system only can be distributing user input packets at a time.

Furthermore, the DistributedGameLauncher manages the network, specifically it keeps the network session alive, receives[3], and processes all sent packets in every update step. It is doing this to free the incoming data queue of XNA Game Studio, which is handling the network layer. It queues the received GamePadState instances in a queue especially reserved for GamePadState instances. This prevents an overload of the incoming data queue (of XNA) and ensures that it will not reach a performance degrading size [17] by moving them in application memory preserving the incoming order.

Every calculation has to be deterministic, in order to produce the same results on every computer system. The user has to use the gamepad of the serving system to control the executed application, since only its user interaction is serialized and distributed over the network. dXNA ensures that an ActualDistributedGame's update step is always invoked with one copy of the same GamePadState instance on every system. If there is no GamePadState instance available in a DistributedGameLauncher update step, then it skips the invocation of the ActualDistributedGame's update step. Therefore every received GamePadState instance might be considered like a tick command containing information for the next tick calculation (update step). In order to trigger timed events, a tick counter/delta may be applied instead of real time intervals, e.g. representation of a second by 60 ticks when running at 60 Hz. Although this does not solve the synchronization problem completely. For instance, if the server performs update steps more frequently than a client does, then it will distribute GamePadState instances faster than the client can process them. Consequently, the queue size will grow and never shrink. The size of the queue represents the number of pending GamePadState instances to be processed, which may be considered as the distance between a client and the server measured in update steps/ticks. In order to keep the systems synchronized, the DistributedGameLauncher's Update method invokes the ActualDistributedGame's Update method as many times as GamePadState instances were received since the last invocation of its own Update method. The execution of multiple ActualDistributedGame update steps in one DistributedGameLauncher update step might impact the draw invocation frequency (section 5), depending on the applied time step mode.

If the application is designed well, so that it can always run on its specified frame rate, the described performance issue does not appear. Although because of network latency and/or packet losses it might happen that multiple packets were received at once. The application developer has to design his application considering the limitations of the applied hardware to ensure a satisfying application performance.

---

[3] The actual receiving is handled asynchronously by XNA Game Studio which stores the received data in its incoming data queue. It forwards the so far received data to the DistributedGameLauncher when it invokes ReceiveData [17].

All application logic related operations have to be performed within the `Actual-DistributedGame`'s `Update` method, for instance, artificial intelligence or user input related computations, movements, etc. Calculations which are only required to draw the application state have to be performed in its `Draw` method. This rule ensures that no skipping of logic computations occurs, and also avoids unnecessary drawing calculations in an update step, in case its following `Draw` is skipped. In the BPMN diagram in Fig. 8 the runtime workflow of the `DistributedGameLauncher`'s `Update` method on the server and on a client system is depicted.

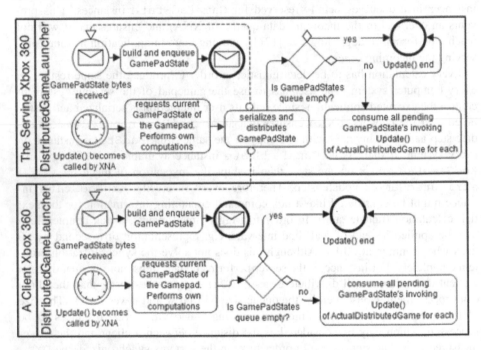

Fig. 8. The runtime workflow of the `Update` method of the `DistributedGameLauncher` on the server and on any client

The illustration in Fig. 8 shows that when XNA Game Studio calls the `Update` method of the `DistributedGameLauncher` in one system (entry point in Fig. 8), it request the current `GamePadState` instance of its connected gamepad and does any calculations necessary. That way an application can be controlled locally independent of the others to adjust parameters which are not supposed to be synchronized. Then if the system is the server it serializes the previously requested `GamepadState` instance and distributes it. After that the `GamePadState` queue is checked for pending `GamePadState` instances. If any contained, they get consumed invoking the `Update` method of the `ActualDistributedGame` for each of them sequentially. Finally the routine terminates and XNA Game Studio takes control back.

6.5   Using Xbox 360 Systems and PCs

Despite the use of gamepad states (GamePadState instances), it is possible to use any kind of input data. The system allows to configure a mixed setup of multiple Xbox 360 systems and PCs, since XNA Game Studio supports cross-platform development. If a PC is used as a server it can serialize any kind of data and distribute it to Xbox 360 systems and other PC clients. Since the Xbox 360 is based on IBM PowerPC architecture, it uses the big endian representation. PC CPUs may use little endian. Therefore a special data structure (CustomUserInput) has been developed for serializing and distributing the input data to different kind of operating computer system architectures. A user of dXNA does not need to consider the endianess of its computer systems; dXNA automatically serializes and deserializes the transmitted values considering the endianess of the underlying machine's architecture. This enables a CustomUserInput instance instantiated on a PC to replicate itself on any other system, considering the underlying architecture. It is a high level data structure which allows the application developer to combine primitive data types (such as bool, char, byte, short, ushort, int, uint, float, long, ulong and double). For instance, in a mixed setup with one PC and two Xbox 360 systems, the PC were used to access data from a Microsoft KINECT® and provided the data to the Xbox 360 systems. The Xbox 360 systems were used for rendering in a stereoscopic fashion, while the PC provided the head and hands positions based on the KINECT® data as CustomUserInput instances. This way head-tracked rendering was realized.

The use of the GamePadState or CustomUserInput is equivalent, since an instance of a GamePadState can also be integrated into a CustomUserInput instance. dXNA supports the serialization and distribution of GamePadState instances natively to allow efficient development of applications, which use the standard Xbox 360 gamepad as input device. It will be continued to mention GamePadState as the standard user input data data structure, although it is no restriction.

6.6   Support of Randomness

Applications based on distributed XNA Game Studio can use the random number generator provided by the .NET framework to generate random number sequences. It is recommended to use a time-dependent initialization value to force the random number generator to calculate different sequences every time a number generator is instantiated [18]. However, it has to be considered that clocks on individual systems may not be synchronized and that the instantiation of the random number generators are unlikely to occur at exactly the same millisecond.

To overcome this problem, the DistributedGameLauncher provides a special method that supports the instantiation and consistent initialization of the random number generators on the individual systems. The serving system chooses a value for initialization and distributes it over the network which the clients receive and use. Therefore the computed random number sequences can be ensured as the same on all systems.

7   Evaluation and Results

To evaluate dXNA, a special tool named EvaluateMe has been developed, which was simultaneously computed on three Xbox 360 systems during the evaluation. EvaluateMe is a distributed application developed with dXNA. In other words, EvaluateMe is a passive component, which can be executed by the `DistributedGameLauncher` of dXNA. It is designed to simulate an `ActualDistributedGame` analyzing the behavior of the `DistributedGameLauncher` in different situations.

The hardware used for evaluation was three Xbox 360 systems, two normal and one slim editions. The normal and slim editions are technically comparable. Other required hardware was three output devices of exactly the same make and type, to ensure that the computed frames would not differ because of the output devices. Therefore, three identical LG L1970HR-BF TFT monitors have been applied with a vertical retrace frequency of 60 Hz. The Xbox 360 systems were synchronizing their output with the vertical retrace of the monitors, so there exists the possibility that the actual values in the Xbox 360 systems are equal, but one system might be waiting for the vertical retrace of its monitor to display it. Therefore, a variation of one on the displayed value of the Counter (C) is not unlikely and might be used as tolerance threshold for setup's architecture. The variation is defined as the difference $= x - y$ of two numbers x and y, where x is the counter of the server and y is the counter of a client.

Fig. 9. EvaluateMe while running on three Xbox 360 systems simultaneously. In the upper part the Counter (C) has a variation of one on both clients, which might mean that the clients are not synchronized with the server. Although, the variation of one is within the tolerated range so that they still are considered as synchronized. In the lower part of Fig. 9 which was captured ~1.3 seconds after the upper part (compare runtime counter (RT)) all counters are the same. This shows that the systems are able to physically run synchronized, which leads to the assumption that in the upper part the Counter is the same on all systems, but not drawn by the screens.

A standard SLR camera is used to document the states on all three screens. The used camera is a Canon EOS 30D, operated with an exposure time of 1/250 seconds. The setup of the camera system was chosen in such a way that the visual field of the camera included all three monitors (Fig. 9). To ensure unblurred images, the exposure time was kept very short, since the screens update their images at 60 Hz. The slim Xbox 360 was connected to the monitor on the left.

The center machine was assigned as host. The output of the serving Xbox 360 system differs from the others through its red text color. The Xbox 360 systems were connected via a LogiLink Hub NS0001B. A router with an internet connection allowed the Xbox 360 systems to connect to Xbox Live permitting them to deploy and execute applications developed with XNA Game Studio.

7.1 EvaluateMe

The evaluation tool EvaluateMe provides a wide variety of customizable settings (see Fig. 9) to explore runtime issues and performance related specifications. In Table 1 the abbreviations used for the visualization are explained.

EvaluateMe uses these settings for update and draw logic simulation. Load mode indicates where LDX and LDM are applied, in the `Update`, `Draw` or in both methods of the `ActualDistributedGame` (which is in this case the EvaluateMe tool). LDX and LDM are measured in milliseconds. To simulate application logic and draw calculations, the method `System.Threading.Thread.Sleep` is applied. The thread that invokes this method sleeps for the specified number of milliseconds, simulating workload. XNA Game Studio waits for `Update` and `Draw` to finish and then depending on how long their computation lasted, it decides whether to invoke `Draw` or to skip following `Draw` invocations.

There is a difference between `Update` and `Draw` workload simulation. Since the purpose of EvaluateMe is to simulate distributed applications, it is most likely that the operations in `Update` will be the same on all computer systems because they have to perform the same logic operations to keep a consistent internal representation of the application state. But the operations in `Draw` can vary because the orientations or positions of the virtual cameras on the individual systems might differ so that different values of the Counter and other parameters might be visible. Therefore, it might happen that `Draw` on one system has to do more than `Draw` on another. Respecting this phenomenon two different workload implementations were applied. Two random number generators are used, one synchronized and a normal one. The synchronized random number generator is realized as described in subsection 6.6 and is used to calculate the sleep intervals for `Update` to ensure that an update step will take the same time on all systems. For `Draw`, an unsynchronized random number generator is applied to ensure that drawing a frame might take more time for one system and less for another but they still work within the same workload ranges. The initialization value of a normal random number generator is the timestamp when it is being instantiated, that way all normal random generators will compute different number sequences. The synchronized ones use the timestamp of the server as initialization value, that way they all compute the same number sequences.

Table 1. Explanation of the abbreviations displayed by EvaluateMe

Screen name	Full name	Description
C	Counter	This value is a counter, which is being incremented on every update step of the `ActualDistribut-edGame` (counts computed actual application update steps).
CStep	Counter Step (rate)	Represents the rate at which the Counter (C) is changing with. This value indicates the update rate of the application (average over the last second).
LM	Load Mode	Indicates the load mode. Values: U, D, UD U: Update D: Draw UD: Update and Draw
GUP	GUP count	Indicates the maximum number of `ActualDis-tributedGame` update steps, within a `Distribut-edGameLauncher` update step over the last 60 `DistibutedGameLauncher` update steps.
LDX	Load Maximum	Indicates the maximum workload in milliseconds that might appear in U, D or U and D.
LDM	Load Minimum	Indicates the minimum workload in milliseconds that can appear in U, D or U and D.
URS, DRS	Update, Draw Running slowly	Indicates whether the XNA Game Studio sets the `IsRunningSlowly` flag in the `GameTime` object of the `Update` or the `Draw` method.
FRR	Frame rate	Indicates the rate the application is being drawn with. The number of times the `ActualDistribut-edGame`'s `Draw` method becomes invoked per second (average over the last second).
S, R	BytesSent, BytesReceived	Indicates the number of bytes which are sent/received per second.
RT	Runtime counter	Elapsed time minutes since the application start.
Z	Send Multiplier	Indicates how often to distribute the user input.

The workload is simulated by instructing the main thread to sleep for a random amount of milliseconds which ranges from LDM to LDX. LM indicates on which method workload simulation is applied to Update (U), Draw (D), or both (UD).

The Counter is a number which gets incremented every update step. This value indicates whether the systems run synchronously or not. The strategy of this evaluation strategy is to increase the Counter on all Xbox 360 systems while recording screenshots using the digital SLR camera. In the recorded screenshots, the value of the Counter between the different systems will be compared, to determine whether the systems run synchronously. A variation of one might be caused by the vertical retrace synchronization between the screens and the Xbox 360 systems and must therefore be tolerated.

The GUP count will be a constant one on the server because it is the one which distributes the GamePadState instances. However, the server can be faster than a client, thus this value indicates the maximum number of actual application update steps which were performed in one of the last 60 update steps of the DistributedGameLauncher. This calculation method is necessary, to avoid a quick change of that value, which would make it unrecordable for the camera. If the GUP count is higher than one that means that the server has distributed the GamePadState instances faster than the client can process them. If the GUP count alternates between one and two, it does not necessarily mean that the server is too fast because it might happen that two GamePadState instances are received almost at the same time due to network latency and packet-losses. They both were then processed on the last update step. If this value is higher than one for a longer time period then the reason might be the client's Update performance. Z was a constant one during these trials.

EvaluateMe applies a target configuration of 60 Hz and runs in fixed time step mode, therefore the values for FRR and CStep should converge to 60.

7.2   Balanced Trials

Different trials have been performed challenging dXNA in different ways. For every trial, several pictures have been taken to examine dXNA runtime performance. The most interesting trials will be presented and described, summing up the results of all pictures taken. Balanced trials model the application domain of dXNA the best. In balanced trials, all Xbox 360 systems have the same workload configuration. One basic trial has shown that if the application is not performing any complex and time consuming calculations, dXNA is capable to run a distributed application synchronously. Making it more interesting, the workload was increased to 10-16ms (milliseconds) for D and U and 0-13ms for UD.

While Draw only was working, not much happened, except for a little decrease of the draw rate to 59.3 Hz. The maximum variation of one was within the accepted tolerance threshold, so it is not certain if that value is caused by dXNA not being fast enough or because it was waiting for the monitor to draw its state. However, having the workload in Update it impacted a little more than it did in Draw only. This happened because Draw was skipped by XNA Game Studio in order to call Update method of the `DistibutedGameLauncher` 60 times per second. Therefore, the FRR decreased to 54 in the worst case to keep the UR (update rate) at 60 Hz.

The next test involved examining the performance in the workload mode "Update" and "Draw", which means the two workload methods which were applied previously individually were then applied simultaneously. The workload ranges from 0 to 13ms. This is less than the previously applied workload (10-16ms), but it is applied twice this time. The FRR decreased to 56 Hz. UR is almost at 60 Hz, it is the limit for this configuration, in order for the application to run almost at the desired frame rate of 60 Hz.

This configuration examined the limits of each workload mode and the point at which the frame rate starts to decrease because of performance issues. Another trial used workload values beyond the hardware's limits, to evaluate its behavior under extreme conditions. It showed that dXNA also executes the actual distributed application synchronously even if it is highly overloaded, although at a decreased FRR[4].

7.3   Results

The purpose of the evaluation was to examine the quality of interactive distributed rendering using dXNA on multiple systems. The assumptions and expectations which were made in the previous sections were fulfilled. The applied approach needs a constant network load which proven by looking at the pictures of the trials. There is a constant network load value for a constant update rate. The synchronization which was the actual challenge to be mastered, is solved in a robust way which is able to recover itself even after a much stressed situation. If the workload is balanced equally on all systems, then all are entirely synchronized over the whole period of execution and all draw their state with the same frequency.

If an Xbox 360 system sees only Object1 at one moment, it might happen that the virtual camera rotates and it will be seeing Object2 in the next. Therefore, it is essential that every Xbox 360 system in the cluster performs exactly the same logic calculations without considering the current view. It was explicitly mentioned, that all application logic like AI, movements, user input and so on, has to be performed within the `Update` method of the `ActualDistributedGame`. Analogously, all operations which are related to rendering have to be accomplished within its `Draw` method. Respecting this rule, dXNA manages interactive distributed rendering satisfyingly. If the same update logic will be executed by all systems the workload for `Update` will be balanced on all systems. Such a balanced trial showed that all systems run synchronously if the workload is equal. If different computer systems have to calculate different views, which is expected in distributed rendering for interactive multi-screen visualization environments, the worst that can happen is that a computer system will skip to draw its state, for one or more update steps, depending on the workload level. So the systems remain synchronized, but those with too much workload in their `Draw` method will supply the same output data to their output device. So instead of 60 frames the overloaded systems provide less, depending on the complexity of the data

---

[4] Depending on the workload mode and the actual workload the UR might also decrease.

they have to render. The other systems will stay unaffected. As soon as the load decreases the overloaded system continues its execution normally.

XNA Game Studio provides a time slice of 16.6 milliseconds for the execution of both, `Update` and `Draw` when running at 60 Hz. dXNA started to skip `Draw` when the simulated workload accounted more than 15 milliseconds which means that dXNA provides more than 15 milliseconds to the actual application for its own computations.

The implementation based on the proposed approach, distributed XNA Game Studio, is a lightweight extension of XNA Game Studio which allows for efficient porting of existing XNA Game Studio projects and needs slightly more than one millisecond per update step to compute the interactive distributed rendering overhead.

Acknowledgements. This work has been partially funded by the Deutsche Gesetzliche Unfallversicherung (grant FP307) and the FHprofUnt program of the BMBF (grant 17028X11). The authors also acknowledge the support and fruitful discussions with Jürgen Wirtgen.

References

1. Melax, S.: A simple, fast, and effective polygon reduction algorithm. Game Developer 11, 44–49 (1998)
2. Johnson, P.B.: Connecting graphics adapters for scalable performance. USA Patent 7477256 (January 13, 2009)
3. ATI, ATI CrossFire™ Technology White Paper (January 2008)
4. Adams, R.: OpenSimulator Virtual World Server Case Study (part 1), Intel (January 17, 2011), http://software.intel.com/en-us/articles/opensimulator-virtual-world-server-case-study/
5. Adams, R.: OpenSimulator Virtual World Server Case Study (part 2), Intel (February 2, 2011), http://software.intel.com/en-us/articles/opensimulator-virtual-world-server-case-study-part-2/
6. spot3d, Distributed rendering, spot3d (January17, 2011), http://www.spot3d.com/vray/help/150SP1/distributed_rendering.htm
7. Zotos, E., Herpers, R.: Interactive Distributed Rendering of 3D Scenes on multiple Xbox 360 Systems and Personal Computers. In: IEEE Proc. Cyberworlds 2012, Darmstadt (2012)
8. Weißmann, S., Gunn, C., Brinkmann, P., Hoffmann, T., Pinkall, U.: A Java library for real-time interactive 3D graphics and audio. In: Proceedings of the 17th ACM International Conference on Multimedia, MM 2009. ACM, New York (2009) ISBN: 978-1-60558-608-3
9. Sahm, J., Soetebier, I.: A Client-Server-Scenegraph for the Visualization of Large and Dynamic 3D Scenes. Journal of WSCG 12(1-3), ISBN: 0-7803-9802-5; WSCG 2004, February 2-6. Copyright UNION Agency Science Press, Plzen (2004)

10. Humphreys, G., Buck, I., Eldridge, M., Hanrahan, P.: Distributed Rendering for Scalabale Displays. In: Proceedings of the 2000 ACM/IEEE Conference on Supercomputing (CDROM), Supercomputing 2000, vol. 5. IEEE Computer Society, Washington, DC (2000) ISBN: 0-7803-9802-5
11. Mircosoft, XNA Framework Overview Mircosoft (January 15, 2011),
    http://social.technet.microsoft.com/wiki/contents/
    articles/xna-framework-overview.aspx
12. Hargreaves, S.: Understanding GameTime, Shawn Hargreaves Blog (September 11 (2010),
    http://blogs.msdn.com/b/shawnhar/archive/2007/07/25/
    understanding-gametime.aspx
13. Mircosoft, NetworkSession Class, Microsoft (July 10, 2010),
    http://msdn.microsoft.com/en-us/library/
    microsoft.xna.framework.net.networksession.aspx
14. IETF, User Datagram Protocol, IETF (November 11, 2011),
    http://tools.ietf.org/html/rfc768
15. Institute of Visual Computing of Bonn-Rhine-Sieg University of Applied Sciences, FIVIS: Bicycle Simulator,
    http://vc.inf.h-bonn-rhein-sieg.de/ivc/?page_id=425
    (accessed February 25, 2013)
16. Mircosoft, Polymorphism, Microsoft (February 17, 2011),
    http://msdn.microsoft.com/en-us/
    library/ms173152(v=vs.80).aspx
17. Mircosoft, LocalNetworkGame.ReceiveData, Microsoft (April 1, 2011),
    http://msdn.microsoft.com/
    en-us/library/microsoft.xna.framework.net.
    localnetworkgamer.receivedata.aspx
18. Microsoft, Random Class (System) (March 5, 2013),
    http://msdn.microsoft.com/
    en-us/library/vstudio/system.random.aspx

Training Interpreters Using Virtual Worlds

Panagiotis D. Ritsos[1], Robert Gittins[1], Sabine Braun[2],
Catherine Slater[2], and Jonathan C. Roberts[1]

[1] Bangor University, Bangor, UK
{p.ritsos,rgittins,j.c.roberts}@bangor.ac.uk
[2] University of Surrey, Surrey, UK
{c.slater,s.braun}@surrey.ac.uk

Abstract. With the rise in population migration there has been an increased need for professional interpreters who can bridge language barriers and operate in a variety of fields such as business, legal, social and
medical. Interpreters require specialized training to cope with the id-
iosyncrasies of each field and their potential clients need to be aware of
professional parlance. We present 'Project IVY'. In IVY, users can make
a selection from over 30 interpreter training scenarios situated in the
3D virtual world. Users then interpret the oral interaction of two avatar
actors. In addition to creating different 3D scenarios, we have developed
an asset management system for the oral files and permit users (mentors
of the training interpreters) to easily upload and customize the 3D environment and observe which scenario is being used by a student. In this
article we present the design and development of the IVY Virtual Environment and the asset management system. Finally we make discussion
over our plans for further development.

Keywords: Interpreting, Virtual Environments, Second Life, Usability.

1 Introduction and Motivation

Nowadays, interpreters are being called to master an ever broadening range of
interpreting scenarios and skills and are required to help in demanding situations
such as courts, police interviews and medical emergencies. However, training for
such situations can be challenging to do through traditional teaching methods.
In addition, efforts to educate potential clients of the realities of working with
an interpreter are scarce and normally separate from interpreter education.

In this paper we present the IVY Virtual Environment (IVY-VE). The aim of
IVY is to address these needs, offering future interpreters (trainees) and future
users of interpreters (clients) a 3D virtual environment that supports the acquisition and application of skills required in interpreter-mediated communication,
focusing on the practice of consecutive and liaison interpreting in business and
community settings. In contrast to many other initiatives in interpreter training,
IVY attempts to integrate the education of interpreters and their clients closer
together by employing working modes which allow the two user groups to engage
with the environment in a variety of ways.

M.L. Gavrilova et al. (Eds.): Trans. on Comput. Sci. XVIII, LNCS 7848, pp. 21–40, 2013.

The specific aims of project IVY are to develop (i) an adaptive 3D virtual environment for interpreting students and future users of interpreters; (ii) a range of virtual interpreting scenarios (e.g., 'business meeting') that can be run in different modes (e.g., 'interpreting mode', where interpreting students can practice using dialogues and monologues as shown in Fig. 1; 'exploration mode', where clients can learn about interpreting; 'live interaction', where both groups can engage in role plays);(iii) integrate into the virtual environment multilingual audiovisual content based on video corpora from the LLP project BACKBONE [1] and (iv) develop two sets of learning activities, one for students and one for clients (e.g., interpreting and awareness-raising exercises).

IVY-VE supports these aims by fusing web-based technologies with Second Life (SL). The concept is to abstract the 3D world (SL) from the assets (the audio and video files and management thereof). This is achieved through web technologies, which offer intuitive means of managing scenarios and resources. We follow an Agile implementation strategy [2] where Interpreters and computer Programmers work closely together to develop several prototypes (each building on the previous), and evaluate the prototype at each iteration.

This article is an extension of a conference publication [3]. In this publication we provide (1) more detailed description of the server-side mechanisms of IVY-VE, including audio playlists and file name conventions. (2) Add greater detail on the functionality of the in-world interface, especially to explain the different modes and operations. (3) Describe a usability evaluation of IVY. In fact, the evaluation focused on expert users, with experience in Virtual Learning Technology, developing Virtual Worlds, computer programming, and computer science research at postgraduate level.

The structure of the paper is as follows: Sect. 2 presents related work of training in Virtual Worlds, technology based interpreting training and the use of web technologies with virtual worlds, Sect. 3 describes several alternative design strategies that we considered, Sect. 4 explains in detail our implementation, Sect. 5 presents a usability evaluation from virtual world and computer-aided learning experts, Sect. 6 discusses our prototypes current limitations and outlines future work and Sect. 7 presents our conclusions.

2   Related Work

Different technologies have been used in training for many years. Technologies such as audio and video streaming, radio, web pages and wikis have all enabled remote learning to occur. Some of these can be used by several users synchronously, while others provide asynchronous learning environments where students can learn remotely and at their own speed. Many of these Information and Communication Technologies (ICT) enable *blended learning* experiences [4] that fuse face-to-face experiences with remote (web) technologies.

In addition, computer games and virtual environments have become a huge industry and educators have been investigating how these systems can be used for training. These so-called *serious games* [5] have a strong appeal to users [6,7] and seem to enhance participant involvement when used for educational and training purposes [8]. A comprehensive presentation of virtual worlds, their history and availability to date is beyond the scope of this paper; the reader can obtain such information from other sources such as Bartle [9] and Duncan et al. [10]. Instead, we focus on (i) ICT-based Interpreter Training, (ii) Pedagogy of Education and training in Virtual Worlds, and (iii) the fusion of web technologies with virtual worlds to provide a remote management.

2.1 ICT-Based Interpreter Training

While virtual worlds have not been adopted in interpreting training programs, other Information and Communication Technologies (ICT) have been successfully used. These systems allow the trainee interpreters to practice and also develop computing literacy skills, which is becoming increasingly important in the interpreter's daily work [11].

Many of the training tools use audio files. The SIMON (Shared Interpreting Materials Online) project [12] contains a database of mp3 audio recordings and transcripts as pdf files. The SIMON project classified the material according to progression level, exercise type language and thematic domain, which helps the users improve their skills and enables materials to be shared between educators.

Video is also used in interpreter training. Hansen and Shlesinger [13] describe a video-based interpreter training initiative. The video clips show tutors and other actors performing monologues and bilingual role-play dialogues. Similarly, the English Language Interview Corpus as a Second-Language Application (ELISA) [14] is a collection of video interviews with native speakers of English which is designed to be a resource for language learning and interpreter training. ELISA was a forerunner of BACKBONE [1] which produced video interviews with native speakers of English, French, German, Polish, Spanish and Turkish, as well as with non native speakers of English. The BACKBONE resource also includes interpreting exercises that can be applied to any of the videos in the BACKBONE corpora.

Apart from serving audio and video materials to the user, another focus is on authoring. Sandrelli and Jerez [15] describe the evolution of authoring programs for interpreters, starting with Interpr-IT, through Interpretations, and finally to Black Box 3.0. They highlight functionalities such as a voice recording feature, on-screen note-pad, pitch-tracker for gauging performance etc. While their focus was on authoring, the need to manage resources is an important challenge in the development of these training systems, and is thus a major feature of our IVY environment.

2.2 Pedagogy of Education and Training in Virtual Worlds

Today's virtual worlds and massively multiplayer online games (MMOGs) are descendants of Multi-user virtual environments (MUVEs) [9,16] of the 1980s.

Second Life is a popular commercial virtual world, often employed by educational institutions [17]. It is used in various fields such as medical and health education [18], environmental education [19] and security [20]. Another virtual world that has attracted the attention of researchers [21,22,23] is Activeworlds launched in 1997 which includes a dedicated educational world, called Educational Universe (AWEDU). OpenSimmulator is a newer virtual world implementation, in the form of an open source multi-platform, multi-user 3D application server. It is almost exclusively used by universities and big companies and has recently attracted the attention of researchers [24,25].

The pedagogic implications of using Virtual Worlds in training and simulation scenarios have been investigated by many researchers. Savin-Baden et al. [26] argue that "technology has led pedagogy" and further technological development should be driven by pedagogy itself. Thackray et al. [27] suggest that different methodologies are used among institutions, disciplines and instructors, which introduces much variety on virtual world implementations and associated practices.

More importantly, Salmon et al. [28] point to challenges of 'familiarity'. Users' unfamiliarity with the world increases challenges inherent to the learning process [29]. In addition student expectations can also effect the learning process. Moschini [30] highlights that users of such environments expect interactive content, rather than a mere passive learning experience. Consequently it is important to structure the tasks appropriately and make them intuitive, especially considering that Second Life can be chaotic and anarchic, as claimed by Carr et al. [29].

Evaluation of the learning environment is obviously an important aspect in any system development. For instance, Tymczyńska [31] describes how the Moodle Learning Management system[32] was integrated into a healthcare interpreting module at Adam Mickiewicz University in Poland. She highlights five different criteria for evaluating the applicability of the learning resources — student learning potential, student and context fit, authenticity, practicality and sense of achievement. These are similar to the findings from the pedagogical considerations emerging from other virtual world projects. However, while researchers are considering the potential positive impact on the broader serious games learning environments [33], none of the studies reported have researched whether the ability to learn improves in virtual worlds. An equally important aspect is that studies to date have predominately focused on students in a higher education environment.

2.3 Web Technologies and Virtual Worlds

One of the drawbacks of most virtual environments is that they are exclusive [34] because they don't have the functions necessary to interact or operate with other learning environments. In addition they often require 'in-world' scripting, even for the simplest examples of communication and mediation. Therefore managing content in these worlds requires knowledge of proprietary scripting languages — such as LSL (Linden Scripting Language) used in Second Life. However these languages do not have the features of established web technologies like Java, or

JavaScript etc. and can thus limit the functionality of potential implementations; especially those requiring frequent content management and material updates.

Some researchers have investigated how virtual worlds and web technologies merge [35] to manage the content better and enable a better in-world experience. For example, Sloodle [36] fuses Second Life with Moodle [32]. It presents information in Second Life using HTTP-requests that communicate with Moodle's PHP-based database front end. Zender et al. [34] present their SOA-based approach, using Web Services to provide lecture streaming and a messaging service in Second Life.

But there are important limitations in establishing communication between Second Life and external entities (e.g., scripts, programs). LSL uses functions that utilize HTTP and XML, such as llHTTPRequest or the older RPC-based llSendRemoteData and llRemoteDataReply for this purpose. However, Linden imposes time delays and limits on these methods, such as request size, number of requests per object, per owner and per period of time, making more demanding communication tasks quite difficult to implement.

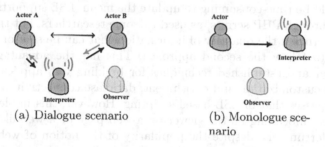

(a) Dialogue scenario   (b) Monologue scenario

Fig. 1. A range of scenarios is created in IVY VE to support interpreting practice in ready-made dialogues (a) and monologues (b) as well as live interaction and other working modes. In the dialogues and monologues, the actors are avatars controlled by the environment (robots), representing the interlocutor(s) in each scenario, and the avatar of the interpreting student. In live interactions, avatars of interpreting students and their 'clients' interact.

3 IVY Design

Our design vision was to create a virtual world where interpreters can be immersed in different scenarios, listen to virtual actors and interpret the conversations. Users need to choose a scenario from a menu of choices, navigate to a room or location that has appropriate appearance and follow exercises and view instructions. Mentors also need to be able to populate the world with training materials, upload audio tracks for the actors and manage the world assets.

Therefore, our first strategic choice concerned the virtual world. We chose to use Second Life (SL), instead of other virtual worlds (such as OpenSimulator), for several reasons. SL provides a large community of users, developers and enthusiasts. These users have created many add-ons, plugins and therefore there are many examples of customizations and vast support for scripting and assets for creating the scenario settings. This is extremely useful to bootstrap the development of a virtual learning environment. SL is a platform for social interaction and education, used by numerous institutions, colleges, universities – thus, using SL increases the chances of exposure and information dissemination of the IVY project. Finally, SL is a managed service with public servers; subsequently, prototypes could be quickly built and shared between the developers and partners in IVY.

With the decision to use Second Life two alternative implementation strategies were considered: whether the IVY-VE interface would be scripted in Second Life, using LSL or implemented as a separate, external component using popular web technologies such as HTML/CSS and Java.

The major advantage of the first solution is that the code can closely integrate with other objects in the scenes and menus and GUI elements built using LSL have comparable aesthetics to the main client GUI. Embedding scripts into objects is common practice and many information display systems make use of such mechanisms. Nonetheless, due to the static nature of including data into scripts it would be time-consuming to update the menu. LSL supports database connections through PHP scripts, as used by some researchers, but the solution is limited in terms of the quantity of information that can be sent or received.

We chose to follow the second approach. This has the advantage of relying on popular and established techniques for building web applications. The level of menu customization and enrichment, database connectivity and overall flexibility surpasses that of LSL-based scripting. However, this implementation requires either embedding an SL viewer on a web page or a web-like, in-world interface. Unfortunately, despite the popularity of the notion of web-based SL viewers, Linden Labs does not officially offer a web client and most of the efforts to implement something similar seem to have ceased. Canvas, from Tipodean Technologies[1] appears to be the only implementation of such a viewer, claiming to support both SL and OpenSim.

4   Implementation

Our chosen implementation strategy therefore is a hybrid solution (see Fig. 2). The scenario manager is independent of SL and is used by content-managers to manage scenarios and user's information, offering basic CRUD functionality. The second part is viewable within Second Life, in the form of a heads-up-display menu (HUD). The information displayed on the HUD is populated from a database and depicts available scenarios to the user. It includes the audio player and methods to initiate in-world teleport events.

Nonetheless, a major consequence of using SL is the lack of mechanisms such as *instancing, replication* and *zoning*, used in massively multiplayer online games (MMOGs)[37] to allow an increasing number of simultaneous users to be present

---

[1] http://www.tipodean.com/

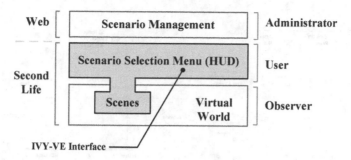

Fig. 2. IVY-VE Architecture - depicting the three main parts of the application: (i) the web-based administration panel, (ii) the in-world HUD, and the scenes associated with the scenarios and the remaining, (iii) the virtual world (SL)

in the game/virtual world. Contemporary MMOGs, such as EVE[2] and World of Warcraft use multiserver architectures to allow access to many users at a given time. However SL is fairly static when it comes to each individual island and the virtual world created on it, resulting in an environment with almost no dynamic scalability.

Of particular interest in our research is instancing; the creation of multiple copies of parts and locations of the virtual world. Several of the interpreting scenarios take place in the same setting, e.g., many language combinations take place in a classroom. Instancing these rooms would allow the world to scale according to users' demands. While it is possible to copy locations, this method has resource implications. Indeed due to limits on the quantity of primitives available to the IVY Island we cannot merely replicate all models in different points on the SL island.

To combat these limitations we use a collection of unique, in-world locations for each type of scenario (e.g., Classroom, Office). We replicate some commonly used models, but lockout any scenarios on the menu that share locations with the ones being used at a given time. Once the user exits the selected scenario, the location, and scenarios executed in it, becomes available. While Holodeck or rez-on-demand scripts exist in SL we decided to maintain consistency in the virtual environment and explore such scalable solutions in future implementations. Fig. 3 shows the relationships and sequence of actions in IVY-VE.

4.1 IVY Scenario Management

The IVY scenario manager application was built using Appfuse 2[3]. Appfuse, built upon the Java platform, uses industry-standard features, such as Apache Maven integration, JPA support for database operations and popular web frameworks such as Spring MVC and Apache Struts, employed in this example. Our prototype is deployed using Apache Tomcat 6.x and uses the MySql 5.x database. Appfuse comes with the following features, used in IVY-VE:

---

[2] http://www.eve-online.com/
[3] http://www.appfuse.org

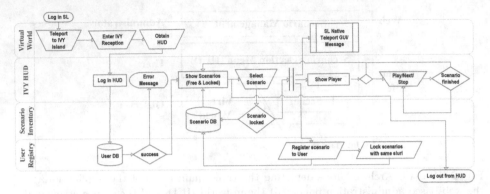

Fig. 3. IVY-VE Cross-functional flowchart - depicting the functions and the process flow, in each tier of the application, from log-in to dialogue selection and playback

- **Generic CRUD backend**, allowing the design and implementation of mechanisms for creating, uploading, editing and deleting scenarios and users.
- **Authentication and authorization**, allowing easy implementation of access control based on Spring Security.
- **User management**, enabling administrators (interpreting tutors) to easily manage the pool of users (students) and their access level.
- **Strong Internationalization support**, providing means of translating the web application in all the languages supported in our corpus.

4.2   Scenario Locations and Actors

The IVY environment was built on a full SL Island using several geometric models and textures. Photorealistic landscaping of both scenario locations and distant views provide a natural-looking environment for users to explore, and a series of buildings and rooms including a reception area, meeting rooms, classroom and offices have been built (see Fig. 4). The goal throughout the build was to use the smallest number of primitives to allow scalability and replication in the future.

The reception area acts as a central focus for visitors (Fig. 4a) where users can obtain the HUD, view introductory videos and read noticeboards with information. Care and effort has been put into the scale of objects [38].

In fact, there are two types of rooms that are used for the scenarios, that match the modes (as discussed in Sect. 1): those, used for the *interpreting mode* and those used in *live mode*.

The interpreting scenarios are actually located on sky platforms. These are modular components that can be readily replicated to expand capacity of a particular scenario, depending on their frequency of usage in the corpus. Also by being located in the sky, users need to teleport to them through our menu, and it is less likely that they are accessed by merely walking to them.

Live mode locations, along with an exhibition hall used in the exploration mode are located on the Island floor. These are necessarily more accessible such

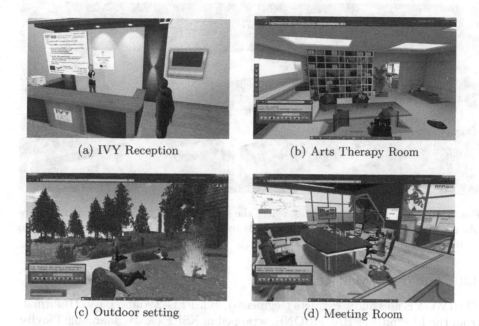

(a) IVY Reception   (b) Arts Therapy Room

(c) Outdoor setting   (d) Meeting Room

Fig. 4. Screenshots of the IVY-VE in use, showing scenario locations in Second Life - The IVY Reception (a) is where visitors are initially teleported and where they pick the HUD from. The locations were designed to match the available scenario themes, maintaining a generic look as much as possible to allow re-use of primitives.

that avatars can walk to them easily and thus permit more opportunities for social interaction.

Each scenario is populated with 'actors'. Currently we manually situate each of these SL 'robots' (bots) in specific locations and match the male/female versions to each scenarios requirements, adding another level of complexity to the management system. The ultimate aim is for the bots to teleport in-situ upon scenario selection, relay sound when it is their turn to speak and perform gesture animations related to the scenario. We use both Pikkubots[4] and Thoys[5] and control them from a separate server. We also use recursive animation overrides (AO) to give them movement.

The exhibition mode has a dedicated *exhibition area* on the IVY island. This area includes information and presentation boards. Different boards are available including those using Microsoft Powerpoint presentations and others that use the HTML-on-a-prim feature, that maps HTML onto virtual objects. The latter are implemented to display textual information arranged in meaningful sections using a jQuery accordion menu, minimizing the need to excessive vertical scrolling. Various informative videos are also embedded on prims, using the same strategy, displaying webpages with embedded media.

---

[4] http://www.pikkubot.de/
[5] http://slbot.thoys.nl/

Fig. 5. Aerial view of the skyboxes, where the locations used for interpreting mode are placed. This view normally is not accessible to users, who are teleported directly into each location/room.

4.3 Audio File Management

The IVY-VE uses audio extracts (segments), in MPEG-2 Audio Layer III format, from the LLP project BACKBONE, wrapped in XSPF (XML Shareable Playlist Format)[39] play-lists (scripts) and played within pre-fabricated scenes. Audio segments are uniquely named (see Fig. 6) and can be interchanged — within each script — to derive further language combinations of that scenario.

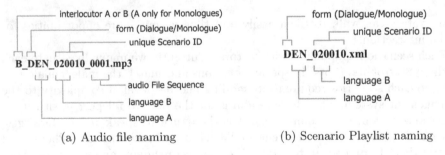

(a) Audio file naming   (b) Scenario Playlist naming

Fig. 6. Audio file and playlist naming convention. The name of each file is unique. Interchanging audio files yields additional language combinations of a particular scenario, which in turn are uniquely named in XSPF playlists.

Each actor may speak for more than one consecutive segments, allowing for scenarios where one talks for extended periods. However, it is assumed that only one actor talks per audio segment and there is no overlap between actors' speech. Each scenario has textual information associated with it, such as brief content information, scene description and domain keywords. XSPF playlist are enhanced upon upload (see Sect. 4.5) with turn counters per interlocutor. The information is places in the XSPF element allocated for the title of each track, corresponding to each scenario turn (see Fig. 7).

```
<?xml version="1.0" encoding="UTF-16" standalone="no"?>
<playlist xmlns="http://xspf.org/ns/0/" version="1">
<title>Bookshop</title>
   <trackList>
   <track>
      <location>/Inventory/mp3/A_DGR_000020_0001.mp3</location>
      <title>Participant A Turn: 1/2</title>
   </track>
   <track>
      <location>/Inventory/mp3/B_DEN_000020_0001.mp3</location>
      <title>Participant B Turn: 1/2</title>
   </track>
   <track>
      <location>/Inventory/mp3/A_DGR_000020_0002.mp3</location>
      <title>Participant A Turn: 2/2</title>
   </track>
   <track>
      <location>/Inventory/mp3/B_DEN_000020_0002.mp3</location>
      <title>Participant B Turn: 2/2</title>
   </track>
   </trackList>
</playlist>
```

Fig. 7. Example of an IVY XSPF playlist, for a scenario about a Bookshop, where Interlocutor A speaks in Greek and Interlocutor B in English

4.4   In-World Head-Up Display

The HUD makes use of the HTML-on-a-prim feature of SL and is built using the jQuery JavaScript library (Fig. 8). It displays the list of the scenarios from a database as a drill-down menu and is placed at the lower left of the user's viewport. By relying on web technologies the text is displayed in-world in the best possible rendering quality, particularly when compared to text rendered on 'prims' using native LSL. Moreover, the extent of character sets supported using web technologies ensures that our system displays properly textual information in all character sets of languages in our corpus (which is particularly for different language combinations). The functionality embedded in the HUD includes:

Navigation. Navigation through the island is achieved using slurls, providing direct url-like teleport links to locations within the virtual world. Each slurl is being called upon a series of events, such as scenario launch in interpreting mode, location selection in live-interpreting mode and launch of the exhibition mode, triggering the native SL-client teleport interface. Fig. 4 shows some screenshots of the IVY-VE.

Mode Selection. Modes are selected in the Mode Selection View by means of icons.

Utility Buttons. Log-off and Modes access buttons are available in all views, whereas a teleport launch button to IVY Reception is available in the Mode Selection View

Audio File Playback. Audio is being played by means of a Flash player, parsing the XSPF playlist upon each dialogue selection. The player control resemble a standard audio player interface allowing users to play, pause, repeat and advance tracks, corresponding to each turn of the scenario.

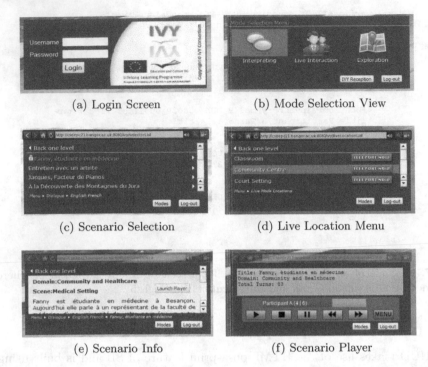

(a) Login Screen (b) Mode Selection View

(c) Scenario Selection (d) Live Location Menu

(e) Scenario Info (f) Scenario Player

Fig. 8. Screen captures of the IVY-VE HUD, depicting the login screen (a), the mode selection view(b), the scenario title selection view (c), the live location selection view (d), the scenario information view (e) and the scenario player (f)

Textual Information. Each mode has textual information and icons to assist users. Particularly in the case of the interpreting mode, launching a scenario allows access to scenario information, in the form of a summary brief, keywords and location description.

Access to SL GUI functions (limited). A limited number of `slurls`, using the prefix `secondlife:///app/`, allows direct control of the native SL client user interface[6]. We make use of such a `slurl` to launch the IVY Group inspection panel, displaying group members, allowing communication by chat, instant messaging as well as means of offering teleports on locations in the IVY Island.

4.5 Administrator's Panel

One of the most important functionality features of the IVY-VE is the scenario and user management console. Content administrators can create, edit and delete scenarios, through a form (shown in Fig. 9) where they provide textual information (title, language combinations, participants gender, scenario brief etc.),

---

[6] http://wiki.secondlife.com/wiki/Viewer_URI_Name_Space

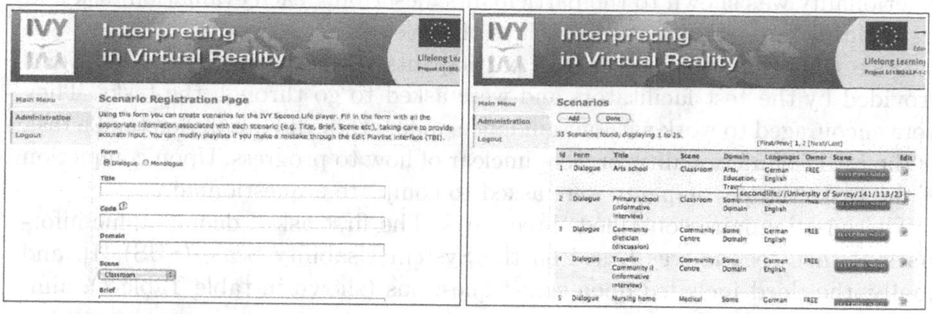

(a) Scenario Upload Form   (b) Scenario Listing View

Fig. 9. The Administrator's panel includes tools to create, edit, delete scenarios and users as well as monitor scenario usage, launch SL client and teleport to scenario locations, using `slurls`

select the scenario location from a series of pre-fabricated scenes and provide an ordered file listing of the audio tracks of the scenario. Textual information is stored in the database and the audio file listing in the aforementioned XSPF playlist format, in the playlist inventory.

In addition, a listing of all the scenarios in the system's inventory allows tutors to see which user is going through which scenario at a given time and teleport to that location, by launching their local SL client. Administrators can choose to use the `slurl` links to launch their SL client and teleport to those locations. Particular attention was paid to extended language support of the forms and database, so that scenario information in different character sets can be entered and displayed properly.

5   Usability Evaluation

The IVY-VE prototype underwent a usability evaluation from experts in virtual environments and computer-aided learning technologies. The purpose of our evaluation was to assess the usability of IVY-VE, focusing on the virtual world and HUD. We chose to follow a formative evaluation approach [40]. The evaluation took place during the Virtual Learning Technologies 2012 workshop, at Bangor University.

5.1   Evaluation Methodology and Tasks

The evaluation methodology was as follows. The participants were formally welcomed and presented with a project introduction, description of the functionality of the HUD and evaluation task overview. The roles of the test facilitators and evaluators was clarified, emphasizing that we were not evaluating the participants' performance but the usability of our prototype. Written consent for their participation was obtained from all participants. A video tutorial of the IVY-VE functionality was shown to the participants, describing each evaluation task and highlighting important features such as the teleporting.

Once the briefing was over, the participants used avatars and HUD logins provided by the test facilitators and were asked to go through the tasks. They were encouraged to work without guidance, unless they did not understand a task or the HUD's functionality, or were unclear of how to progress. Upon completion of the tasks the participants were asked to complete a questionnaire.

The questionnaire contained three parts. The first asked demographic information, then second was based on the System Usability Scale (SUS)[41], and finally, the third included open-ended questions (shown in table Table 1), aiming to collect general comments.

As Lindgaard and Chattratichart [42] demonstrated the number of issues discovered in a usability evaluation correlate significantly with the evaluation task coverage and not with the number of participants. It was important therefore to ensure that the tasks cover the complete functionality spectrum of the evaluated system, compared to having a large pool of participants. In that respect, four evaluation tasks were designed around obtaining the HUD from the IVY reception hub and going through all the functionality modes, i.e., interpreting, live interaction and exploration. All tasks were to be performed in Second Life, using the HUD, much like the end users would.

5.2 Evaluation Conditions, Apparatus and Participants

The evaluation was carried out, for reasons of convenience and availability, using laptops, with Intel i5 CPUs, 8GB RAM and Nvidia NVS4200M GPUs. All laptops used the official SL client (v. 3.4.1 - 266581). Laptops were connected over a wireless connection to Bangor University's infrastructure. SL Client Lag meter indicated 'normal lag' throughout the experiment. We set the SL client's graphics settings to the lowest possible settings, as our evaluation did not focus on the graphical quality of the locations or the resulting sense of immersion.

We used a convenience sample [43] of twelve participants, nine male and three female, between 23 and 59 years of age. Seven of them reported they have had little familiarity with interpreters, mostly from the vocational meetings, conferences and presentations. The remaining five reported no familiarity with interpreters and their practice. In addition we recorded their perceived expertise in computers, virtual worlds and environments, Second Life and computer games, shown in Fig. 10a.

5.3 Results

The average SUS score, rating overall usability, was 65.5/100, with individual scores from participants ranging between 32.5 and 87.5. The scores for each participant are shown in Fig. 10a and we discuss answers to each question.

Q1,2. When participants were asked to list positive features of IVY-VE they commented favourably on the HUD interface and the "*simplicity of controlling audio*", the "*multiple of different locations*", the ease of selecting modes and

Table 1. Open-ended questionnaire, used in our IVY-VE evaluation

Q.1 Describe some positive aspects of the IVY Virtual Environment
Q.2 Describe some negative aspects of the IVY Virtual Environment
Q.3 Briefly describe any type of enhancement that you would like to see in IVY Virtual Environment
Q.4 Our design model is to fuse web technologies with Second Life, and to provide a content management system for users. Is this an effective approach and where could it be applied?
Q.5 Explain whether you think IVY Virtual Environment will be a useful tool for interpreters and their clients?
Q.6 What is your opinion of using an immersive three-dimensional Virtual Learning Environment, such as the IVY Virtual Environment

scenarios and the good aesthetics of some locations. When participants were asked to list negative aspects five reported that *"the lack of visual cues on who is speaking is an important limitation"*. In addition, two participants said that IVY-VE is *"not as interactive as modern games"* and *"needs a bit of training to get used to*, mostly due to movement and interaction with objects (panels etc.) in SL .

Q3. Participants were also asked to discuss possible enhancements they would like to see in IVY-VE in the future. The most common enhancements included: better visual cues to assist interpreters on who is speaking, *"a facility to record one's interpreting for future assessment"* and that directional sound may enhance usability. One user mentioned that *"the environment is not used in a dynamic way"* (see Sect. 4) and that implementing such mechanisms would enhance usability. In addition, the same user argued that *"getting an emotional connection with the situation, characters and narrative could make things more interesting, making situations tense or pressured etc."*.

Q4. All participants expressed positively that the web technologies rendered 'text' better and could display different character sets (in-world text renderings are traditionally of low quality). More importantly, they expressed that a web-based scenario management system is the best way to update content in such a system. However, controlling virtual assets and modifying the world aesthetics requires access to the world and can not be easily done using an external, say web-based, system.

Q5. Regarding the usefulness of such an environment for interpreters, most users responded that if the enhancements they suggested were implemented they system would be an effective tool of simulation and training. Some appeared sceptical on whether such systems would be popular with students as *"they take some getting used too"*.

Q6. Finally participants saw much potential on the use of Virtual Learning Environments (such as IVY-VE) for training, particularly for situations which are hard to recreate with other means. Two of the participants argued that because computer games can be educating so can VLEs in general. Three

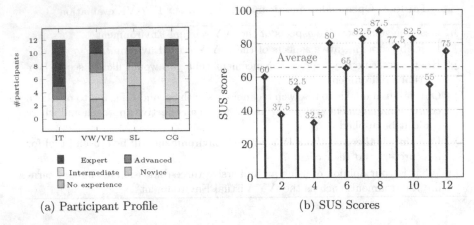

(a) Participant Profile   (b) SUS Scores

Fig. 10. Participant expertise in Computers in general (IT), Virtual Worlds and Environments (VW/VEs), Second Life (SL) and Computer Games (CG) is shown in Fig. 10a. System Usability Scores for each participant along with the average score is shown in Fig. 10b.

participants pinpointed that as VLEs become more accessible on the web or through mobile devices they will be more common place and become traditional educational tools.

6 Discussion

The results of the usability evaluation as well as the preliminary functional assessment [3] were positive. The average score in our evaluation was 65.5/100. This corresponds well with SUS scores of other web-based applications that have a mean score of 60 [44]. From this feedback we classify useful features and limitations of our current prototype, in five categories: scenario management, interface design, virtual world scalability, actor management and scenario execution.

As far as **scenario management** is concerned our web-based scenario management system, compared to the alternative of scripting content in the world, arguably, ensures ease of access and good level of control from interpreting tutors with no programming experience. Additionally, relying on web technologies to render text properly and support all the character sets required in our corpus yields good results and is simpler than enabling such a feature in bespoke systems.

We developed the HUD **interface** using web technologies, such as HTML/CSS and jQuery. By separating the virtual world from the functionality of the HUD results in a very flexible solution. Scripting similar functionality using LSL would be possible but hard. In addition, our approach allows us to experiment in the future with various other designs and explore the resulting user experience. There are certainly improvements that can be made, such as improving the visual cues to highlight the current speaking actor. But, as most evaluators mentioned, the current HUD was easy to use, informative and provided good control for teleporting and choosing modes and scenarios

Scalability issues are still a concern (see the discussion in Sect. 4) especially over *zoning*, *instancing* and *replication*. Our solution works exceptionally well, but we have a limit on the number of such scenarios the SL island can support. Moreover, **actor management** is affected, both in terms of populating scenarios as well as making them more interactive.

Finally, the **execution** and use of SL also provides challenges of quality. Newer modern computer games include high quality renderings with complex shadows, physics engines and caustic light models. Overall, it is evident that SL introduces important limitations, despite being relatively straightforward to develop and create an operational prototype.

7 Conclusions

In this article we present the design, implementation and evaluation of IVY-VE, a 3D virtual environment that supports the acquisition and application of skills required in interpreter–mediated communication.

One of our overarching successes is the separation of the content and manipulation of the learning material from the virtual world. This paradigm has many benefits: not only can the educator easily upload materials to a web interface, but the abstraction affords extensibility (where a new virtual reality environment could be used instead). The system is based on the fusion of Second Life and web technologies such as HTML/CSS, Appfuse, jQuery and JavaScript.

We have performed a usability evaluation (based on the SUS methodology), and have collected feedback from experts and researchers of Virtual Worlds and Computer Science. The evaluation of the work has been positive. Indeed, by following the SUS methodology we can compare the usability of this system to the scores of similar systems [44]. With a SUS score of 65.5/100 our usability compares favourably to other web-based tools.

We discuss various limitations with IVY-VE in this article. In fact, many of these limitations could be overcome by developing a bespoke virtual environment such as by using a game engine (such as Unity). Features such as directional and localized sound, more elaborate actor movement and interaction and in-world communication and collaboration could be included in a single application. Moreover, we could use our current scenario management system. Indeed other modalities such as haptics [45,46] could be added to the environment to develop a more realistic interactive experience. However, the use of SL has several advantages: it enables other views to readily access the world, enables quick building of rooms and buildings

In conclusion, we have developed a usable virtual environment for interpreting students and clients and our evaluation of the tool suggests it to be useful and valuable. However more work is required to develop IVY further, as a bespoke system, with enhanced scalability and tighter integration to the virtual world, allowing us to investigate further the resulting sense of presence. Our aspiration is to explore such a solution, based on the findings of using the current prototype and the feedback that we have collected, regarding the associated user experience of interpreter students and clients.

Acknowledgements. We are grateful to all the members of the IVY consortium, for their assistance and contribution to the project. This work was supported by the European Commission through project 511862-LLP-1-2010-1-UK-KA3-KA3MP in the Lifelong Learning Programme. This publication reflects the views only of the authors and the Commission cannot be held responsible for any use which may be made of the information contained therein.

References

1. Kohn, K., Hoffstaedter, P., Widmann, J.: BACKBONE - Pedagogic Corpora for Content & Language Integrated Learning. In: Eurocall Conference Proceedings. Macmillan ELT (2009)
2. Highsmith, J.: Agile software development ecosystems. Addison-Wesley Longman Publishing Co., Inc. (2002)
3. Ritsos, P.D., Gittins, R., Roberts, J.C., Braun, S., Slater, C.: Using Virtual Reality for Interpreter-mediated Communication and Training. In: 2012 International Conference on Cyberworlds (CW), pp. 191–198. IEEE (2012)
4. Bonk, C., Graham, C.: The handbook of blended learning: Global perspectives, local designs. Pfeiffer (2012)
5. Johnson, W., Vilhjalmsson, H., Marsella, S.: Serious games for language learning: How much game, how much AI. In: Artificial Intelligence in Education: Supporting Learning Through Intelligent and Socially Informed Technology, pp. 306–313 (2005)
6. de Noyelles, A., Seo, K.K.J.: Inspiring equal contribution and opportunity in a 3D multi-user virtual environment: Bringing together men gamers and women non-gamers in Second Life. Computers & Education 58(1), 21–29 (2012)
7. Yee, N.: The demographics, motivations, and derived experiences of users of massively multi-user online graphical environments. Presence: Teleoperators and Virtual Environments 15(3), 309–329 (2006)
8. Jarmon, L., Traphagan, T., Mayrath, M., Trivedi, A.: Virtual world teaching, experiential learning, and assessment: An interdisciplinary communication course in Second Life. Computers & Education 53(1), 169–182 (2009)
9. Bartle, R.: From MUDs to MMORPGs: The history of virtual worlds. In: International Handbook of Internet Research, pp. 23–39 (2010)
10. Duncan, I., Miller, A., Jiang, S.: A taxonomy of virtual worlds usage in education. British Journal of Educational Technology (2012)
11. Collins, C.: Looking to the future: Higher education in the Metaverse. Educause Review 43(5), 51–63 (2008)
12. Seeber, K.: SIMON: An online clearing house for interpreter training materials. Technology and Teacher Education Annual 4, 2403 (2006)
13. Hansen, I., Shlesinger, M.: The silver lining: Technology and self-study in the interpreting classroom. Interpreting 9(1), 95–118 (2007)

14. Braun, S.: ELISA-a pedagogically enriched corpus for language learning purposes. In: Corpus Technology and Language Pedagogy: New Resources, New Tools, New Methods (2006)

15. Sandrelli, A., Jerez, M., et al.: The impact of Information and Communication Technology on interpreter training. The Interpreter and Translator Trainer 1(2), 269–303 (2007)

16. Warburton, S.: Second Life in higher education: Assessing the potential for and the barriers to deploying virtual worlds in learning and teaching. British Journal of Educational Technology 40(3), 414–426 (2009)

17. Jennings, N., Collins, C.: Virtual or Virtually U: Educational Institutions in Second Life. International Journal of Social Sciences 2(3), 180–186 (2007)

18. Boulos, M., Hetherington, L., Wheeler, S.: Second Life: an overview of the potential of 3D virtual worlds in medical and health education. Health Information & Libraries Journal 24(4), 233–245 (2007)

19. Ye, E., Fang, Y., Liu, C., Chang, T., Dinh, H.: Appalachian tycoon: an environmental education game in second life. In: Second Life Education Workshop 2007, vol. 72 (2007)

20. Ryoo, J., Techatassanasoontorn, A., Lee, D.: Security education using Second Life. IEEE Security Privacy Magazine 7(2), 71–74 (2009)

21. Ang, K., Wang, Q.: A case study of engaging primary school students in learning science by using Active Worlds. In: Proceedings of the First International LAMS Conference 2006: Designing the Future of Learning (2006)

22. Dickey, M.: Three-dimensional virtual worlds and distance learning: two case studies of Active Worlds as a medium for distance education. British Journal of Educational Technology 36(3), 439–451 (2005)

23. Prasolova-Førland, E.: Analyzing place metaphors in 3D educational collaborative virtual environments. Computers in Human Behavior 24(2), 185–204 (2008)

24. Zhao, H., Sun, B., Wu, H., Hu, X.: Study on building a 3D interactive virtual learning environment based on OpenSim platform. In: 2010 International Conference on Audio Language and Image Processing (ICALIP), pp. 1407–1411. IEEE (2010)

25. Konstantinidis, A., Tsiatsos, T., Demetriadis, S., Pomportsis, A.: Collaborative learning in opensim by utilizing sloodle. In: 2010 Sixth Advanced International Conference on Telecommunications (AICT), pp. 90–95. IEEE (2010)

26. Savin-Baden, M., Gourlay, L., Tombs, C., Steils, N., Tombs, G., Mawer, M.: Situating pedagogies, positions and practices in immersive virtual worlds. Educational Research 52(2), 123–133 (2010)

27. Thackray, L., Good, J., Howland, K.: Learning and teaching in Virtual Worlds: Boundaries, challenges and opportunities. In: Researching Learning in Virtual Worlds, pp. 139–158 (2010)

28. Salmon, G., Nie, M., Edirisingha, P.: Developing a five-stage model of learning in Second Life. Educational Research 52(2), 169–182 (2010)

29. Carr, D., Oliver, M., Burn, A.: Learning, teaching and ambiguity in virtual worlds. In: Learning in Virtual Environments International Conference, vol. 83 (2008)

30. Moschini, E.: The Second Life Researcher Toolkit–An exploration of in-world tools, methods and approaches for researching educational projects in Second Life. In: Researching Learning in Virtual Worlds, pp. 31–51 (2010)

31. Tymczynska, M.: Integrating in-class and online learning activities in a healthcare interpreting course using Moodle. The Journal of Specialised Translation (12), 148–164 (2009)

32. Dougiamas, M., Taylor, P.: Moodle: Using learning communities to create an open source course management system. In: Proceedings of World Conference on Educational Multimedia, Hypermedia and Telecommunications, vol. 3 (2003)
33. Connolly, T., Boyle, E., MacArthur, E., Hainey, T., Boyle, J.: A systematic literature review of empirical evidence on computer games and serious games. Computers & Education (2012)
34. Zender, R., Dressler, E., Lucke, U., Tavangarian, D.: Pervasive media and messaging services for immersive learning experiences. In: IEEE International Conference on Pervasive Computing and Communications, PerCom 2009, pp. 1–6 (2009)
35. Blais, C., Brutzman, D., Horner, D., Nicklaus, M.: Web-based 3D technology for scenario authoring and visualization: The SAVAGE project. In: Interservice/Industry Training, Simulation & Education Conference (I/ITSEC), NTSA (2001)
36. Kemp, J., Livingstone, D., Bloomfield, P.: SLOODLE: Connecting VLE tools with emergent teaching practice in Second Life. British Journal of Educational Technology 40(3), 551–555 (2009)
37. Glinka, F., Ploss, A., Gorlatch, S., Müller-Iden, J.: High-level development of multiserver online games. Int. J. Comput. Games Technol. 2008, 3:1–3:16 (2008)
38. Roberts, J.C., Gittins, R., Thomas, R.: Scale and the construction of real-world models in Second Life. Journal of Gaming & Virtual Worlds 2(3), 259–279 (2010)
39. Gonze, L., Friedrich, M., Kaye, R.: XML shareable playlist format version 1 (2008)
40. Hix, D., Hartson, H.: Developing user interfaces: ensuring usability through product & process. John Wiley & Sons (1993)
41. Brooke, J.: SUS - A quick and dirty usability scale. In: Usability Evaluation in Industry, pp. 189–194. Taylor & Francis (1996)
42. Lindgaard, G., Chattratichart, J.: Usability Testing: What Have We Overlooked? In: Conference on Human Factors in Computing Systems (CHI 2007), pp. 1415–1424. ACM Press, San Jose (2007)
43. Scholfield, P.: Quantifying language: A researcher's and teacher's guide to gathering language data and reducing it to figures. Multilingual Matters Limited (1995)
44. Bangor, A., Kortum, P.T., Miller, J.T.: An empirical evaluation of the system usability scale. International Journal of Human-Computer Interaction 24(6), 574–594 (2008)
45. Panëels, S.A., Ritsos, P.D., Rodgers, P.J., Roberts, J.C.: Prototyping 3D haptic data visualizations. Computers & Graphics 37(3), 179–192 (2013)
46. Panëels, S.A., Roberts, J.C.: Review of designs for haptic data visualization. IEEE T. Haptics 3(12), 119–137 (2010)

Mathematical Foundations for Designing a 3-Dimensional Sketch Book

Kenji Ohmori[1] and Tosiyasu L. Kunii[2]

[1] Hosei University, Computer and Information Sciences
3-7-2 Kajino-cho, Koganei-shi, Japan
ohmori@hosei.ac.jp
[2] Morpho Inc
Iidabashi First Tower 31F
2-6-1 Koraku, Bunkyo-ku, Tokyo 112-0004 Japan
kunii@ieee.org

Abstract. This paper describes mathematical foundations for designing a 3-dimensional sketch book and the development of an experimental system. The system helps a non-professional user draw a mountain from a rough image to a fine image using filtration. The user draws important critical points (summits, ravine bottoms and saddles), which are used to obtain a 0-dimensional approximation. The system generates a Reeb graph to provide height information of the saddles with a partial order in height. Then, the contours are provided from the Reeb graph. The user draws ridges and ravines by pushing and pulling contours. The system generates a 1-dimensional approximation from these curves. Finally, NURBS surfaces are generated to give a 2-dimensional approximation and a 3-dimensional rendering image is obtained. The above procedure is repeated until a satisfactory result is obtained by giving the most important points and curves at the first stage and adds less important points and curves, later.

Keywords: 3D sketch, Morse theory, Reeb graph, Voronoi diagram, manifold, critical points.

1 Introduction

As a computer tablet is excellent in mobility and handiness, new applications are being explored. Among them, a 3-dimensional sketch book is a promising application. A non-professional user may hold the delightful dream that he draws landscapes as skillfully as a professional painter. The dream has never been realized by conventional vector graphic editors [8], such as Inkscape [3], Illustrator and Rhinoceros [5]. These applications provide fundamental tools for drawing curves and surfaces. But, these tools are not sufficient for a non-professional painter, who has difficulty in drawing curves and surfaces properly.

ILoveSketch [1], [2], [4] is a challenging work. ILoveSketch was developed using a desk top computer with a styles pen since the research started before the tablets came in the market. A user can get the sketch of a car, an airplane or a spider

M.L. Gavrilova et al. (Eds.): Trans. on Comput. Sci. XVIII, LNCS 7848, pp. 41–60, 2013.

by drawing the characteristic curves. As the user can view the sketch from any direction by rotating it, curves that he has drawn can be modified if those are not proper. ILoveSketch is a good tool for a professional painter since he can draw curves accurately. However, a non-professional user feels difficulty in using it since he has problems of drawing curves properly even when he feels that these are not suitable. A non-professional user who is not good at drawing has to be equipped by different technology, which covers his inability.

As a preparatory research for developing a 3-dimensional sketch book for landscapes, we have studied mathematical foundations for drawing mountains since mountains are typical landscapes that a painter wants to draw. A mountain is considered as a manifold [15], [7], [14] mathematically, which is a topological space and locally equivalent to a Euclidean space, to which a lot of mathematical theories can be applied.

Mathematical backgrounds including manifolds, homotopy [6], [12], [13], topology, filtration [9], Morse theory [10] and Reeb graphs [11] are extensively studied to provide a 3-dimensional sketch book for a non-professional user. This paper proposes a new theoretical procedure, which generates a pretty sketch from summits, ravine bottoms, saddles, ridges and ravines, and explains the experimental system equipped with the mathematical foundations.

A topological space, which forms the mathematical basis of a mountain as a manifold, is represented by a filtration, a series of skeletons. The filtration gives an approximation process. The first skeleton of the series is the 0-dimensional space composed by points. The second skeleton is the 1-dimensional space in which curves are added to the first skeleton. The nth skeleton is obtained in the same way by adding n-dimensional topological balls to the $(n-1)^{th}$ skeleton.

On the other hand, the sketches drawn by different professional painters are amazingly similar, in which the positions of lines and curves for the landscape are precise. It is the first step for the development of a 3-dimensional sketch book to study methods of drawing the lines and the curves of a mountain as accurately as possible.

Most of the lines and the curves that the professional painter draws are characterized as summits, cradles (passes), ravine bottoms, ridges and ravines (valleys). Our theoretical procedure is composed by repeated stages. At the first stage, a user supplies the most valuable points and curves. The first image that is generated from these points and curves is presented to the user. If the user does not satisfies the result, he gives the second most valuable points and curves. An alternative image that is more precise than the previous one is generated. The process is repeated until the user satisfies the result.

In each stage, the image of a mountain is constructed using a filtration. The points that the user has supplied create the 0-dimensional skeleton. Then, the curves that the user has supplied are added to the 0-dimensional skeleton and the 1-dimensional skeleton is generated. Finally, the surfaces that fit to these points and curves are automatically generated and the 2-dimensional skeleton is generated. The skeleton is rendered to obtain a 3-dimensional image that the user can review.

Each stage is carried out based on mathematical foundations so that points, curves and surfaces are drawn precisely.

2 Sketching Procedure

A user accomplishes his sketch by incrementally supplying invariant data such as summits, ravine bottoms, saddles, ridges and ravines. He repeats a stage until a satisfactory 3-dimensional image is obtained. More valuable data are supplied in an early stage and more concrete data in a later stage. In each stage, a series of skeletons is generated from the supplied data and the 3-dimensional image is proposed to the user. Each stage starts by providing critical points of summits, ravine bottoms and saddles and is followed by supplying invariant curves of ridges and ravines.

1. **Providing summits, ravine bottoms and saddles**
   Using the top view of the sketch book, summits, ravine bottoms and saddles are allocated. Their heights are not given at this stage. The top-view positions of the critical points are allowed inaccurate. In a later stage, the user may move these points to set on the right positions. The main purpose of allocating these points is to obtain a satisfactory rough 3-dimensional image of the mountain. The summits, the ravine bottoms and the saddles constitute the 0-dimensional skeleton in the filtration of the mountain.

2. **Creating a Reeb graph**
   A critical point (a summit, a ravine bottom and a saddle) forms seeds to create a Voronoi diagram. The Voronoi diagram gives information of how each saddle is formed by neighboring summits or ravine bottoms. From the Voronoi diagram, a Y shape branch or a reversed Y shape branch is provided for each saddle. The junction of the branch is the position of the saddle. A top end point of the branch shows a summit or the direction to a summit. A bottom end point of the branch shows a ravine bottom or the direction to a ravine bottom. A Y shape branch shows that there are two choices of summits to climb up when arriving at the saddle. A reversed Y shape branch shows also two choices. One choice is climbing up the mountain. The other choice is going down a ravine or a canyon.
   From the Voronoi diagram, the neighboring branches are obtained and they are connected each other to form a Reeb graph. The Reeb graph is a quotient space of contours, each of which is a closed line of the same height. In the Reeb graph, each contour is represented by a representative point. The Reeb graph gives a partial order of the saddles in height, so that it is an important mathematical background to provide height information for the user. Using the Reeb graph reversely, (usually, the Reeb graph is constructed from the contours), we can also obtain a set of contours that forms the 1-dimensional skeleton of the mountain.
   If the Reeb graph is disconnected graphs, some critical points are missing. The system promotes the user to provide the necessary points.

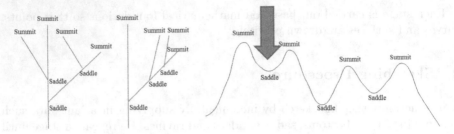

Fig. 1. A four shape mountain and its Reeb graph

3. Giving height information

Multiple Reeb graphs, which are different from each other in topology, may be possible from the supplied summits, ravine bottoms and saddles. An example is shown for a 4-peak mountain. As height information is not provided, there may be several types of Reeb graphs for the mountain, which are different from each other in topology. The two figures of the left-hand side in Figure 1 show possible Reeb graphs for the 4-peak mountain. The system proposes one of them. Suppose that the system proposes the left-hand side figure, which corresponds to the mountain shape of the right-hand side of Figure 1. However, the user does not prefer it. The user likes the other Reeb graph, which is obtained by moving down the saddle of the most left-hand side. This operation is achieved by manipulating the saddle on the Reeb graph.

Even though the Reeb graphs are different in topology, it is possible to provide a homotopy map morphing from any Reeb graph to any other Reeb graph if those are constituted from the same number of summits, ravine bottoms, and saddles, respectively.

By defining a homotopy map, we can morph from one Reeb graph to another. Adjunction maps $f : X \rightarrow Y$ and $g : X \rightarrow Y$ are defined as shown in Figure 2. On the graph, there is a route that can move the saddle from the point (source) of f and to the point (destination) of g. Assuming that the length of the route from the source to the destination is L, we can define an adjunction map f_t such that it attaches the saddle to the point whose distance from the source is $L \times t$ where $t \in I$ and I is an interval $[1, 0]$. As f_t is continuous, we can define a homotopy $H : X \times I \rightarrow Y$, where $H(x, 0) = f$ and $H(x, 1) = g$. Therefore, along H, the user can morph form the suggested Reeb graph to the one that he wants.

As the Reeb graph shows a partial order of saddles in height, the user can change the height relation of saddles by moving saddles.

4. Generating contours

A contour is a closed curve whose points have the same height. Contours are automatically generated for the summits, the ravine bottoms and the saddles. Around a summit or a ravine bottom, a simple closed curve is provided. Around a saddle, a closed curve with a double point is provided, where a double point is set at the saddle. We call these curves principal contours.

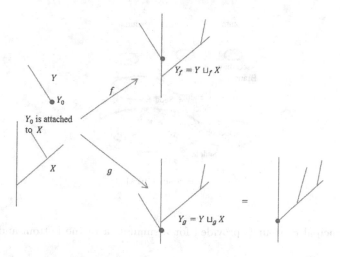

Fig. 2. The homotopy map morphing from one Reeb graph to another Reeb graph

A Y shape branch or a reversed Y shape branch is provided for each saddle when generating the Reeb graph. The junction of a branch is the place for the saddle. A branch has three line segments. One line segment A goes to the bottom (foot) of the mountain. Other two lines B and C go to summits or ravine bottoms.

As the contour provided at a saddle point is a closed curve of a double point, the contour has two loops b and c. Each line segment B or C going to summits or ravine bottoms corresponds to either of the two loops b and c, separately. Suppose B corresponds to b and C to c. The other end of B is a summit or a ravine bottom, its contour is surrounded by b. If B is connected to another branch, its contours are also surrounded by b. It is also the same to C and c.

If the other end of A is the bottom of the mountain, its contour a surrounds b and c. If A is connected to another branch, its contours also surround b and c. An example is shown in Figure 3. As the mountain is surrounded by its bottom, only one contour is provided for the bottom of the mountain. The contour surrounds all the rest contours of the mountain.

5. **Drawing ridges and ravines**

Ridges and ravines are drawn by manipulating contours. The principal contours are too rough for this purpose. Therefore, auxiliary contours are supplied between two neighboring principal contours. An auxiliary contour is configured so that it surrounds the inner principal counters and is surrounded by the outer principal contours. Each auxiliary contour either surrounds or is surrounded by another auxiliary contour. The height of an auxiliary contour is proportional to the heights of the principal contours. Using these contours,

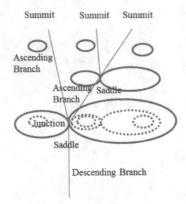

Fig. 3. A principal contour is provided for a summit, a ravine bottom and a saddle, respectively

a ridge is drawn by pushing contours and a ravine by pulling contours. An example is shown in Figure 4.

The ridges, the ravines and the contours constitute 1-dimensional curves of the mountain. By attaching the 1-dimensional curves to the 0-dimensional skeleton, a 1-dimensional skeleton is generated.

6. **Creating surfaces**

A closed surface surrounded by the 0-dimensional points and the 1-dimensional curves is automatically created. The closed surfaces created here are attached to the 1-dimensional curves and the 0-dimensional points to generate a 2-dimensional skeleton. The space obtained here is a CW complex, which can be easily transformed to a NURBS surface and rendered. By checking the 3-dimensional rendering image, the user can repeat the above procedure until he satisfies the result.

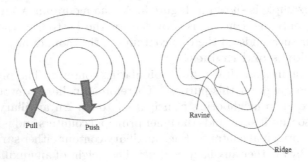

Fig. 4. Pulling and pushing contours for making a ravine and a ridge, respectively

3 Mathematical Backgrounds

3.1 Adjunction Maps

An adjunction map is defined as follows. Assuming that X and Y are topological spaces, consider attaching Y to X by an adjunction map f.

$$Y_f = Y \sqcup_f X = Y \sqcup X/ \sim \tag{1}$$

is an adjunction space obtained by attaching Y to X by f (or by identifying each point $y \in Y_0|Y_0 \subseteq Y$ with its image $f(y) \in X$ by a surjective and continuous map f). $\sqcup$ denotes a disjoint union. f is a continuous map such that $f : Y_0 \to X$, where $Y_0 \subseteq Y$. Thus, the attaching space $Y_f = Y \sqcup X/ \sim$ is a case of quotient spaces

$$Y \sqcup X/ \sim = Y \sqcup_f X = Y \sqcup X/(x \sim f(y)|\forall y \in Y_0). \tag{2}$$

3.2 Creating the CW Complex Using a Filtration Space

A filtration gives a way to construct a manifold or a topological space step by step.

1. **Filtrations**
   A filtration space is a sequence of cells used to represent a topological space. It is defined as follows. For any topological space X, we can obtain a finite or infinite sequence of skeletons X^p, where p is an integer, such that

   $$X = \cup_{p \in Z} X^p,$$
   $$X^0 \subset X^1 \subset .... \subset X^p .... \subset X. \tag{3}$$

   A skeleton X^p consists of cells whose dimensions do not exceed n. A cell is a topological space, homeomorphic to an n-dimensional open ball $IntB^n$, where n is an arbitrary integer. A sequence of skeletons is called a filtration. If it is finite, it becomes a CW-complex.
   Using the filtration, a topological space is constructed as a CW-complex. A skeleton X^p is obtained from the skeleton X^{p-1} by attaching $\sqcup_i B_i^p$ to X^{p-1} through an adjunction map f where B_i^p is a p-dimensional closed ball.

   $$f : \sqcup_i \partial B_i^p \to X^{p-1},$$
   $$X^p = X^{p-1} \sqcup (\sqcup_i B_i^p)/(x \sim f(x)|x \in \sqcup_i \partial B_i^p). \tag{4}$$

2. **The CW complex for a tetrahedron**
   As a tetrahedron is a very rough sketch of a mountain, it is worthwhile to see how the CW complex is organized using a filtration. A function $\mathcal{F}$, called a characteristic function, is introduced to transfer an internal space of a closed ball into a cell, which is an open set, of a CW complex. If a filtration space is represented using polygons, then

   $$X^p = \mathcal{F}(\sqcup_i B_i^p). \tag{5}$$

If $Int\mathcal{B}_i^p$ is transformed to a cell e_i^p and X^p is attached to X^{p-1} by an adjunction function f, then

$$X^p = \mathcal{F}(\sqcup_i \mathcal{B}_i^p) = \mathcal{F}((Int \sqcup_i \mathcal{B}_i^p) \sqcup (\partial \sqcup_i \mathcal{B}_i^p)) = \{e_1^p, e_1^p, ..., e_n^p, X^{p-1}\}, \quad (6)$$

where $f : \partial \sqcup_i \mathcal{B}_i^p \to X^{p-1}$ and $\partial \mathcal{B}$ is the boundary of $\mathcal{B}$.

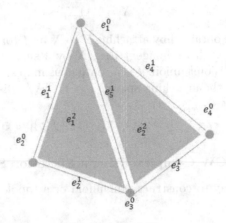

Fig. 5. The CW complex of a tetrahedron

The filtration space of the tetrahedron of Figure 5 is obtained as follows. As the tetrahedron has four vertexes, X^0 is represented by four 0-dimensional cells as follows,

$$\begin{aligned} X^0 &= \mathcal{F}(\sqcup_i \mathcal{B}_i^0) \\ &= \{e_1^0, e_2^0, e_3^0, e_4^0\}. \end{aligned} \quad (7)$$

The tetrahedron has six edges. The boundary of each edge is connected to two vertexes. Each edge is represented as a 1-dimensional cell. X^1 becomes

$$\begin{aligned} X^1 &= \mathcal{F}(\sqcup_i \mathcal{B}_i^1) \\ &= \mathcal{F}((Int \sqcup_i \mathcal{B}_i^1) \sqcup (\partial \sqcup_i \mathcal{B}_i^1)) \\ &= \{e_1^1, e_2^1, e_3^1, e_4^1, e_5^1, e_6^1, X^0\}. \end{aligned} \quad (8)$$

where $f : \partial \sqcup_i \mathcal{B}_i^1 \to X^0$ means that the boundary of e_1^1 is attached to e_1^0 and e_2^0, e_2^1 to e_2^0 and e_3^0, and so on.

Though the tetrahedron has four surfaces, we exclude the bottom surface since we are considering a mountain that does not have a bottom surface. Each surface is represented by a 2-dimensional cell. The boundary of a surface is attached to three edges and three vertexes. X^2 becomes

$$\begin{aligned} X^2 &= \mathcal{F}(\sqcup_i \mathcal{B}_i^1) \\ &= \mathcal{F}((Int \sqcup_i \mathcal{B}_i^2) \sqcup (\partial \sqcup_i \mathcal{B}_i^2)) \\ &= \{e_1^2, e_2^2, e_3^2, X^1\} \end{aligned} \quad (9)$$

where $f : \partial \sqcup_i \mathcal{B}_i^2 \to X^1$ means that the boundary of e_1^2 is attached to $e_1^0, e_1^1, e_2^0, e_2^1, e_3^0$ and e_5^1, and so on.

3.3   Critical Points

Summits, ravine bottoms and saddles characterize the shape of the mountain and give the roughest skeleton in the filtration. These points are called critical points in mathematics. Suppose that the shape of a mountain is a manifold. A manifold is a space in which every point on its surface is locally defined as a Euclidean space. A spherical surface like the earth is an example of a manifold. An area of the earth is represented by a real valued function $z = f(x, y)$ where x, y are latitude and longitude, and z is height. This is generalized to a n-variable function $y = f(x_1, x_2, ..., x_n)$. For example, x_1, x_2, x_3 are latitude, longitude and time and y is wave height, then $y = f(x_1, x_2, x_3)$ represents time changes of wave height.

Given a multiple variable function f, if all second partial derivatives of f exist, the neighbor of x is represented by

$$y = f(x + \Delta x) = f(x) + J(x)\Delta x + \Delta^T H(x)\Delta x, \tag{10}$$

where $J(x)$ and $H(x)$ are a Jacobian matrix and a Hessian matrix, respectively. If the Jacobian matrix is zero, x is a critical point. Critical points are divided into cases depending on the determinant of the Hessian matrix. If the determinant is not 0, x is a non-degenerate point. If it is 0, x is a degenerate critical point.

For a real valued function $z = f(x, y)$ with two variables, the following things are known. If a point (x, y) is a critical point and the determinant of the Hessian matrix is positive, f attains a local maximum value (if both of eigenvalues are positive) or a local minimum value (if both of eigenvalues are negative) at (x, y). If the Hessian matrix is negative, f takes a saddle at (x, y). If the determinant of the Jacobean matrix takes 0 not at a point but a continuous curve, the curve is a ridge or a ravine.

3.4   Voronoi Diagrams

A Voronoi diagram is the partition of a plane with n points (called seed) into convex polygons such that each polygon contains exactly one seed and any point in the polygon is closer to the seed of its polygon than any other seed. To generate the Reeb graph of a mountain, a Voronoi diagram is created such that each summit and each ravine bottom become a seed, respectively, and each saddle provides four seeds close to the saddle. The cell containing a summit (ravine bottom) seed is the region of contours surrounding the summit (ravine bottom). If a cell of a saddle is the neighbor of a summit cell (ravine bottom cell), the contours in the region are connected to contours of the summit (ravine bottom).

An example is shown at the left-hand side of Figure 6. The figure shows summit and saddle cells. The summit cell is surrounded by contours, some of which are connected to the contours of the neighbor. A saddle, which is depicted by a symbol "+", provides four seeds. Around the left-hand side saddle, the upper cell and the lower cell are ascending regions to the summits. The right and left ones are descending ones to the bottom of the mountain. The contours of these cells are connected to their neighbors.

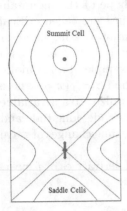
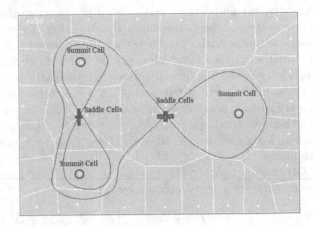

Fig. 6. The Voronoi diagram created from the summits, ravine bottoms and saddles

The saddle is usually the minimal height point of a ridge connecting two neighboring summits. However, sometimes a saddle appears between two neighboring ravine bottoms or between a summit and a ravine bottom adjacent to each other.

To simplify discussion in this section, we will consider a mountain that is constructed only by summits and saddles. As the Reeb graph is obtained by connecting Y shape branches, each of which is provided for a saddle, we have to find Y shape branches from the Voronoi graph. This process is carried out step by step.

1. For each saddle, the most neighboring two summits are selected and the total length from the saddle to the two summits is calculated. Among the saddles, the saddle that has the shortest total length is selected as the first candidate.
2. A Y shape branch is provided to the first candidate. The end point of an ascending line segment is the place for one of the summits. The end point of the descending line segment is the place for the bottom of the mountain or the direction to the mountain bottom. The saddle and the summits are grouped together and regarded as a virtual summit from now. The summit of the virtual summit is regarded as the position of the saddle.
3. Next candidate is selected among the rest saddles using the same procedure described above. The next procedure depends on the selected summits.
   Case 1) None of the summits are not virtual summits. A new Y shape branch is provided for this candidate.

Case 2) One of the summits is a virtual summit. A new Y shape branch is provided and one of the ascending line segments is connected to the descending line segment of the virtual summit branch.

Case 3) The two summits are virtual summits. A new Y shape branch is provided and the ascending line segments are connected to the descending line segments of the virtual summits, respectively.

4. This procedure is continued until all the saddles are selected.

From the Voronoi diagram of Figure 6 , the following Reeb graph of Figure 7 is obtained. This procedure is easily extended to the case in which ravine bottoms are included.

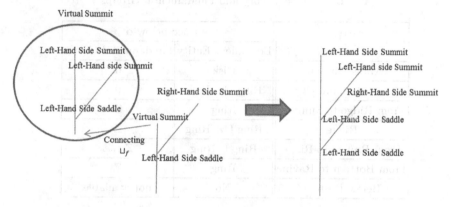

Fig. 7. The Reeb graph is obtained from the Voronoi diagram

3.5   Morse Theory

Suppose that the shape of a mountain is a manifold $\mathcal{M}$ and a real valued function $f : \mathcal{M} \to \mathbb{R}$. The inverse function f^{-1} at a point (x, y) gives a contour. A contour is a simple closed curve of the same height or a closed double-point curve of the same height. A closed double point curve gives a saddle at the crossing point. If f is a non-degenerate real valued function,

$$M^\alpha = f^{-1}(-\infty, \alpha) \tag{11}$$

is called a Morse function.

Using the Morse function, consider topological properties of the mountain of a somma volcano, which is a volcanic caldera that has been partially filled by a new central cone. This type of a mountain consists of a somma, a caldera and a central cone as shown in Figure 8. The bottom of the mountain is supposed to be open.

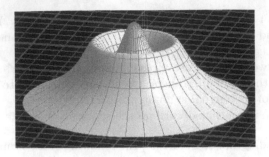

Fig. 8. A somma volcano

Table 1. Morse Theory and Fundamental Groups

α	Surface below α	
	Equivalent Entity	Fundamental Group
Above Summit	Disk	0
Summit	Ring $\sqcup_{f_2}$ Disk	0
From Ridge to Summit	Ring	$\mathbb{Z}$
Ridge	Ring $\sqcup_{f_1}$ Ring	$\mathbb{Z}$
From Ravine to Ridge	Ring $\sqcup$ Ring	$\mathbb{Z} \sqcup \mathbb{Z}$
From Bottom to Ravine	Ring	$\mathbb{Z}$
Below Bottom	No	not available

When the height α reaches to the bottom of the mountain, M^α is homotopy equivalent to a ring since the bottom is surrounded by a cylinder. This situation continues until α reaches to the ravine of the caldera. When it reaches to the ravine of the caldera, another cylinder appears in the caldera. This situation continues until α reaches to the ridge of the somma volcano. At the ridge, two cylinders are connected and constitute one cylinder, which is homotopy equivalent to a ring again. This situation continues to the summit of the central cone. At the summit, the top of the cylinder is closed and becomes an object that is homotopy equivalent to a disk. These changes are shown in Table 1. In the table, the fundamental groups are also depicted.

Morse theory gives a set of the fundamental groups of a manifold. The fundamental groups are the most basic properties of the manifold. Even when the manifold is topologically morphed, the fundamental groups do not change. As a set of fundamental groups is determined only by the critical points, it is worthwhile to allocate the critical points of the mountain at the beginning. The basic property determined at the beginning is preserved in the process of creating the curves and the surfaces. As a fundamental group gives a homotopy-equivalent cell, a set of the fundamental groups also shows how the manifold is constructed using the cells.

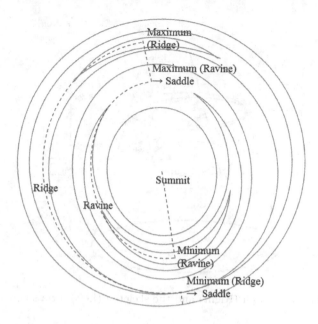

Fig. 9. A summit, a ridge, a ravine and contours for a somma volcano

3.6 Reeb Graphs

A Reeb graph is defined as follows. Let $f : \mathcal{M} \to \mathbb{R}$ be a real valued function defined on a compact manifold $\mathcal{M}$. The Reeb graph of f is the quotient space of f in $\mathcal{M} \times \mathbb{R}$ by the equivalence relation

$$(p_1, f(p_1)) \sim (p_2, f(p_2)), \tag{12}$$

if and only if, $f(p_1) = f(p_2)$, and p_1 and p_2 belong to the same connected component of $f^{-1}(f(p_1))$.

Consider making a Reeb graph for the mountain of Figure 8. Suppose that the ridge of the somma volcano and the ravine of the caldera are horizontal circles. That is, the height is the same at any point of the ridge. It is the same for the ravine. To provide a slope to the ridge and the ravine, the mountain is slightly slanted to the front right. As shown in Figure 9, the ridge and the ravine provide the maximum points at the front and the minimum points at the back, respectively. The contour lying at the minimum point of the ridge or the maximum point of the ravine becomes a closed double-point curve, which crosses at the minimum or maximum point, respectively. Therefore, these points constitute saddles. The minimum point of the ravine is a bottom and the maximum point of the ridge is a summit.

For the slanted mountain, consider making a Reeb graph. As all the points on a connected contour are equivalent each other, the representative point is selected among them. The Reeb graph for the mountain is shown at the right hand side of Figure 10. The obtained Reeb graph is composed by three line

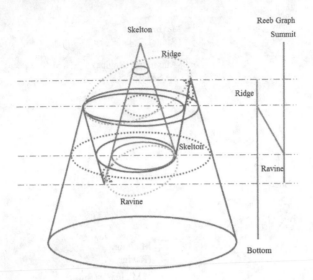

Fig. 10. The Reeb graph (Right) and the skeleton (Left) for a somma volcano

segments. One line segment represents the outline of the somma volcano, which ranges from the bottom of the mountain to the maximum point of the ridge. Another line segment shows the outline of the central cone, which ranges from the minimum point of the ravine to the top of the central cone. The last line segment represents the outline of the caldera, which ranges from the maximum point of the ravine to the minimum point of the ridge.

Now, we will consider finding the 0-dimensional, the 1-dimensional and the 2-dimensional skeletons from the Reeb graph. Utilizing an end point or a junction of the Reeb graph, we can find the critical point, which is an element of the 0-dimensional skeleton. For each end point or a junction, we can also find its contour, which is an element of the 1-dimensional skeleton. From these critical points and the principal contours, the 1-demensional skeleton is obtained as shown in the left-hand side of Figure 10, where a solid line segment is a component of the 1-dimensional skeleton. A dotted line is a ridge, a ravine or an auxiliary contour, which is used to obtain a surface, an element of the 2-dimensional skeleton.

Table 2 shows the number of contours and its homotopy fundamental group. The homotopy structure of the mountain changes at the maximum and minimum points of the ridge and the ravine. The maximum point of the ridge has the same property as a summit. The minimum point of the ridge and the maximum point of the ravine have the same property as a saddle. The minimum point of the ravine has the same property as a bottom.

In the previous discussion, it is explained how to make a Reeb graph from the contours surrounding the manifold and how to find the principal contours among them. However, our method for the automatic landscape generation from the critical points uses the Reeb graph in an opposite way so that the Reeb graph generates contours. It is required that the generated contours are adequate to

Table 2. A Reeb graph and invariants

Critical Points (Invariants)		Contours (Invariants)	
		Number	Fundamental Group
Summit		1	0
		1	$\mathbb{Z}$
Ridge	Maximum	2	$0 \sqcup \mathbb{Z}$
		2	$\mathbb{Z} \sqcup \mathbb{Z}$
	Minimum	2	$2\mathbb{Z} \sqcup \mathbb{Z}$
		3	$\mathbb{Z} \sqcup \mathbb{Z} \sqcup \mathbb{Z}$
Ravine	Maximum	2	$\mathbb{Z} \sqcup 2\mathbb{Z}$
		2	$\mathbb{Z} \sqcup \mathbb{Z}$
	Minimum	2	$\mathbb{Z} \sqcup 0$
		1	$\mathbb{Z}$
Bottom		1	0

form a mountain. The generation rules are determined as follows. 1) An upper contour is surrounded by a lower contour on the somma volcano and the central cone. 2) An upper contour surrounds a lower contour on the caldera volcano.

3.7   Generating Contours at Critical Points

Principal contours are obtained from the Reeb graph. As the Reeb graph is composed by branches, contours are generated by tracing the branches. When a new branch is found, simple closed curves are provided as contours around the three end points of the branch and a closed double-point curves are provided as a contour at the junction of the branch. The relation of the contours provided for the new branch is determined by its structure. When a branch is a Y shape, there are two cases.

1. The junction shows the minimal point of a ridge. Both sides of the ridge ascend to separate summits. At the junction, a closed double-point curve, whose shape resembles 8, is provided. Around each upper end point, a simple closed curve is provided so that it is surrounded by one of loops of the closed double-point curve. Around the lower end point, a simple closed curve is provided so that it surrounds the closed double-point curve. An example is a two peak mountain as shown in Figure 11.
2. The junction shows the maximum point of a ravine. Both sides of the ravine descend to the same ravine bottom. At the junction, a closed double-point curve, where one loop is enclosed by another loop, is provided. The area between the two loops constitutes a hole such as a caldera. Around the upper end points, two simple closed curves are provided. One curve is surrounded by the other curve. The outer curve also surrounds the double-point curve.

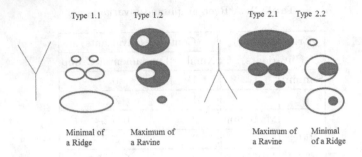

Type 1.1   Type 1.2   Type 2.1   Type 2.2

Minimal of   Maximum of   Maximum of   Minimal
a Ridge   a Ravine   a Ravine   of a Ridge

Fig. 11. Junctions and their contours (A contour covered by the gray area is descending)

The inner curve is surrounded by the inner loop of the double closed curve. Around the lower end, which may be a ravine, a simple closed curve is provided so that it is included in the area between the two loops of the double point curve. An example is the ravine that appears in a somma volcano as shown in Figure 11.

When a branch is a reversed Y shape, it is explained as a dual to the above situation.

1. The junction shows the maximum point of a ravine. This is opposite to the first case of a Y shape. Both sides of the ridge descend to separate ravine bottoms as shown in Figure 11.
2. The junction shows the maximum point of a ridge. Both sides of the ridge ascend to the same summit. This is opposite to the second case of a Y shape. An example is the ridge that appears in a somma volcano as shown in Figure 11. Another example is a hole in the middle surface of a mountain.

A contour around a top (bottom) end point is called a top (bottom) contour. A contour that is ascending (descendig) is called an ascending (descending) contour. When two branches are connected, both contours at the connected point are either ascending or descending. One of them is a top contour and the other a bottom contour. Using this rule, the type of a branch is determined by the depth search algorithm. An example is shown in Figure 12. Two summits, one ravine bottom and two saddles are allocated by the user. The system finds two branches and creates a Reeb graph. Using the Reeb graph, the system determines the type of each branch. Finally, the descending bottom contour of the left branch and the descending top contour of the right branch are merged together. The principal contours obtained here are further used to create auxiliary contours. The contours generated here are the same as ones of a somma volcano.

4   The Experimental System

Before developing a practical system for drawing a general landscape, an experimental system for drawing the landscape of a mountain has been developed using

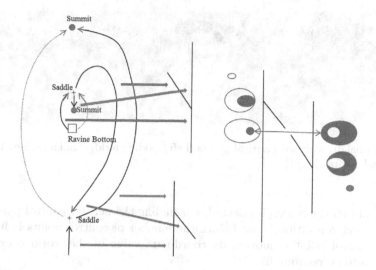

Fig. 12. Contours are generated from the Reeb graph

a desk top computer instead of a tablet. To shorten development time, Ruby and OpenGL is utilized. The shape of a mountain is drawn by NURBS curves and surfaces. At the first stage, a user allocates invariants such as summits, ravine bottoms and saddles and adjusts their heights, while the system automatically generates a closed contour around a summit and a ravine bottom. The system also creates a closed double-point contour for a saddle where the contour crosses at the saddle. Furthermore, the system generates auxiliary fine contours that support to draw ridges and ravines. By pushing or pulling contours, a ridge or a ravine is configured.

In OpenGL, three kinds of coordinate systems exist: a local coordinate system that is given to an object, the world coordinate system that is given to allocate the object in the world system, and the screen coordinate system that projects the object to the screen. By changing the position of the object, or moving or rotating the object in the world coordinate system, the objects can be observed from any direction. When using a tablet, an object can be moved or rotated by the operation of moving or rotating the tablet itself. In the experimental system, these operations are carried out using a mouse. In OpenGL, a transformation from the local coordinate system to the world coordinate system is defined by *Modelview* matrix and one from the world coordinate system to the screen coordinate system is operated by *Projection* matrix.

When drawing a ridge or ravine, the mountain is possibly moved and rotated so that a user can easily draw it. By pushing or pulling contours, a ridge or ravine is drawn. As OpenGL does not provide interpolation points that lie on a contour, control points are instead used in the experimental system. Therefore, by moving a control point, the contour is pushed or pulled. To let the mouse move a control point, the system has to make the point of mouse correspond to a control point. When the right side button of a mouse is clicked, the nearest

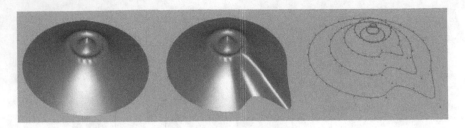

Fig. 13. Initial drawing with critical points (Left), adding a ridge and a ravine (Middle) and control points (Right)

control point on the screen is selected. For finding the nearest control points, an exhaust search algorithm is used since the number of control points is limited. When a control point is moved, its coordinate value of the world coordinate system has to be computed.

In general, a point (wx, wy, wz) of the world coordinate system is transformed to the point (mx, my, mz) of the screen coordinate system using $Modelview$ matrix M and $Projection$ matrix P as follows.

$$[mx \ my \ mz \ 1] = [wx \ wy \ wz \ 1]PM \tag{13}$$

where dz is the depth of the z coordinate. The depth is used not to display hidden surfaces or curves since many points may be projected into the same point in the screen coordinate system. By moving the mouse, the control point moves to a new point (mx', my'). By this movement, the depth is also changed. Assuming that it becomes dz' and the new point is located at (wx', wy', wz') in the world coordinate system. As the new point lies on the same contour, $wz' = wz$. Therefore, wx' and wy' are obtained by the following expression.

$$[wx' \ wy' \ wz \ 1] = [mx' \ my' \ dz' \ 1]M^{-1}P^{-1} \tag{14}$$

In OpenGL, the point is further transformed by $Viewport$. It is related to the size and the position of the screen. At the above expression, $Viewport$ is neglected since it is not essential. The left-hand side of Figure13 shows the initial drawing where critical points for summits and ravine bottom are defined and the middle of Figure13 does the final drawing where ridges and ravines are provided. The right-hand side of Figure 13 shows the NURBS curves and their control points.

The left-hand side of Figure 14 shows another example, where two summits and one saddle are defined. Firstly, the critical points are defined by a user. In this case, two summits and a saddle are defined. The contours around the summits are automatically provided by the system. Also, the contour crossing at the saddle is also provided. The skeleton of this mountain is shown at the middle of Figure 14. There are three branches in the Reeb Graph. One branch represents the bottom area of the mountain and the other two line segments the two peaks. The three branches are connected at the saddle. Along with the

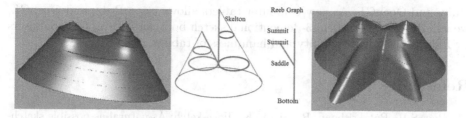

Fig. 14. A two-peak mountain (Left), the skeleton and the Reeb graph (Middle) and a ridge and a ravine (Right)

skeleton, contours that will be generated by the system are depicted. The right-hand side of Figure 14 shows a picture after the user draws ridges and ravines. By drowning these ridges and ravines, the summits and the saddles are not affected since these points are invariants.

1. Control points are used to draw ridges and ravines in the experimental system. However, as these points do not lie on a contour, a user feels uncomfortable in an indirect way of drawing. Interpolation points that lie on a contour are more desirable for direct and comfortable drawing.
2. When drawing ridges and ravines, it is desirable that the length of these curves is determined not by pushing or pulling control or interpolation points but by the speed or pressure of drawing for giving comfortable user interface.

5 Conclusions

Mathematical backgrounds for designing 3-dimensional sketch book have been discussed. A user is only required allocating summits, ravine bottoms and saddles and drawing ridges and ravines by pulling and pushing automatically generated contours. Based on user supplied data, the landscape image is presented. If it is not satisfactory, the user supply less important critical points and curves until a satisfactory image is obtained.

The method for generating a landscape image is based on mathematics. A mountain, which is handled in this paper as an example of landscapes, is represented as a manifold. The manifold is characterized by critical points, ridges and ravines. These characteristic entities are utilized to create a series of skeletons, filtration, which gives a series of approximation of a mountain. The roughest skeleton is created from the critical pints. The second roughest skeleton is generated from the characteristic curves and the critical points. By repeating this process, a 2-dimensional skeleton is created and rendered to obtain its image. Morse theory gives the mathematical foundation to the roughest skeleton. A Reeb graph gives the mathematical foundation to the second roughest skeleton. The 2-dimensional skeleton is based on NURBS curves.

The experimental system has been developed based on the above mathematical backgrounds. Usefulness of the mathematical backgrounds is clarified through the experimental system. The experimental system has been developed using

Ruby and OpenGL. As new computer tablets allows using Ruby and OpenGL, we will develop a practical 3-dementional sketch book for non-professional users by fully utilizing the mobility and handiness of tablets.

References

1. Bae, S.H., Balakrishnan, R., Singh, K.: Ilovesketch: As-natural-as-possible sketching system for creating 3d curve models. In: Proc. ACM Symp. User Interface Software and Technology (UIST 2008), pp. 151–160 (October 2008)
2. Bae, S.H., Balakrishnan, R., Singh, K.: Everybodylovessketch: 3d sketching for a broader audience. In: Proc. ACM Symp. User Interface Software and Technology (UIST 2009), pp. 59–68 (October 2009)
3. Bah, T.: Inkscape: Guide to a Vector Drawing Program. Prentice Hall, Boston (2011)
4. Brixius, L.: Google SketchUp Workshop: Modeling, Visualizing, and Illustrating. Focal Press, Burlington (2010)
5. Cheng, R.K.: Inside Rhinoceros 4. Thomson/Delmar Learning, Clifton Park, NY (2007)
6. Dodson, C., Parker, P.E.: A User's Guide to Algebraic Topology. Kluwer Academic Pub., Boston (1997)
7. Fomenko, A.T., Kunii, T.L.: Topological Modeling for Visualization. Springer, New York (1998)
8. Glitschka, V.R.: Vector Basic Training: A Systematic Creative Process for Building Precision Vector Artwork. New Riders, Berkeley (2011)
9. Kunii, T.L.: Valid computational shape modeling: Design and implementation, pp. 123–133 (December 1999)
10. Morse, M.: The calculus of variations in the large. American Mathematical Society Colloquium Publication 18, 173–188 (1934)
11. Reeb, G.: On the singular points of a completely integrable pfaff form or of a numerical function. Comptes Randus Acad. Sciences Paris 222, 847–849 (1946)
12. Sieradski, A.J.: An introduction to topology and homotopy. PWS-Kent Publishing Company, Boston (1992)
13. Spanier, E.H.: Algebraic topology. Springer, New York (1966)
14. Takahashi, S., Ikeda, T., Shinagawa, Y., Kunii, T.L., Ueda, M.: Algorithms for extracting correct critical points and constructing topological graphs from discrete geographical elevation data. Computer Graphics Forum 14, 181–192 (1995)
15. Tu, R.W.: An Introduction to Manifolds, 2nd edn. Springer, New York (2010)

Image-Based Virtual Palpation

Shamima Yasmin and Alexei Sourin

Nanyang Technological University, Singapore
{syasmin,assourin}@ntu.edu.sg

Abstract. In this paper, we propose a new approach to virtual abdominal palpation. Firstly, we describe palpation as a medical procedure. Then, we analyze the necessity of virtual palpation. Next, we present our survey on the existing work on virtual palpation. Then, we propose a new image-driven function-based approach to virtual palpation to address the weakness of the previous works. Lastly, we discuss the advantages of our method over other existing works.

Keywords: Palpation, respiration, virtual reality, haptic device, function based, haptic interaction point.

1   Introduction

Palpation is a medical investigation performed by pressing fingers on a particular part of a patient's body to locate abnormalities of internal organs. Palpation is mainly used for detection of painful areas in the patient's body, swelling of organs, or presence of tumors inside the organs. Palpation is widely used by chiropractors, physical therapists and massage therapists to assess muscle tenderness, stiffness, elasticity, quality of joints of bones, etc. Palpation can be light or deep [1]. Light palpation is usually done by one hand. Deep palpation is used to find out abnormalities inside the body. Both hands then may be engaged to exert pressure on the area of interest.

Medical students need a long practice to learn palpation, while there are rather limited possibilities of obtaining these skills. Regular medical palpation training is mostly based on observing the instructor or working with dummy patients. However actual palpation is a dynamic and versatile procedure. Therefore, haptic interaction with a simulated human body in a virtual space can be very helpful. With a haptic device, a medical trainee would be able to palpate the virtual body, which could be more flexible, realistic and scalable than dummies. Haptic devices would allow the trainee to feel force feedback between the virtual palm and virtual tissues in 3D virtual modeling space while assessing properties of any particular organ, i.e., malignant or normal. Also, different physical properties, such as muscle elasticity, skin tenderness, etc., can be attributed to different virtual patients according to their age and gender, giving eventually practically unlimited sets of educational cases. This virtual training may therefore efficiently augment the actual training on real patients in medical clinics.

M.L. Gavrilova et al. (Eds.): Trans. on Comput. Sci. XVIII, LNCS 7848, pp. 61–80, 2013.
© Springer-Verlag Berlin Heidelberg 2013

2   Background

Research and development works on virtual palpation have been carried out since early nineties. Virtual palpation can be classified by a number of contact points between the virtual body and the haptic device as *single point palpation* and *multiple point palpation*.

Single point palpation is carried out by representing a fingertip/palm as a point in a virtual space, which is called Haptic Interaction Point (HIP). As the fingertip/palm is reduced to a virtual point, the position and orientation of the point give the position and orientation of the palm or the fingertip. Some early work on single point palpation were carried out using the PHANTOM haptic interface which provided real time force feedback to the trainees index finger [2]. Here, the handle of a 3 DOF Phantom desktop device was replaced with a thimble-gimbal where a trainee's index finger was inserted in. Early works were carried out in a much simpler environment where rotation and torque of the virtual point had not been addressed. Later, Chen et al. [3] used volumetric tetrahedral mass spring model to simulate different kinds of tissues, i.e., skin, muscle, ligament, bone, etc., but they did not address palpation of inner organs. Ullrich et al. [4] developed multi-object algorithm for pulsation simulation.

Meanwhile, Virtual Haptic Back simulator [5] was developed to give to the trainee the feeling of touching human vertebrae. Two Phantom 3.0 devices were used, each having three degrees of freedom. By using both hands, a particular vertebrae stiffness and tenderness could be examined. A layered haptic model was used with different spring stiffness, which let the trainee feel the skin and underlying tissue on his/her way to touching the vertebrae.

To give the impression of using multiple fingertips, instead of generating a number of HIPs from different haptic devices, *multiple contact points* need to be generated from a single haptic device, which can be mounted on a virtual palm. At first, haptic data gloves were used for virtual palpation with a number of key-points, which had a very little capacity of exerting pressure [6]. They were only able to detect some key points of the fingers while a virtual object could be hold or deformed at those contact points. Data gloves, like Rutgers Master I, were used for position measurement [7]. Rutgers Master II was later developed to generate better force feedback [8]. Rutgers Master II consisted of custom pneumatic cylinders extending from a palm-mounted platform to the fingertips. Each finger in Rutgers Master II was given four degrees of freedom with three flexions/extensions and one adduction/abduction. Contact forces were simulated at the fingertips, and different tissues were deformed locally under different fingertips. Rutgers Master II was used for detecting tumors, as well as for palpation with a variable number of input fingers.

In order to give more realistic simulation of touching with human fingers, Haptic Interface Robot (HIRO) was developed and described in [9, 10]. HIRO II consisted of five fingers, each having three DOF. Fingers were mounted on a wrist having three DOF. The first DOF of the wrist was controlling the forearm supination/pronation, the second DOF was used for the wrist flexion/extension, and the third DOF was assigned for the wrist abduction/adduction. The wrist was connected to a robot arm. HIRO considered deformation caused by multiple fingers contacting the surface and the interaction between the forces exerted by all contact points. HIRO had reportedly been used to detect tumor in a haptic immersive environment [11].

Haptic Interface Area was considered to generate distributed pressure (tactile information) that occurs in real world between the surface of the hand and the skin [12]. Here, a single point in a thimble-gimbal had been replaced with a number of pins in a small area at the finger tips to give the illusion of surface. All contact points from the pins generated spring forces, which interacted with virtual organ with constant spring stiffness. It has been reported that due to its large contact area, Haptic Interface Area (HIA) can detect tumor more readily than HIP.

An abdominal palpation haptic device, consisted of sphygmomanometer bladder as the haptic interface, was developed for colonoscopy simulation where the bladder pressure can be regulated [13]. Integration of haptics with augmented reality allows the users to feel a virtual patient with their own hands [14, 15, 16].

We found some shortcomings in the existing projects. Most of the virtual palpation works are dealing with detecting tumors in a particular organ, i.e., liver, breast, prostate, etc. The real palpation is not only done for detecting tumors but also for determining:

- how different a malignant organ feels from a normal organ;
- whether a malignant organ is more elastic than a normal organ;
- whether the organ has become enlarged due to prolonged inflammation or it has been displaced from its original position;
- whether the abdominal wall feels more elastic when a particular organ becomes inflamed;
- how different and less elastic an old patient's abdomen feels than that of a young patient, etc.

It would be an advantage if a medical trainee could toggle between a normal and a malignant organ to feel the difference between them. The trainee may need to examine different types of malignancy for the same organ. The trainee may also need to differentiate the feeling according to the age and the gender of the patient. It is difficult to obtain different real-life polygonal models of different organs, each showing all different types of malignant characteristics and properties.

In the previous works, force feedback for palpation was generated by colliding with the primitives, i.e., triangles or quads forming the polygonal models. When the data size becomes large, the number of primitives can exceed a number, above which haptic devices fail to update at an interactive rate. Large polygonal models also prevent from making web-enabled and collaborative distributed software. We address these issues in the following sections.

3   Proposed Approach in Brief

The implementation of the proposed approach required us to generate visual and haptic feedback from the abdominal portion of the patient's body. At the same time, haptic force feedback needs to be generated from the underlying internal organs. In our approach, any 3D polygonal modeling has been avoided.

Firstly, a 2D image of the patient generates visual feedback which is further enhanced to produce 3D visual effect. Secondly, the 2D body-image plane needs to be augmented with haptic data so that the displayed body feels three-dimensional. We also need to have some haptically defined internal organs which can be perceived inside the image-guided haptic body while exerting pressure on the abdominal area. We identify a suitable function-based modeling technique to haptically define the human body and the internal organs. Thirdly, our basic image-driven approach has been combined with the function-based modeling to simulate abdominal deformation and respiratory simulation. Lastly, overall visual and haptic feedback has been combined to simulate palpation in virtual space.

Each of the above mentioned modules will be further detailed in the following sections.

4   Visual Feedback from the Patient's Body

Virtual patient is displayed by mapping a photograph of the patient onto the xy-plane located in the virtual space. Hence, the depth of the patient's body is going along the negative z-axis. Figure 1 shows the image of the patient lying on an examination bank. The position of haptic device tool is displayed as a 3D model of a hand located above the image of the patient. The virtual hand has 6 DOF controlled by the haptic device (three directions of displacements and three rotations, i.e., roll, pitch, and yaw).

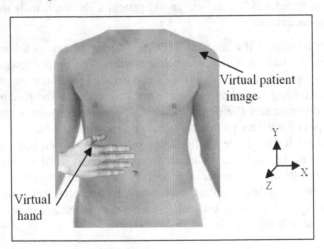

Fig. 1. Virtual hand and body

When the virtual hand is touching the surface of the image plane, visual deformation will take place. Since the deformation of the abdominal area of the patients body with the doctor's hand is local, not very deep, partially covered by the hand, and happens with the pressure exerted vertically down or sideways, it can be successfully simulated without going to full 3D modeling of the body. This is performed by subdividing the image of the patient into a regular grid of 2D cells with corner grid points fixed. As the virtual palm touches the body image plane, a sub-grid is formed within the main gridded image plane where the grid point nearest to the virtual palm is considered as the center sub-grid point. Figure 2 shows the gridded body image plane, the HIP and the formation of a sub-grid (marked with red line) as the HIP touches the image plane.

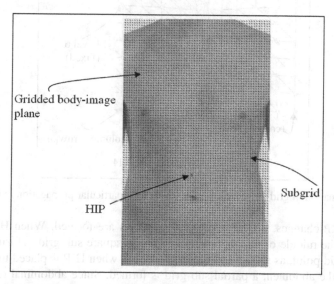

Fig. 2. The gridded body image plane, the HIP and the formation of the sub-grid as the HIP touches the image plane

The sub-grid points surrounding the center grid point are selected according to the propagation radius. For a propagation radius of value 'n', a $(2n + 1) \times (2n + 1)$ sub-grid is created and the propagation takes place in $(n+1)$ tiers. The center grid point is given the maximum amount of displacement, which is determined by the position of the virtual palm and is considered as 'Level 1' displacement. Its immediate neighboring eight grid points are considered to be displaced at 'Level 2'. With the information on the relocation of the center vertex, the displacement required for each grid point at different levels is calculated using a weighted propagation. The neighbors of the 'Level 2' grid points, which have not yet been considered, are selected as 'Level 3' grid points. Grid points at 'Level $n+1$' form the bordering grid points and are given zero displacement. A displacement at each level takes place along the direction of the proxy touch normal. The higher the level of grid points, the lower is the amount of displacement. Figure 3 shows the formation of a sub-grid with propagation radius '5'. The corresponding deformation of grid points at different levels for a particular position and direction of HIP has been shown. For ease of visualization, all sub-grid points at a particular level have been marked with the same color.

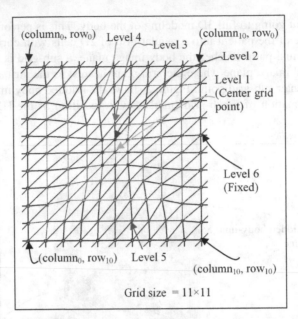

Fig. 3. Deformation of grid points at different levels for a particular propagation radius, i.e., '5'

As the HIP changes, different sub-grid windows are formed. When HIP is positioned near the middle of the abdomen, a complete square sub-grid is formed around the center grid point, as shown in Figure 2, whereas when HIP is placed to the left or the right of the abdomen, a partial sub-grid is formed. Since abdominal deformation depends on the underlying internal organs and their physical properties, more on abdominal deformation will be discussed after discussing the modeling of the internal organs.

5   Haptic Feedback Simulation

In our virtual palpation method, all haptic models have been defined in terms of implicit mathematical functions. Models representing sphere, ellipse, elliptical supercylinder, etc., can be represented by some pre-defined mathematical functions. On the other hand, in order to construct models of any arbitrary shape, so-called blobby function can be used [17]. Each blob can be defined as follows

$$f_i = e^{-\sqrt{(s_{xi}x-x_i)^2+(s_{yi}y-y_i)^2+(s_{zi}z-z_i)^2}} \tag{1}$$

where s_{xi}, s_{yi} and s_{zi} are inverse scaling factors along x, y and z direction, and x_i, y_i and z_i define the coordinates of the center of the blob. A solid haptic organ model made of several blobs is then defined as the following FRep function [18]:

$$F = k_1f_1 + k_2f_2 + \ldots\ldots\ldots + k_nf_n - c \geq 0 \tag{2}$$

where $k_1....k_n$ are overall scaling factors determining the size of each blob, $f_1 .... f_n$ are individual blobby functions, and 'c' defines a threshold for the tangible surface of the model. In Figure 4, a human liver model has been constructed with four blobs.

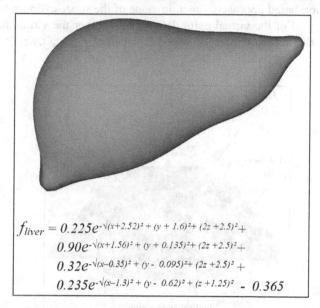

$$f_{liver} = 0.225e^{-\sqrt{(x+2.52)^2 + (y + 1.6)^2 + (2z +2.5)^2}} +$$
$$0.90e^{-\sqrt{(x+1.56)^2 + (y + 0.135)^2 + (2z +2.5)^2}} +$$
$$0.32e^{-\sqrt{(x-0.35)^2 + (y - 0.095)^2 + (2z +2.5)^2}} +$$
$$0.235e^{-\sqrt{(x-1.3)^2 + (y - 0.62)^2 + (z +1.25)^2}} - 0.365$$

Fig. 4. A human liver model has been constructed with four blobs

We have used the function-based FRep approach [18] for modeling internal organs to avoid calculation of collision detection with a large number of triangles or quads in commonly used 3D polygonal models. The HIP with coordinates x_i, y_i and z_i will be considered located inside the organ if the respective evaluated function is greater than zero. It is on the surface of the model if the function value is zero, and outside the organ model if it is negative.

If organs can be defined in terms of blobs, they can be easily deformed or scaled in various directions by adjusting their scaling parameters. Efficient Boolean operations (union, difference or intersection) can also be performed on the function-based models to carve out different human organs [18].

5.1   Haptic Feedback from the Patient's Body

When the virtual hand is pressing the surface of the image, the elastic force feedback has to be rendered. In order to produce realistic effect of sliding of the virtual palm over a virtual body, an invisible model of a haptic elliptical super-cylinder is wrapped around the body-image plane (Figure 5). This elliptical super cylinder represents the virtual human abdomen and its functional representation is as follows:

$$f_{abdomen}(x, y, z) = \left(\frac{x}{a}\right)^6 + \left(\frac{y}{b}\right)^6 + \left(\frac{z}{c}\right)^6 - 1 \geq 0 \qquad (3)$$

The functionally defined elliptical super-cylinder closely resembles a human abdomen in shape as it is flat and its corners are blunt and smooth. Hence, if properly haptically defined, the elliptical super-cylinder can replicate human abdomen in virtual space. With our function-based approach, function value of the super-cylinder for a particular position (x, y, z) of the virtual palm determines whether the virtual hand touches the surface of the super-cylinder or not, i.e., whether $f_{abdomen}(x,y,z) \geq 0$ or $f_{abdomen}(x,y,z) < 0$.

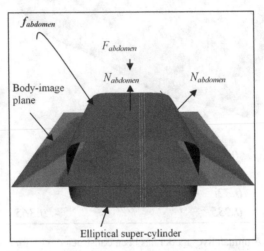

Fig. 5. An invisible elliptical super-cylinder is wrapped around the patient image plane to replicate 3D virtual body

If the virtual hand touches the super-cylinder, an initial location of the HIP is generated. This is shown as $P_{initial\ HIP}$ in Figure 6(a) for a particular iteration of virtual palpation. The corresponding nearest point (center grid point) on the image plane is marked as 'P', as shown in Figure 6(b). In Figure 6(a), while exerting pressure, a certain location of the current HIP has been marked as $P_{current\ HIP}$. This moves the center grid point P to P' (Figure 6(c)). Thus, as the virtual palm becomes interactive with the haptic abdomen, a corresponding deflection of the image plane takes place.

The abdominal elastic force $F_{abdomen}$ is simulated with respect to $P_{initial\ HIP}$ along the direction of the surface normal of the super-cylinder. The surface normal of the super cylinder is computed at $P_{initial\ HIP}$. The surface normal is defined by the gradient or the first derivative of the function $f_{abdomen}(x, y, z) \geq 0$ and it is represented as $\nabla f_{abdomen}(x, y, z)$ where

$$\nabla f_{abdomen}(x, y, z) = \frac{\partial f_{abdomen}}{\partial x} + \frac{\partial f_{abdomen}}{\partial y} + \frac{\partial f_{abdomen}}{\partial z} \qquad (4)$$

defines the surface normal at any point (x, y, z). The magnitude of the abdominal elastic force $F_{abdomen}$ increases with the depth of penetration inside the body. As the abdominal wall tissue feels soft, this elastic force is given a very little stiffness so that the tenderness of the abdominal wall can be perceived.

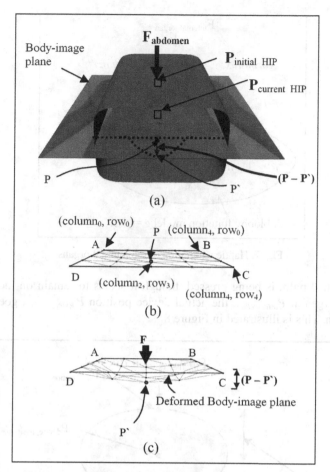

Fig. 6. Visual deformations following the haptic interaction

5.2   Haptic Simulation of the Internal Organs

While the virtual hand is being pressed against the super-cylinder, internal organs are encountered through the soft haptic abdomen. For haptic simulation of the internal organs defined in terms of functions, the function value of the model for a particular HIP location is calculated. If the function value is greater than zero, the current HIP is considered inside the organ and the force feedback for that particular organ is simulated. Figure 7 illustrates haptic simulation of an internal organ defined by function $g = f(x, y, z) \geq 0$. The elastic force $F_{internal\ organ}$ is simulated along the normal at the intersection point $P_{intersection}$ on the surface, as shown in the figure. For a particular ray cast from point P_{start} towards point P_{end}, the intersection point $P_{intersection}$ is approximated through several iterations by the method of binary subdivision. The surface normal at the intersection point is calculated from the first derivative of the function model, as described in the previous subsection.

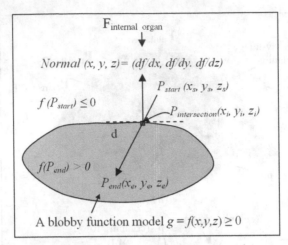

Fig. 7. Haptic simulation of the internal organs

As the virtual palm is being pressed, though it seems to remain on the surface of the internal organ at $P_{intersection}$, the actual device position $P_{device\_position}$ goes down inside the organ. This is illustrated in Figure 8.

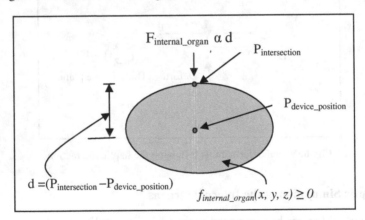

Fig. 8. Elastic force feedback simulation by the internal organs

In Figure 8, it is shown that the actual device position $P_{device\_position}$ goes directly below the surface of the organ. The difference between the position of the virtual palm and the device position generates the elastic force with respect to the intersection point $P_{intersection}$. Hence the magnitude of $F_{internal\ organ}$ is calculated proportionally to the difference between $P_{intersection}$ and the actual device position $P_{device\_position}$ inside the organ. Hence, $F_{internal\ organ}$ can be defined as follows:

$$F_{internal\_organ} = k_{internal\_organ} \bullet (P_{intersection} - P_{device\_position}) \qquad (5)$$

where $k_{internal\_organ}$ represents the stiffness of the internal organs. To model different internal organs haptically, we need to set different values for k.

5.3   Popping through Prevention

While continuously pressing the abdomen with a virtual hand, pop-through effect can
take place if the depth of the internal organ is small and generated haptic force feedback is comparatively low. In order to alleviate this effect, the internal organ models
need some modification. At first, the internal organs are generated as shown in Figure
9(a). Here, the original model of a human liver is generated by a blobby function f_{liver}.
Then, each generated organ is extruded in the direction from its center and orthogonal
to the image of the patient's body. As the original image is mapped onto the xy-plane,
the extrusion is done along the negative z-axis. This generates a hollow tube-like
structure with a constant cross section. In Figure 9(b), the liver model has been extruded. Hence the final model of the liver is constructed as a union of two objects: the
original model of the liver defined by f_{liver} and the extrusion function of the original
model inside the virtual body defined as $f_{extrusion}$, as shown in Figure 9(c). The union
of the two functions is defined with function 'max', while the intersection – with
function 'min' [18]. Thus the final model of the liver is a combination of both functions, which can be calculated as follows:

$$f_{liver\_fina\ l} = max(f_{liver}, f_{extrusion}) \geq 0 \qquad (6)$$

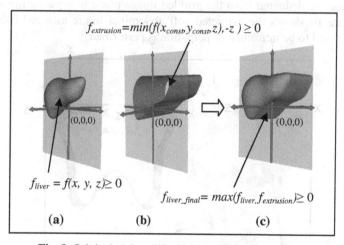

Fig. 9. Original and modified blobby model of the liver

6   Combining Image-Based and Function-Based Modeling

This section discusses further enhancement of the 2D image plane with the help of the
function-based modeling. Any kind of visual deformation simulation of the visible
part of the patient's body depends a great deal on the positioning, shape and physical
properties of the underlying internal organs. For example, if ribcage is encountered
while palpating with a virtual palm, no further deformation of the skin takes place as
the ribcage feels hard and stiff and does not let the virtual palm probe further. On the

other hand, soft abdominal tissues produce noticeable visible deformation while prob-ing them with the virtual palm. Again, during respiration, the portion of the body comprising ribcage moves forward and backward when breathing in and out, respec-tively. In order to simulate respiration, the 2D image plane needs to be augmented with proper visual and haptic feedback. The following two subsections discuss abdo-minal deformation and respiration simulation during palpation, respectively.

6.1   Abdominal Deformation Simulation

For abdominal deformation simulation, firstly, we need to identify and separate the abdominal portion in the image. Soft abdominal portion is extracted from the gridded body-image plane. This is performed with the help of a functionally defined ribcage. A blobby model of a ribcage is defined by a function $f_{ribcage}(x, y, z) \geq 0$, as shown in Figure 8. Then, the ribcage is properly positioned on the xy-image plane, and it is projected onto it. A ribcage model projected onto the xy-plane is defined in terms of function as $f_{ribcage}(x, y) \geq 0$. The intersected portion of the ribcage with the gridded image plane is separated by calculating the function value of the grid points for $f_{ribcage}(x, y) \geq 0$. If the function value of any grid point is greater than zero for $f_{ribcage}(x, y) \geq 0$, then that grid point lies inside the ribcage. Then, the grid points form-ing the ribcage are deducted from the gridded image plane to separate the abdominal portion. Figure 10 shows the extracted soft abdominal tissue as a red-colored grid, which is supposed to be deformed as palpation is performed.

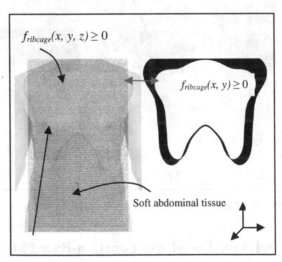

Fig. 10. Extraction of soft abdominal portion from the gridded image

All grid points, except those forming the deformable abdomen area, are considered fixed. Hence, the sub-grid points, which form the ribcage, are also considered fixed. As the force is applied on the abdominal wall, the center grid point follows the virtual palm while the other sub-grid points displace at relatively smaller values according to their distances from the center grid point, as discussed in Section 4. Depending on the position of the virtual palm, complete or partial sub-grid windows are formed. For a particular position of the virtual palm pressing the virtual body, both the deformed grid and the corresponding deformed image (without grid) are shown in Figure 11.

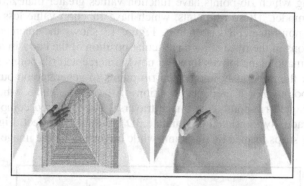

Fig. 11. Deformed grid and the corresponding deformed image during palpation

6.2   Respiration Simulation

Simulation of respiration during palpation has been performed by moving the ribcage forward and back to the normal position as the patient is breathing in and out. Figure 12 (a) shows the position of the ribcage with respect to the body-image plane in the normal position. Both front and side views have been shown in the figure. In normal (breathe-out) position, the ribcage lies behind the body image plane. While breathing in, the ribcage moves forward. This position of the ribcage with respect to normal body image plane is illustrated in Figure 12(b).

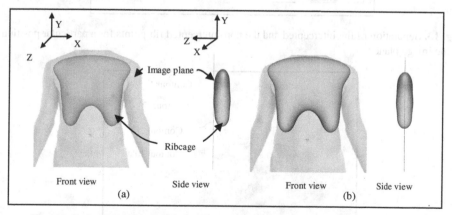

Fig. 12. Deformed grid and the corresponding deformed image during palpation

As the ribcage moves forward while breathing in, we need to wrap the image around the protruding ribcage to simulate 3D effect. In order to do this, grid-points forming the ribcage are extracted from the projection of the grid points onto the *xy*-plane, as illustrated in Figure 10. Then, keeping the position of the protruding ribcage constant, as shown in Figure 12(b), the image plane is gradually moved forward. This translates the z-coordinates of the rib-points along the positive z-direction. For a particular image position, the intercepted rib-points are separated from the original rib-points. This is done by checking which rib-points have function values greater than zero for the protruding ribcage model. Those rib points, which have function value less or equal then zero, are called non-intercepted rib points. Figure 13 shows the intercepted and non-intercepted portions of the ribcage for a particular position of the body-image plane.

Thus, as the image plane moves forward, newly intercepted rib-points are formed by subtraction from the previously intercepted rib-points to generate contour for the non-intercepted rib-points. For a particular position of the image plane, when there is no remaining intercepted rib-points, the image traversal is considered complete. Thus the rib-points are gradually translated to simulate 3D breathing in effect. Figure 14 shows different contour strips formed by rib-points while traversing by the image plane.

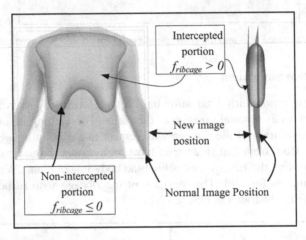

Fig. 13. Separation of the intercepted and the non-intercepted rib-points for a particular position of the image plane

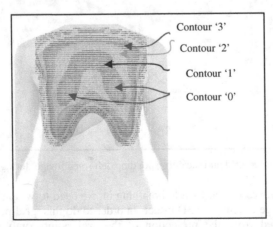

Fig. 14. Formation of different contour strips by rib-points as the image gradually traverses the protruding ribcage

7   Overall Visual and Haptic Feedback Implementation

In virtual space, the haptic models of the organs are placed behind the body-image plane at a distance and with a location consistent with the proper positioning of different internal organs in a human body. Figure 15(a) shows the cross section of the virtual body along its depth. It is shown that the internal organs are placed under the body-image of the patient while a super-cylinder encapsulates the body image as well as the internal organs. Figure 15 (b) shows the cross section along the longitudinal direction of the patient's body, which helps to visualize the internal organs with the semi-transparent body-image plane. In order to simulate realistic palpation, we need to combine this visual effect with the force feedback to get the resultant immersive effect. We have introduced two haptic force feedbacks: one is $F_{internal\ organ}$ directly generated by the internal organs, and the other one comes out from the visible part of the body, i.e., soft skin tissue and abdominal muscle defined as $F_{abdomen}$.

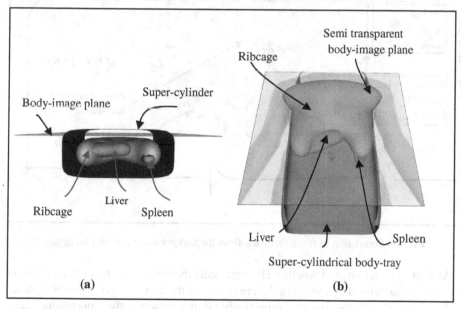

Fig. 15. X-sections of the virtual body along its (a) depth and (b) longitudinal direction

While palpating, soft skin tissue is encountered first. This has been simulated using the built-in effect provided by the Haptic Library API (HLAPI, *http://www.sensable.com/openhaptics-toolkit-hlapi.htm*). As the haptic palm touches the surface of the super-cylinder, a force effect starts along the direction of the surface normal of the super-cylinder. As the palm goes further down, this force effect increases and updates accordingly. As long as no internal organs are encountered while pressing down the abdomen, only the abdominal force $F_{abdomen}$ is active. This has been described in Figure 14. Figure 16 shows a partial cross section of a simplified virtual body along its depth where a functionally defined abdomen encloses a functionally defined organ. It is shown that up to a certain depth, only the force $F_{abdomen}$ remains active and the resultant force F equals to abdominal force $F_{abdomen}$. As any internal organ is encountered, $F_{internal\ organ}$ gets activated. Figure 16 illustrates this case when both abdominal force, as well as the force generated by internal organ, are engaged. A custom shape defined by extended HLAPI has been used for haptic modeling of the internal organs.

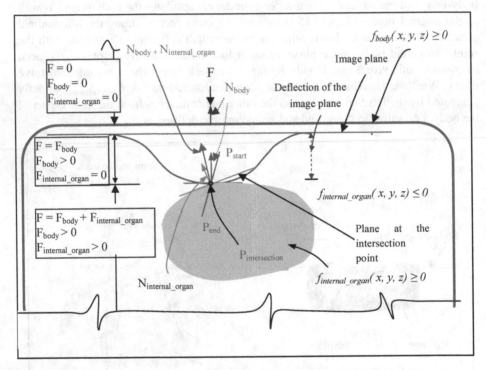

Fig. 16. Simulation of force feedback from the abdomen and the internal organ

At first, it is determined whether HIP intersects the surface of the internal organ or not. This is calculated by checking the previous and the current device position shown as P_{start} and P_{end} in the figure, respectively. If it intersects, the intersection point $P_{intersection}$ and the normal built at it represented by $N_{internal\_organ}$ are calculated. With the help of the intersection point and the surface normal, a plane is generated which passes through the intersection point and whose normal is perpendicular to the surface. Thus, as the virtual palm keeps moving while being pressed on the internal organ, a sequence of planes is returned. This helps to form the so-called "god object" [19] for a functionally-defined shape, which eventually allows the virtual palm slide along the surface of the organs. As the virtual palm touches the internal organ, $F_{internal\ organ}$ becomes active and the resultant force F is calculated as the summation of $F_{abdomen}$ and $F_{internal\ organ}$.

In our design, only one active organ has been considered at a time, which is derived using the set theoretic operations between the functionally defined models, as described in Figure 17. Different stiffness and friction values are assigned to different active organs, as shown in the figure.

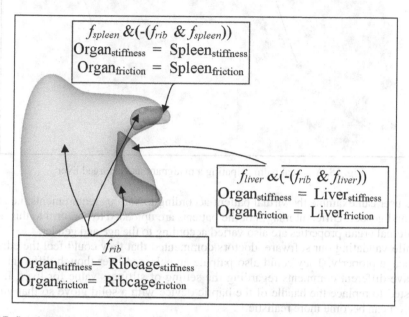

$$f_{spleen} \& (-(f_{rib} \& f_{spleen}))$$
$$\text{Organ}_{stiffness} = \text{Spleen}_{stiffness}$$
$$\text{Organ}_{friction} = \text{Spleen}_{friction}$$

$$f_{liver} \propto (-(f_{rib} \& f_{liver}))$$
$$\text{Organ}_{stiffness} = \text{Liver}_{stiffness}$$
$$\text{Organ}_{friction} = \text{Liver}_{friction}$$

$$f_{rib}$$
$$\text{Organ}_{stiffness} = \text{Ribcage}_{stiffness}$$
$$\text{Organ}_{friction} = \text{Ribcage}_{friction}$$

Fig. 17. Set-theoretic operation is performed among the organs in order to determine the active organ

8   Results

We have implemented a layered haptic model. On the upper half of the body, a rib cage lies just beneath the skin. In the abdominal area, soft abdominal muscles and tissues are located beneath the skin. While assigning haptic properties, we have used a very high stiffness value to represent the bone-like feeling of the rib cage. As the abdominal tissues feel very soft, we model it with a very low stiffness value.

We have tested our virtual abdominal palpation method on two organs: liver and spleen. While modeling the internal organs, we avoided complex definition and design. We have generated any particular model with a maximum number of six blobs. While modeling inflamed organs, scaling factors of the functions used in normal organs were adjusted to replicate the inflammatory case.

In normal case, usually liver and spleen are not palpable while the user can only feel the corners of the rib cage and the soft elastic abdominal tissues. Hence, the internal organs like liver and spleen are given very low elastic value. However, when the organ is inflamed, it can become enlarged, more elastic and palpable.

Figure 18 shows palpation of an enlarged and malignant liver of an adult male patient where a virtual palm is detecting the edge of the liver so that the extent of the enlargement can be determined. The degree of roughness of a malignant organ can also be measured during palpation. A transparent view helps to clarify the position and shape of the organ.

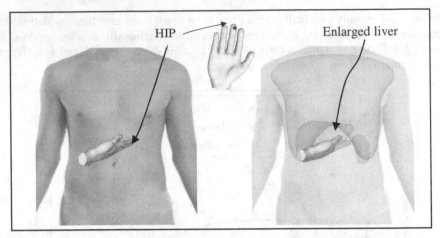

Fig. 18. A virtual palm palpating a malignant and enlarged liver

The user can examine the virtual patient according to various requirements, i.e., age, group and gender. Different images of the patients are uploaded to conform to this need. The internal organ properties are also varied according to the age and gender.

While validating our software, doctors commented that they could feel the edge of the ribcage properly. They could also palpate an enlarged liver though different doctors gave different comments regarding the setting of stiffness value for liver. It was suggested to replace the handle of the haptic device with a solid glove so that virtual palpation can become more realistic.

We have simulated respiration with our image-guided function-based approach. Figure 19 compares the breathe-out (left) and breathe-in (right) conditions with our approach. While breathing in, clavicle or collar bone moves upward. This difference between breathe-out and breathe-in images is marked 'A' in the figure. The patient's chest expands and moves upward, as shown with mark 'B' and mark 'C', respectively.

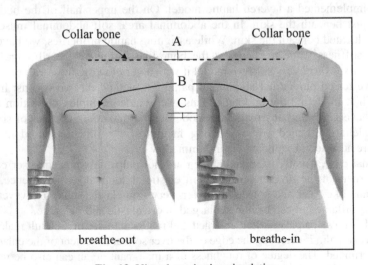

Fig. 19. Virtual respiration simulation

9   Conclusion and Future Work

We have implemented a new approach to virtual palpation. For visualization, we have used 2D images rather than 3D polygonal models. A number of patients of different age and gender can be generated just by replacing the images. We have represented internal organs by implicit functions. This has made collision detection much easier to compute as only a single function value determines the case. On the other hand, we have avoided colliding with a number of primitives, as it is required when using a polygonal model. With our function-based modeling of internal organs, we do not need to construct every model independently. Instead, we can adjust different scaling parameters of the respective defining functions to represent various conditions, i.e., normal or inflammatory, for a particular organ. Thus, our method is simple but, at the same time, very flexible. As the size of the data coming with the application is very small, the application can be easily portable for deploying over the internet in various educational cyberworlds.

Future work includes extending palpation to other abdominal organs, such as appendix, etc. We would also like to deploy our method for the palpation of non-abdominal organs, such as breast for breast tumor detection. While we have successfully elicited palpation during respiration, our goal is to explore another clinical examination called "percussion" in virtual environment.

Acknowledgements. This project is supported by the Singapore National Research Foundation Interactive Digital Media RD Program Grant NRF2008IDMIDM004-002 and by the Ministry of Education of Singapore Grant MOE2011-T2-1-006. The authors are very thankful to NTU Lee Kong Chian School of Medicine staff for invaluable consultations, especially to Martyn Partridge and Dinesh Kumar Srinivasan.

References

1. Walker, H.K., Hall, W.D.: Clinical Methods: The History, Physical, and Laboratory Examinations. In: Hurst, J.W. (ed.). Butterworths, Boston (1990)
2. Burdea, G., Patounakis, G., Popescu, V., Weiss, R.E.: Virtual Reality-Based Training for the Diagnosis of Prostate Cancer. IEEE Trans. Biomedical Engg. 46(10), 1253–1260 (1999)
3. Chen, H., Wu, W., Sun, H., Heng, P.: Dynamic touch-enabled virtual palpation. Computer Animation and Virtual Worlds 18, 339–348 (2007)
4. Ullrich, S., Kuhlen, T.: Haptic Palpation for Medical Simulation in Virtual Environments. IEEE Transactions on Visualization and Computer Graphics 18(4), 617–625 (2012)
5. Robert, I., Williams, L., Srivastava, M., Howell, J.N., Robert, J., Conaster, R.: The Virtual Haptic Back for Palpatory Training. In: Proc. Sixth Int'l Conf. Multimodal Interfaces, pp. 191–197 (2004)
6. Ma, L., Lau, R.W.H., Feng, J., Peng, Q., Wong, J.: Surface Deformation Using the Sensor Glove. In: ACM Symposium on Virtual Reality Software and Technology, pp. 189–195 (1997)

7. Burdea, G., Zhuang, J., Roskos, E., Silver, D., Langrana, N.: A portable dextrous master with force feedback. Presence: Teleoperators and Virtual Environments 1(1), 18–28 (1992)

8. Gomez, D., Burdea, G., Langrana, N.: Integration of the Rutgers Master II in a Virtual Reality Simulation. In: Proc. Virtual Reality Annual International Symposium, pp. 198–202 (1995)

9. Kawasaki, H., Takai, J., Tanaka, Y., Mrad, C., Mouri, T.: Control of multi-fingered haptic interface opposite to human hand. In: Proc. Intelligent Robots and Systems, pp. 2707–2712 (2003)

10. Kawasaki, H., Mouri, T., Alhalabi, M.O., Sugihashi, Y., Ohtuka, Y., Ikenohata, S., Kigaku, K., Daniulaitis, V., Hamada, K.: Development of five-fingered haptic interface: HIRO-II. In: Proc. International Conference on Augmented Tele-Existence, pp. 209–214 (2005)

11. Alhalabi, M.O., Daniulaitis, V., Kawasaki, H., Kori, T.: Medical Training Simulation for Palpation of Subsurface Tumor Using HIRO. In: Proc. EuroHaptics, pp. 623–624 (2005)

12. Kim, S., Kyung, K., Park, J., Kwon, D.: Real-time area-based haptic rendering and the augmented tactile display device for a palpation simulator. Advanced Robotics 21(9), 961–981 (2007)

13. Cheng, M., Marinovic, W., Watson, M., Ourselin, S., Passenger, J., Visser, H., Salvado, O., Riek, S.: Abdominal palpation haptic device for colonoscopy simulation using pneumatic control. IEEE Transactions on Haptics 5, 97–108 (2012)

14. Jeon, S., Knoerlein, B., Conatser, R., Harders, M., Choi, S.: Haptic Simulation of Breast Cancer Palpation: A Case Study of Haptic Augmented Reality. In: Proc. IEEE International Symposium on Mixed and Augmented Reality, pp. 237–238 (2010)

15. Jeon, S., Knoerlein, B., Conatser, R., Harders, M.: Rendering Virtual Tumors in Real Tissue Mock-Ups Using Haptic Augmented Reality. IEEE Transactions on Haptics 5(1), 77–84 (2012)

16. Coles, T., John, N.W., Gould, D., Caldwell, D.: Integrating haptics with augmented reality in a femoral palpation and needle insertion training. IEEE Transactions on Haptics 4(3), 199–209 (1995)

17. Wyvill, B., McPheeters, C., Wyvill, G.: Animating soft objects. The Visual Computer 2(4), 235–242 (1986)

18. Pasko, A., Adzhiev, V., Sourin, A., Savchenko, V.: Function representation in geometric modeling: concepts, implementation and applications. The Visual Computer 11(8), 429–446 (1995)

19. Zilles, C.B., Salisbury, J.K.: A constraint-based god-object method for haptic display. In: Proc. International Conference on Intelligent Robots and Systems, pp. 146–151 (1995)

Asynchronous Immersive Classes in a 3D Virtual World: Extended Description of vAcademia

Mikhail Morozov[1], Alexey Gerasimov[1], Mikhail Fominykh[2], and Andrey Smorkalov[1]

[1] Multimedia Systems Laboratory, Volga State University of Technology, Yoshkar-Ola, Russia
[2] Program for Learning with ICT, Norwegian University of Science and Technology,
Trondheim, Norway
{morozovmn,gerasimovav,smorkalovay}@volgatech.net,
mikhail.fominykh@ntnu.no

Abstract. vAcademia is a 3D virtual world designed for collaborative learning. It enables a new approach to educational activities in virtual worlds, which is based on a new vision of content and learning process. The most distinct feature of vAcademia is 3D recording which allows capturing everything in a given virtual world location in dynamics. The resultant recordings can be not only watched later, but also visited, providing students with a collaboration space and giving a sense of presence. 3D recording is conceptually different from video recording or screen capturing. In such a manner, vAcademia supports a new type of digital content – 3D recording or virtcast which is created based on synchronous activities. In addition, this platform has an integrated set of tools for collaborative learning which substitute those commonly used in physical classrooms, but also allows implementing new learning scenarios that are not possible or costly in reality. In this paper, we present the functionality, scenarios of use, and the initial evaluation results of the vAcademia virtual world.

Keywords: 3D recording, vAcademia, learning in virtual worlds, virtcast.

1   Introduction

Many studies report the potential of three-dimensional virtual worlds (3D VWs) for educational activities [1]. This technology can benefit educational process in many ways. Most of them are considered to exploit advantages of the 3D VWs, such as low cost and high safety, three-dimensional representation of learners and objects, and interaction in simulated contexts with a sense of presence [2,3]. However, this technology is far from becoming a mainstream in education, as there are a number of challenges in applying it for learning.

Despite the demand and interest from educators, in most cases, 3D VWs are adopted for educational purposes, but not specially created for them [4]. Cooperation and co-construction in 3D VWs is a complex task, it needs to be supported and requires additional tools [2]. The design of environments or 'learning spaces' within 3D VWs is considered to be important, however, there are no strong guidelines [5]. In

M.L. Gavrilova et al. (Eds.): Trans. on Comput. Sci. XVIII, LNCS 7848, pp. 81–100, 2013.

addition, 3D VWs are mostly used for synchronous activities and lack support for learning in the asynchronous mode.

In this paper, we present a new vision and approach to educational activities and content in 3D VWs. This approach is based on an original technological feature – 3D recording. The nature of this feature is difficult to grasp. 3D recording is often misunderstood and treated as an embedded screen capture mechanism. However, it is conceptually different from the video recording or screen capturing. A replayed 3D recording does not only delivers a virtual camera image and a synchronized communication messages, but much more. A 3D recording contains the entire 3D scene with all 3D objects and avatars. It can be entered by a group of avatars. All the actions of the avatars and in the environments are also saved in a 3D recording. These actions happen again when a 3D recording is replayed or, better to say, visited. In such a way, this feature allows creating a new type of content that comprises both space and time.

Traditional learning approaches require resources, such as teacher time, textbooks, and auditoriums. However, in traditional learning there are little problems with creating content. The product of traditional learning is a live synchronous face-to-face class. Countless classes are conducted in universities and companies all the time, but, unfortunately, most of the classes disappear after ending together with information and experience created by the participants.

E-Learning offers some technologies for getting content out of traditional classes, such as video recording of face-to-face lectures or recording of web conferences (or webinars). These methods allow creating cheap educational content for asynchronous learning [6,7]. However, video lectures and web conferences change the context of learning. These technologies do not provide the same level of immersion or sense of presence, a possibility for collaborative work or a method for further developing the content, except for commenting and annotating it.

3D VWs are also used for generating educational content. Even though this technology allows creating full context of the real-life educational process, it is usually recorded as 'flat' 2D video, which eliminates many advantages of the technology, such as sense of presence [3]. For example, this approach is used in Machinima – collaborative film making using screen capture in 3D VW and games [8].

As presented above, educators are trying to use various technologies for creating content out of synchronous learning activities. However, there is a clear possibility for improvement. In addition, new theoretical approaches to learning also need to be developed. As of now, there are no systematic approaches for combining synchronous and asynchronous learning paradigms [9].

We propose that 3D recording in 3D VW may solve the challenge presented above, as it offers an easy way for creating advanced content out of synchronous activities. This feature allows capturing and saving all educational information together with the context. It allows the students to come back into an immersive environment with more participants, experience the class like a live event, and continue the discussion in both synchronous and asynchronous modes. Using 3D recording, the students can refine acquired knowledge. In such a way, the approach combines rich interactivity of the 3D space and convenience of the video. Besides that, in practice, 3D recording of classes in 3D VWs can provide an unlimited source of educational content.

2   Related Work

2.1   Learning in 3D Virtual Worlds

3D VWs have been attracting attention of educators and researchers since their appearance. This technology provides a unique set of features that can be used for educational purposes, such as low cost and high safety, three-dimensional representation of learners and objects, interaction in simulated contexts with high immersion and a sense of presence [2,3].

Possibilities for synchronous communication and interaction allow using 3D VWs by various collaborative learning approaches [10]. In addition, possibilities for simulating environments on demand and for active collaborative work on the content allow applying situated learning [11] and project-based learning [12] approaches.

Constructivist approaches, such as problem-based learning, are also popular among the adopters of 3D VWs [13]. Social constructivism is often called an ideal approach for learning in a 3D virtual environment, as the technology allows learners to construct their understanding collaboratively [14,15]. In addition, 3D VWs are used for educational simulations [16] and demonstrating complex concepts [17,18].

2.2   Recording in 3D Virtual Worlds

The demand for methods supporting asynchronous activities in 3D VWs and creating content out of synchronous activities was acknowledged as early as in the late 90s, e.g. by developers of CAVE and MASSIVE systems. MASSIVE-3 supported a mechanism called 'temporal links', which allowed "real-time virtual environments to be linked to recordings of prior virtual environments so that the two appear to be overlaid" [19]. CAVE Research Network soft system had an application called Vmail which supported recording of an avatar's gestures and audio together with surrounding environment [20].

Another example is the system called Asynchronous Virtual Classroom or AVC. The developers were focused on solving the problem of time-sharing in distance learning. AVC allowed learners to watch a video image of a certain lecture and to control it, while software agents were playing some of the displayed participants and created a presence effect [21].

Later, N*Vector (Networked Virtual Environment Collaboration Trans-Oceanic Research) project was focused on developing a virtual reality technology for overcoming time-zone differences and time management problems. Within the project, there were developed three approaches to support annotations for asynchronous collaboration in virtual reality. These approaches included: VR-annotator – an annotation tool that allows collaborators to attach 3D VR recordings to objects; VR-mail – an email system built to work entirely in virtual reality; VR-vcr – a streaming recorder to record all transactions that occur in a collaborative session [22].

More recently, an Event Recorder feature was implemented (however, not developed further) within the Project Wonderland (later, Open Wonderland™, http://openwonderland.org/). Event recorder provides an implementation of the recording and playback of the 'events' caused by activities of users or agents in such a way that during playback a user is able to view the activities that those events caused. It achieves this by recording the 'events' in the world into an external form that can then be replayed to all the users that are engaged in the world. The invention also includes a mechanism to record the current state of a virtual world to use it as the starting point to play back the recorded events. In addition, a specialized plugin mechanism records the state and transitions of objects, which cannot be represented in terms of events, for example, the audio conversations.

2.3   Tools for Collaborative Work on 2D Content in 3D Virtual Worlds

One of the most serious challenges in adapting 3D VWs for learning is the lack of features that educators use in everyday teaching [4]. The integration of such features is of high value, as they ease collaborative process and reduce the necessity of using additional software or web services. Implementing tools that are familiar to educators can facilitate the process of adapting the system into practice. In such a way, a set of tools for collaborative learning can have a significant value. It is so, even though the strongest reason for using 3D VWs as learning environments is often referred as simulating situations that are difficult or impossible to implement in reality, and not replicating the real-world educational structures [23].

Processing large amounts of images in 3D VW is mostly required when working on 'serious' tasks, such as collaborative work and learning. In other tasks, displaying images, video or flash is also often required. However, the amount of the content is smaller. Usually, an image is calculated on a CPU on client side (for example, in Blue Mars™) or server side (for example, in Open Wonderland™) and then loaded into the stream processor memory as a texture.

2.4   Web and 3D Virtual World Integration

Educational process is not usually limited with activities in a 3D virtual environment. It requires a web-based complement, since in some cases a web tool is preferable, especially in organization and management. There exists a significant demand for integrating virtual worlds with web-based learning systems [24]. There were attempts at integrating a web support for educational process conducted primary in a 3D VW. A well-known example is Sloodle™ – a free and open-source project that integrates the multi-user virtual environments of Second Life™ and/or OpenSim™ with the Moodle Course/Learning Management System (CMS/LMS).

3   Virtual Academia

Virtual Academia (vAcademia) is an educational 3D VW developed by Virtual Spaces LLC in cooperation with the Multimedia System Laboratory at the Volga State University of Technology (former Mari State Technical University), Russia. The system is currently under beta testing and free to use, however, it is planned to be commercialized.

3.1   Functionality of the 3D Virtual World: 3D Recording

The most distinctive feature of vAcademia is 3D recording, which allows capturing everything in a given location in the VW in process, including positions of the objects, appearance and movement of the avatars, contents on the whiteboards, text and voice chat messages. Similar functionalities were realized earlier in few VWs or desktop virtual reality systems. However, 3D recording was never developed into a convenient tool and never adopted for specific use as in vAcademia. In addition, no convenient tools for working with the resultant recordings were developed.

3D recording of classes allows getting a new type of learning content and involving students in new types of activities. We propose to call it 'virtcast' – a 3D recording of activities in virtual reality or a series of such recordings [25]. This type of content is user-generated, since the process of creating and sharing 3D recordings is fully automated and simple.

A user can attend and work at a recorded class, not just view it as a spectator. In addition, any recorded classes can be attended by a group of users. A new group can work within a recorded class and record it again, but with their participation. Thus, there is an opportunity to build up content of recorded classes and layer realities on top of each other.

Fig. 1. 3D recording in vAcademia

From the user point of view, 3D recording control is very similar to the regular video player (Fig. 1, top). A 3D recording can be fast-forwarded and rewound, paused, and played again from any point of time. A replayed 3D recording looks exactly like a real class. Of cause, the recorded avatars will always act the way they were recorded. However, it is possible to use all the functionality of the VW inside a recording. Moreover, a replayed 3D recording can be recorded again together with new actions. In such a way, new recordings and new content can be created based on the same original event.

Some of the 3D recordings (for example, the most interesting ones, featured or advertised) can be made 'periodical' and replayed constantly in the locations. This feature makes it possible to create a better atmosphere in the VW, since a visitor of vAcademia does not observe empty constructions, which often happens in other 3D VWs. Instead, visitors can explore some of the classes going on with teachers and students involved. This might attract their attention and trigger curiosity.

3.2　Functionality of the 3D Virtual World: Teaching Tools

Interactive Whiteboard. Interactive whiteboard is the main tool for collaborative work on 2D graphical content in vAcademia. It can be used for displaying and annotating slides, sharing the desktop, sharing the application that runs on the teacher's or student's computer, sharing the web camera image, drawing figures, typing text, and inserting text or graphics from the clipboard.

Image generation and processing is implemented with stream processors in order to free the CPU for supporting other functions of the system. Stream processors are highly parallel computing devices designed for various tasks in 3D graphics. These devices have many hardware constraints [26,27] and their cores have relatively simple architecture [28]. Therefore, most of the classical algorithms that can be executed on CPU cannot be executed on stream processors without modification.

Image processing on stream processors is implemented by using shaders and an original programming model, which is based on four main objects (Texture, Drawing Target, Filter, and Filter Sequence). *Texture* is an image stored in the streaming processor memory. *Drawing Target* is an object that defines the resultant image, color mask, and settings of other configurable features of stream processors. *Filter* is a function in GetColor language which returns the color of a point for the given coordinates and defines the transformation of the image in the form of XML. *Filter Sequence* is a sequence of filters with parameters for complex transformations.

The design of the interactive whiteboard is based on using a dynamic texture with two independent layers which are combined in one static texture when rendering. vAcademia tools for collaborative work on 2D graphical content can be classified into three groups by the method of generating the resultant image. The tools in the first two groups generate a dynamic image, while those in last group – a static image.

Sharing changing blocks group of tools uses the lower layer of the interactive whiteboard and processes a dynamic image. The list of tools is presented below.

- Sharing of an application window
- Sharing screen area
- Sharing web-camera image

The implementation of this group of tools is based on an algorithm for discrete wavelet transformations for image compression with quality reduction which is adapted for stream processors. It identifies the changing rectangular parts of the image by using occlusion query [29]. The algorithm is based on a cascade of filters that allows implementing the direct discrete wavelet transformation in one pass.

Sharing attributed vector figures group of tools uses the upper layer of the interactive whiteboard and processes a dynamic image. The tools are presented below.

- Drawing figures and typing text on the whiteboard
- Inserting text from the clipboard

The drawing support is implemented based on triangulation of vector primitives with attributes for one- or two-way rasterization. Displaying (both typed and inserted) text is implemented by using font textures, rasterizing each symbol on demand.

Processing static images group of tools is implemented by resizing the source image, applying filters, asynchronous unpacking, and uploading it. The list of tools is presented below.

- Slide presentations
- Area print screen
- Pasting images from clipboard on a whiteboard

Multiple whiteboards of different sizes and designs can be used in any locations, and users can focus their view on them, by special controls. In addition, every participant can set up an extra whiteboard during the class and present some content on it. A colored pointer can be used for focusing attention on a certain element of the board.

Content Storages. Conducting learning activities in 3D VWs often requires sharing different types of educational content. The two tools that vAcademia offers for these purposes are described below.

- *Object Gallery* allows extending educational environment by locating additional objects. The Object Gallery of each user contains a choice of 3D objects that are usually required for conducting simple virtual classes. These include the interactive whiteboard (with different design and same functionality) and various objects for accommodating participants, such as chairs.
- *Resource Collection* can be used for uploading, storing, and sharing educational materials. This is an individual repository where each user can store presentations in PPT format, documents in PDF, pictures in PNG and JPEG, test templates in XML, test results in CSV (can be opened in Excel), and 3D objects in Collada and 3DS. In addition, the Resource Collection is able to store any other types of files, however, only for uploading and downloading. The files can be accessed from the interface of the vAcademia VW and from the website.

Control and Feedback Tools. vAcademia has a set of tools for classroom control and feedback. These tools reduce the workload of the teacher, help keeping the students engaged, and make the interaction more efficient.

- *Class Control* tool gives a teacher the ability to control students' access to the interactive whiteboards, ability to use their microphones, and ability to use virtual laser pointers. In addition, this tool allows the teacher to expel a disturbing student.

- *Notes* allow enhancing classes and 3D recordings with additional information. vAcademia supports three types of notes: textual, graphical, and sound. A note may be posted on any object in the 3D environment, during a live class or in a 3D recording. In addition, users can post comments to any note.
- *Backchannel* allows displaying text-chat messages on an interactive whiteboard. This tool helps the teacher to have a better contact with the audience during classes without being interrupted.
- *Clicker* allows conducting quizzes (polling or voting) based on single-choice and multiple-choice techniques. In addition, the tool allows displaying the results immediately on any interactive whiteboard in the form of several types of diagrams.
- *Testing tool* supports several types of tests, such as multiple choice with one or several correct answers, and allows assessing the students. Educators can create tests using the Test Designer tool and save them in their Resource Collections. Each test question can be supplemented with a picture. The results are available in the form of tables, bar charts, and pie charts. They can be displayed on an interactive whiteboard board or saved in text format for further use.

3.3   Functionality of the 3D Virtual World: Locations

Common Space, Temporary, and Standard Locations. vAcademia VW has a single island 600 by 600 meters called *Common Space*. It can be used for communication between classes and serendipity meetings. If necessary, users can create their own *Temporary Locations* in the Common Space, by drawing a rectangle anywhere on the ground. Such a location can hold any objects from the Object Gallery or the Resource Collection. However, it is removed when the user who created it goes offline.

The Common Space has over 80 different preliminary-made *Standard Locations* on it. These locations are different in their thematic design, setup, and size. This provides a possibility to conduct formal and informal activities, lectures and active classes, and accommodate small and large groups. Some of the *Standard Locations* have plenty of empty space to be augmented with user objects or, for example, additional interactive whiteboards.

The *Standard Locations* can be used on different levels of reality. A teacher can create an instance of a Standard Location, so the number of live classes in each of them is not limited.

Locations "My Home". In addition to the Standard Locations, each vAcademia user has a personal location, called *My Home*. This location is separated from the Common Space and has a size of 100 by 100 meters. Such location is created automatically and individually for each new registered user. Initially, there are no objects in a *My Home*, just a flat surface. However, users can build their own educational arenas for conducting classes taking standard objects from their Object Galleries or upload own objects. The owner can set the properties of *My Home* to make it accessible only if there is a class scheduled to be held there or to allow or disallow other users to visit it.

Each *My Home* is technically implemented as an independent reality and on a separate island that significantly reduces the restrictions on the total amount of polygons of the user 3D objects, as they do not interfere with the activities of other users in other locations. In addition, much less computational power is required to display a *My Home*, as it has no nearby locations, which is the case in the Common Space.

Location Templates. All types of locations in vAcademia can be customized. Users can add objects to the locations for creating the necessary settings and context for a particular course or a single class. However, such customization does not affect the original set up in the Standard Locations and exists only in the particular instances of virtual reality. Location template is a tool that allows saving the custom setup and applying it later. Location template remembers all custom objects placed in the location with all their properties. A location can be saved at a certain point, and applied when necessary (objects from the template will be re-created and placed in accordance with their properties). This tool allows to change or recover the whole 3D-scene quickly during a class.

A location template is technically created by serializing the list of objects and their properties into a JSON-object (JavaScript Object Notation). Simultaneously, a 2D preview of the template is automatically rendered and uploaded to the Resource Management Server (see section 3.8). Serialized data, path to the preview, and the name of the template are saved in the database.

When applying the template, the serialized object list is requested from the object placement service (see section 3.5). After receiving the list, the data is deserialized, then the objects are created, synchronized, and finally their properties are applied.

Communication Areas. In vAcademia, voice communication is available for the users that are in the same location or within 50 meters in the Common Space. This approach suits most of the learning activities when all the students should be in one place and hear each other. However, some of the learning scenarios require forming groups of students which should work separately for some time.

In order to ease the implementation of such scenarios, vAcademia offers the tool called Communication Areas. Using this tool, users can create areas inside a location that do not allow sound to pass in or out. Such an area can be created by simply drawing a rectangle on the ground. The users inside a Communication Area are provided with an additional text chat that works only in the area. When attending a 3D recording of a class where the Communication Areas were used, visitors get the text and voice communication from the area in which their avatars are located.

3.4   Functionality of the 3D Virtual World: Navigation

vAcademia has two types of maps. The mini-map provides an overview of the nearest space around the avatar and helps navigating within the current location. The large map of the VW displays the entire Common Space and helps navigating between the locations. It also displays two numbers for each currently running live or recorded class – the number of live and recorded participants in the location. Users can teleport to any place of the Common Space or a location by clicking on the map.

Several mechanisms are available to help managing the users and raising awareness. The *Visitors* menu displays the locations which have live or recorded avatars, allows seeing public profiles of these avatars, sending messages or teleporting to them. Another service allows searching for online users and inviting them to a certain location or a scheduled class. In addition, while in the Common Space, each user is notified about the nearby classes that are currently running or periodically played.

3.5   Functionality of the 3D Virtual World: User Objects

Setting up a new place for classes, users can take advantage of the models in their Resource Collections. They can upload own 3D objects, set up their properties, and use for creating specific learning environments.

User Objects Uploading Subsystem. vAcademia allows uploading 3D objects in Collada and 3DS formats. Resource Management Server (see section 3.8) supports the upload and passes the model for recognition and after that to the 3D model converter. The 3D model converter is a separate application that converts the model into BMF5 format and the textures to PNG and JPEG formats with the resolution up to 1024 to 1024 pixels. These formats are natively supported in vAcademia. The converter also checks if the model satisfies the requirements for maximum polygons (up to 50000) and number of textures (up to 12).

If the model is converted successfully, it is registered in the Resource Management Server and becomes available for placing in the 3D space of the VW. The legitimacy of the uploaded content is regulated by the user agreement; however, in addition, it is controlled by moderation.

Supporting user objects in Collada format allows using the Google 3D Warehouse™ library. 3DS format is considered one of the most popular on the Internet – many free models can be found in online libraries. If the required model cannot be found in free access, it can be designed from scratch using any popular 3D-modelling software. For example, Google SketchUp can export to Collada, while 3ds Max, Maya, and Blender can export to 3DS, without installing additional plugins.

User Objects Placing Subsystem. User objects may be placed only in a scheduled class (in a Standard or My Home location) or in a Temporary Location of the Common Space. This limitation is caused by the fact that user 3D objects may be not optimized in the number of polygons. Simultaneous use of several such objects is the Common Space may lead to a serious performance degradation of the VW.

There is another limitation for setting user objects in locations – the platform supports a maximum of 50000 polygons for all objects in instances of Standard Locations and 100000 polygons in My Home locations.

In order to reduce the risk of the overloading by (possibly inappropriate) user content, it is allowed only in instances of Standard and My Home locations. In such a manner, user content can affect only visitors of certain classes.

User Objects Properties Subsystem. User objects have many properties that can be set up. The general properties include enabling/disabling shadows, selecting collision type (no collisions, bounding box, sphere, or polygonal model), and allowing/disallowing other users to move, rotate, scale, remove or change any other properties of the object. It is also possible to set up sitting places on a user object, change or modify the textures, setup autorotation, and make the object play a 3D sound.

In addition, several interaction properties are available. They allow triggering one or several actions by clicking on the object. Assigning interactive properties disables the default action for clicking – moving the avatar to the point. Some of these actions are executed only for the person who clicks on the object. They are presented below.

- Displaying a text message
- Teleporting the user into a specific location in the Common Space
- Teleporting the user into a specific 3D recording
- Opening a URL link in a web browser

The other actions are executed for everyone in the current location.

- Replacing any texture on a surface of the object with pictures uploaded in advance
- Playing a previously uploaded or recorded sound
- Automatic rotation of the objects around three axes with the defined rotation speed
- Rotating the object along the vertical axis by holding the left mouse button

Once set, the specific interactive properties are saved in a template of this object in the Resource Collection. This allows creating different interactive objects from a single 3D model and re-using them at any time. The above list of standard interactive actions is created based on the user feedback and will be extended.

3.6   Functionality of the 3D Virtual World: Avatars

The platform provides a set of preliminary-made avatars which can be customized. The skeleton-skin approach is used for the design of the avatars. The skeleton allows playing motion capture animations, such as common gestures. The skin allows creating and modifying avatars easily. The avatar is divided into parts: body, face, hair, clothing, and shoes. Their shapes can be modified by morphing geometry. vAcademia supports generation of avatars with random selection of all available parameters.

Lip synchronization system is automatically adjusted to the avatar. Voice volume decreases with distance, and cuts off automatically when an avatar leaves a location.

3.7   Website Support

vAcademia has strong web support. While the main function of the 3D environment is offering tools for online classes, the website provides support for planning and managing classes and courses, and searching and organizing 3D recordings. In addition, the website has social networking functionalities (http://www.vacademia.com/).

The main page of the website has the *Activity* section, which syndicates what happens in the vAcademia community. It displays the main activities of vAcademia users, including scheduling meetings, publishing 3D recordings, and sharing text messages written directly into the section, plus messages from Twitter™ and Facebook™. Activity messages appear on the front page after moderation. Registered users can subscribe and follow activities of other users.

The website provides support and information about the VW. In addition, a CMS/LMS is developed and available through the site. The website has several sections that provide particular functionalities.

The *My Account* section contains personal information and provides access to the friend list, the list of communities, access to the Resource Collection, internal messages, and the list of 3D recordings created by the user. The users can also fill in additional information oriented toward the community of teachers and learners. The *Study* section gives the learners access to the list of all attended classes, lists of peer participants, the list of favorite classes, and the schedule. The *Teach* section provides a tool for planning classes and courses, lists of conducted classes and their 3D recordings, the register of classes' attendance, and a tool for managing groups of learners.

In addition, vAcademia provides a possibility for integration with external CMS/LMS. This allows introducing new possibilities that 3D VWs can provide in an already smoothly working learning process. The following plugins were developed to allow using some of the vAcademia functionality in any Moodle-based course.

- A plugin for scheduling vAcademia classed and binding them with Moodle classes allows adding a vAcademia class as a resource for a Moodle class and set parameters directly from Moodle, including class topic, description, date and time, location in the VW, number of allowed participants, and expected duration of the class.
- A plugin for inserting vAcademia 3D recordings as resources into Moodle courses

In order to have a flexible way to work with 3D recordings, each of them is complemented with a 2D Flash-based preview that is recorded automatically. Such a preview consists of the audio of the class, synchronized text-chat messages, and a series of pictures, which are taken from different cameras: for each whiteboard, for the stage, and for the audience. The previews are available on the vAcademia website, but can also be embedded in any web page, blog or a social networking website. The preview player has a toolbox which allows opening recordings in the 3D mode if the vAcademia client is installed.

3.8   System Architecture

vAcademia was developed from scratch using previous experience in developing educational 3D environments. Most of the system components were also developed from scratch. However, many well-known libraries and components, such as audiere, freetype, freeimage, and curl, were used for programming the networking, image processing, and sound. vAcademia has a client-server architecture (Fig. 2) and works on Windows operating system. The main components of the system are briefly described in the list below.

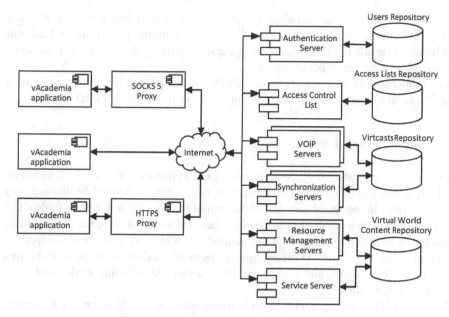

Fig. 2. vAcademia system architecture

- vAcademia application – client software that visualizes the VW and provides all functionality for conducting classes.
- vAcademia servers – a scalable system that supports network interaction. In order to ensure stability and data processing speed, the platform uses multiple servers.
  - Authentication Server supports registration and authorization of the users.
  - Resource Management Servers support access to the VW data and user objects in the Resource Collections.
  - Synchronization Servers support networked interaction between users.
  - VOIP servers support voice communication.
  - Service Server implements mechanisms of scalable services based on SOAP model (Simple Object Access Protocol). These servers are used for several components, such as text chat, Resources Collection, and list of recordings.
- Access Control List (ACL) – a system that manages user access permissions for the resources, such as scheduling and accessing classes, 3D recordings, number of objects in My Home locations, and capacity of Resource Collections.
- Virtual World Content Repository – a storage system for the 3D world data (geometry and textures) and user objects. These resources are divided into separate entities called modules. For example, all the resources that are uploaded by a specific user are stored in a separate module.
- Virtcast Repository – a storage system for 3D recordings. This storage is distributed to a number of different servers and stores all media resources of the 3D recordings, such as the state of objects and avatars, text and voice communication.

The graphical engine of vAcademia was developed specially for the project based on OpenGL. vAcademia has four levels of the graphics quality. The quality changes according to these levels, including the number of objects and polygons in them, quality of textures, antialiasing, and the distance of visibility. In addition, vAcademia uses levels of details for 3D objects and avatars, simplifying the geometry of the long-distance objects for better performance.

For implementing interactivity in vAcademia, a Jscript-based scripting language is used. It can later be given to the users for programing the behavior of 3D objects.

4   Scenarios of Use

In this section, we elaborate some scenarios of use to illustrate the current functionality of vAcademia. The application domain of vAcademia is defined by the teaching tools integrated in the world and the 3D-recording feature. While teaching tools allow using approaches that are used in the face-to-face and virtual modes, the 3D recording opens a new direction in e-Learning the methods for which are yet to be developed.

Learning activities with 3D recordings can be conducted in two basic formats: first – visiting a 3D recording, and second – creating a new 3D recording while conducting activities being inside one.

Visiting a 3D recording is similar to working with a recorded lecture or a webinar. A 3D recording can be watched at any time focusing on specific parts, but it can also be visited by a group of learners who can actively work inside. All the objects are on the same positions in the 3D recording as they were in the live class at any point of time. All the interaction can be observed in the same way as in the live class. The only limitation is that the visiting avatars cannot interact with the recorded ones.

The second format – creating a new 3D recording being inside one – is even more different and promising. A teacher can enhance a 3D-recorded class by visiting it with another group of learners and recording over again. As a result, another 3D recording can be created, containing new discussions, questions, and comments. Working inside a 3D recording, users can set up and use additional tools and materials.

In addition, the teacher can guide learners only through some parts of the original class, for example, the unclear ones. It is possible to fast-forward a 3D recording through the places that should be skipped (see red pieces in Fig. 3). In such a way, the skipped places of the original recording will not appear in the new one (Fig. 3).

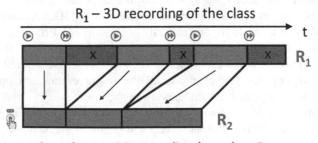

Fig. 3. New 3D recording with skipped parts

Alternatively, the teacher can pause the original 3D recording and add some missing material or discuss a particular part with the students (see green pieces in Fig. 4). Some parts of the original 3D recording can also be replaced. The new 3D recording will contain this additional material (Fig. 4).

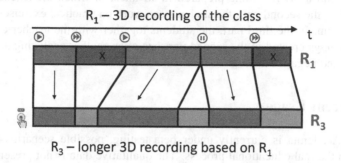

Fig. 4. New 3D recording with additional and replaced parts

In addition, 3D recordings can be enhanced with notes. Being in a 3D recording, users can add notes to any object in the recorded location. These notes can contain questions or additional clarifying material. When re-visiting the new 3D recording, the notes will appear in the same place and in the same moment of time (Fig. 5).

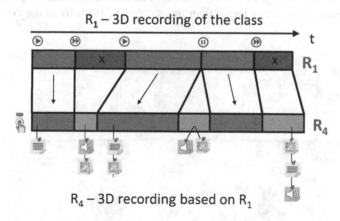

Fig. 5. New 3D recording enhanced with notes

Recording new activities being inside 3D recordings, the teacher will have additional virtual classes focused on specific parts which extend and improve the original class. In such a way, vAcademia allows editing the content of asynchronous recordings of synchronous activities. This feature is especially useful in the cases when a certain class has to be repeated frequently. For example, educators can create a template of a class with demonstrations but perform live discussions with each group of students reusing the content and avoiding unnecessary duplication.

3D recording creates new possibilities for combining synchronous and asynchronous activities within one scenario. Students might not even notice that they experience a recorded session which can be followed by another one which is live and interactive. For example, a class template can consist of three parts. In the first part, the students can attend a 3D recording prepared in advance, in which the teacher explains the material. In the second part, the students can work on practical exercises in groups and record them. In the third part, the students together with the teacher can visit all the 3D recordings created in the second part one after another analyzing and discussing positive and negative aspects.

5   Current Usage

Although vAcademia is currently under beta testing, possible scenarios of use are evaluated in the real educational process. The qualitative data is not presented in this paper but will soon be available.

The VW is used by university teachers for augmenting regular face-to-face classes. For example, vAcademia is used in several IT courses at the Volga State University of Technology. A number of different activities are conducted, such as lectures, seminars, project presentations, and study group discussions. Interactive whiteboards are used for live demonstrations of work in software development environments and the performance of resultant applications (Fig. 6). The number of visits to a 3D recording is approximately three times larger than the number of students in the corresponding live class.

Fig. 6. Developing Scratch applications class in vAcademia

Another example is the use of vAcademia at the Norwegian University of Science and Technology for teaching Cooperation Technology course in 2012. It was used as a platform for one of the lectures (3D VWs as a cooperation technology) and a virtual seminar with student presentations (Fig. 7). Attending the lecture in vAcademia allowed the students to get some practical knowledge on the topic. The virtual seminar pursued the same goal of providing students with experience of using one of the cooperation technologies (3D VWs), but it required active participation. The teacher made a tutorial about the vAcademia features. The students studied the tutorial visiting the 3D recording and practiced the features immediately. Half of the student groups pre-recorded their presentations, while the others performed live during the seminar. The feedback from the students indicated that vAcademia can be used as a cooperation technology, but a number of technical problems were mentioned.

Fig. 7. Cooperation Technology seminar in vAcademia

The VW is also used by several independent educators from around the world who are exploring new ways of collaborative learning or searching for a new platform. For example, vAcademia had been used for language learning by several professors who taught English courses. Students and teachers from different countries took part in the courses. The teachers often provide positive feedback on the integrated CMS/LMS, convenient interactive whiteboards, and many other tools.

vAcademia is used in schools and as a distance learning platform. A number of courses and separate classes were conducted mostly as trials for science and language subjects. In these classes, both teachers and students were actively using whiteboards for displaying multimedia resources, presentations, and practical exercises. The user experience shows that classes in vAcademia are engaging for students, however, the possibilities of the new types of activities require more exploration.

6   Future Directions

Further development of vAcademia project will be focused on widening its use in education and will include the development of additional functionality for the 3D world, extending possibilities for accessing the platform, improving the social and community support, adopting new interfaces, and designing new learning scenarios which would benefit from integrating synchronous classes and 3D recordings.

The development of additional functionality for the 3D worlds of vAcademia will be focused on extending possibilities for using custom 3D objects uploaded by users and programming the behavior of such objects. This will allow creating custom learning environments which can be used, for example, for simulations. Another direction is improving the workspace and teaching tools to make them more convenient.

Extending possibilities for accessing the vAcademia platform includes developing client applications for different operating systems and a light version for mobile devices. The second direction is developing a browser-based client.

Improvements in socializing support include a text chat across the website and the 3D world and integration with popular social networking websites.

Adopting new interfaces includes two main directions that are currently being developed. The first direction is translating classes in the physical world into the virtual world by using input devices such as motion capture and (physical) interactive whiteboards. The first Kinect-based prototype is being developed. This will allow conducting classes with participants from both physical and VWs. vAcademia is also being adapted for CAVE facilities (cave automatic virtual environment).

The second direction of adopting new interfaces is transferring part of the functionality to the mobile devices, for example, allowing to control the interactive whiteboard located in the 3D space by using an auxiliary mobile application.

Designing new learning scenarios is necessary for discovering all the possibilities of 3D recording in VWs. There will be a possibility for creating a library of class patterns, which can be based on certain pedagogical scripts. Such patterns could provide a 3D environment, all necessary tools, and a timeline. Some scenarios can be based on 3D recorded classes playing the role of a new type of user-generated content. Educational simulations and serious games will provide additional value, for example, for later analysis, if they are 3D-recorded.

7 Conclusion

In this paper, we propose a new approach to learning in 3D VWs, which is based on virtcast – a new type of content that can be created by using the 3D recording mechanism and is available in vAcademia. We also present an extended description of the vAcademia system and its major functions.

3D recording of classes in vAcademia expands the educational potential of the 3D VWs by combining advantages of synchronous and asynchronous modes. It allows using new approaches that were not available before.

Acknowledgments. The authors wish to thank their colleagues from the Multimedia Systems Laboratory at the Volga State University of Technology, especially Tanakov A., Bystrov D., Rozenkov M., and Sinitsin A. for their contribution to the vAcademia project. In addition, the authors would like to thank the teachers who actively use vAcademia Beta and help in exploring the possibilities of 3D recording.

References

1. de Freitas, S., Rebolledo-Mendez, G., Liarokapis, F., Magoulas, G., Poulovassilis, A.: Developing an Evaluation Methodology for Immersive Learning Experiences in a Virtual World. In: 1st International Conference in Games and Virtual Worlds for Serious Applications (VS-GAMES), Coventry, UK, March 23-24, pp. 43–50. IEEE (2009)

2. Warburton, S.: Second Life in higher education: Assessing the potential for and the barriers to deploying virtual worlds in learning and teaching. British Journal of Educational Technology 40(3), 414–426 (2009), doi:10.1111/j.1467-8535.2009.00952.x
3. Mckerlich, R., Riis, M., Anderson, T., Eastman, B.: Student Perceptions of Teaching Presence, Social Presence, and Cognitive Presence in a Virtual World. Journal of Online Learning and Teaching 7(3), 324–336 (2011)
4. Kluge, S., Riley, E.: Teaching in Virtual Worlds: Opportunities and Challenges. The Journal of Issues in Informing Science and Information Technology 5(1), 127–135 (2008)
5. Minocha, S., Reeves, A.J.: Design of learning spaces in 3D virtual worlds: an empirical investigation of Second Life. Learning, Media and Technology 35(2), 111–137 (2010), doi:10.1080/17439884.2010.494419
6. Brusilovsky, P.: Web Lectures: Electronic Presentations in Web-based Instruction. Syllabus 13(5), 18–23 (2000)
7. Engstrand, S.M., Hall, S.: The use of streamed lecture recordings: patterns of use, student experience and effects on learning outcomes. Practitioner Research in Higher Education (PRHE) 5(1), 9–15 (2011)
8. Barwell, G., Moore, C., Walker, R.: Marking machinima: A case study in assessing student use of a Web 2.0 technology. Australasian Journal of Educational Technology 27(special issue, 5), 765–780 (2011)
9. Zender, R., Dressler, E., Lucke, U., Tavangarian, D.: Bi-directional Distribution of eLearning Content for Cross-technology Learning Communities. In: Erfurth, C., Eichler, G., Schau, V. (eds.) 9th International Conference on Innovative Internet Community Systems, Jena, Germany, June 15-17, pp. 70–84. GI (2009)
10. Lee, M.J.W.: How Can 3d Virtual Worlds Be Used To Support Collaborative Learning? An Analysis Of Cases From The Literature. Society 5(1), 149–158 (2009)
11. Hayes, E.R.: Situated Learning in Virtual Worlds: The Learning Ecology of Second Life. In: American Educational Research Association Conference, pp. 154–159. AERA (2006)
12. Jarmon, L., Traphagan, T., Mayrath, M.: Understanding project-based learning in Second Life with a pedagogy, training, and assessment trio. Educational Media International 45(3), 157–176 (2008), doi:http://dx.doi.org/10.1080/09523980802283889
13. Bignell, S., Parson, V.: A guide to using problem-based learning in Second Life. University of Derby, Derby (2010)
14. Coffman, T., Klinger, M.B.: Utilizing Virtual Worlds in Education: The Implications for Practice. International Journal of Human and Social Sciences 2(1), 29–33 (2007)
15. Molka-Danielsen, J.: The new learning and teaching environment. In: Molka-Danielsen, J., Deutschmann, M. (eds.) Learning and Teaching in the Virtual World of Second Life, pp. 13–25. Tapir Academic Press, Trondheim (2009)
16. Falconer, L., Frutos-Perez, M.: Online Simulation of Real Life Experiences; the Educational Potential. In: Siemens, G., Fulford, C. (eds.) 21st World Conference on Educational Multimedia, Hypermedia & Telecommunications (Ed-Media), Honolulu, Hawaii, June 22-26, pp. 3564–3569. AACE (2009)
17. Dekker, G.A., Moreland, J., van der Veen, J.: Developing the Planck Mission Simulation as a Multi-Platform Immersive Application. Paper presented at the 3rd World Conference on Innovative Virtual Reality (WINVR), Milan, Italy, June 27-29 (2011)
18. Youngblut, C.: Educational Uses of Virtual Reality Technology. Institute for Defense Analyses, Alexandria, VA, USA, D-2128 (1998)
19. Greenhalgh, C., Flintham, M., Purbrick, J., Benford, S.: Applications of Temporal Links: Recording and Replaying Virtual Environments. In: Virtual Reality (VR), Orlando, FL, USA, March 24-28, pp. 101–108. IEEE (2002), doi:10.1109/VR.2002.996512

20. Leigh, J., Ali, M.D., Bailey, S., Banerjee, A., Banerjee, P., Curry, K., Curtis, J., Dech, F., Dodds, B., Foster, I., Fraser, S., Ganeshan, K., Glen, D., Grossman, R., Heil, Y., Hicks, J., Hudson, A.D., Imai, T., Khan, M.A., Kapoor, A., Kenyon, R.V., Park, K., Parod, B., Rajlich, P.J., Rasmussen, M., Rawlings, M., Robertson, D., Thongrong, S., Stein, R.J., Tuecke, S., Wallach, H., Wong, H.Y., Wheless, G.: A Review of Tele-Immersive Applications in the CAVE Research Network. In: International Conference on Virtual Reality (VR), Houston, TX, USA, March 13-17, pp. 180–187. IEEE (1999), doi:10.1109/VR.1999.756949

21. Matsuura, K., Ogata, H., Yano, Y.: Agent-based Asynchronous Virtual Classroom. In: Cumming, G., Okamoto, T., Gomez, L. (eds.) 7th International Conference on Computers in Education (ICCE), Japan, pp. 133–140. IOS Press (1999)

22. Imai, T., Qiu, Z., Behara, S., Tachi, S., Aoyama, T., Johnson, A., Leigh, J.: Overcoming Time-Zone Differences and Time Management Problems with Tele-Immersion. In: 10th Annual Internet Society Conference (INET), Yokohama, Japan, July 18-21 (2000)

23. Twining, P.: Exploring the Educational Potential of Virtual Worlds – Some Reflections from the SPP. British Journal of Educational Technology 40(3), 496–514 (2009), doi:10.1111/j.1467-8535.2009.00963.x

24. Livingstone, D., Kemp, J.: Integrating Web-Based and 3D Learning Environments: Second Life Meets Moodle. European Journal for the Informatics Professional (UPGRADE) IX(3) (2008) (published bimonthly)

25. Morozov, M., Gerasimov, A., Fominykh, M.: vAcademia – Educational Virtual World with 3D Recording. In: Kuijper, A., Sourin, A. (eds.) 12th International Conference on Cyberworlds (CW), Darmstadt, Germany, September 25-27, pp. 199–206. IEEE (2012), doi:10.1109/CW.2012.35

26. Kirk, D.B., Hwu, W.-M.W.: Programming Massively Parallel Processors: A Hands-on Approach. Morgan Kaufmann, New York (2012)

27. Fatahalian, K., Houston, M.: A closer look at GPUs. Communications of the ACM 51(10), 50–57 (2008), doi:10.1145/1400181.1400197

28. Fatahalian, K.: From Shader Code to a Teraflop: How a Shader Core Works. Beyond Programmable Shading Course. In: ACM SIGGRAPH, New York, NY, USA (2010)

29. Wimmer, M., Bittner, J.: Hardware Occlusion Queries Made Useful. In: Pharr, M. (ed.) GPU Gems 2: Programming Techniques for High-Performance Graphics and General-Purpose Computation, pp. 91–108. Addison-Wesley Professional, Boston (2005)

Real-Time Fractal-Based Valence Level Recognition from EEG

Yisi Liu and Olga Sourina

Nanyang Technological University
Singapore
{LIUY0053,EOSourina}@ntu.edu.sg

Abstract. Emotions are important in human-computer interaction. Emotions could be classified based on 3-dimensional Valence-Arousal-Dominance model which allows defining any number of emotions even without discrete emotion labels. In this paper, we propose a real-time fractal dimension (FD) based valence level recognition algorithm from Electroencephalographic (EEG) signals. The FD-based feature is proposed as a valence dimension index in continuous emotion recognition. The thresholds are used to identify different levels of the valence dimension. The algorithm is tested on the EEG data labeled with different valence levels from the proposed and implemented experiment database and from the benchmark affective EEG database DEAP. The proposed algorithm is applied for recognition of 16 emotions defined by high/low arousal, high/low dominance and 4 levels of valence dimension. 9 levels of valence states with controlled dominance levels (high or low) can be recognized as well. The proposed algorithm can be implemented in different real-time applications such as emotional avatar and E-learning systems.

Keywords: EEG, emotion recognition, Valence-Arousal-Dominance model, valence levels recognition.

1 Introduction

Recognition of the user's emotions from Electroencephalographic (EEG) signals is attracting more and more attention since new wireless portable devices became easily available and could be used in human-computer interfaces. The integration of emotion detection in human computer interfaces could be applied in many fields such as entertainment or education. Traditionally, detection of emotions could be done by analyzing biosignals such as EEG, skin temperature, and heart rate [8]. Now, more research is needed on recognition of emotions from EEG. The development of brain-computer interface (BCI) gives a new way to enhance the interaction between computer and human. The mental states such as concentration levels and emotions could be detected from the EEG signal in real time and serve as a feedback to trigger certain commands in different applications, e.g. to modify the difficulty levels of video games or adjust teaching methods in E-learning systems.

M.L. Gavrilova et al. (Eds.): Trans. on Comput. Sci. XVIII, LNCS 7848, pp. 101–120, 2013.

There are subject-dependent and subject-independent emotion recognition algorithms. Subject-dependent algorithms have much better accuracy than subject-independent ones but the subject-dependent algorithms need the system training session implemented in real-time applications. Generally, the available algorithms consist from two parts: feature extraction and classification. A classifier should be trained with features extracted from EEG data labeled with emotions. Thus, in the case of subject-dependent algorithm implementation, the user/player needs to train the classifier by recording the EEG data and labeling the data with emotions. For example, to recognize 8 emotions in Valence-Arousal-Dominance model, we need to have 8 training sessions which collect the EEG data labeled with 8 emotions such as happy (positive valence/high arousal/high dominance), surprised (positive/high arousal/low dominance), satisfied (positive/low arousal/high dominance), protected (positive/low arousal/low dominance), angry (negative/high arousal/high dominance), fear (negative/high arousal/ low dominance), unconcerned (negative/low arousal/ high dominance), and sad (negative/low arousal/low dominance) [22]. Valence recognition is important in the applications such as neuromarketing and entertainment where different levels of positive and negative states are needed to be differentiated. It could be useful to recognize, for example, 2 levels of positive feelings and 2 levels of negative feelings with arousal-dominance combinations to define 16 emotions. In such case, the training sessions could become difficult to implement.

Therefore, in this paper, we propose a fractal dimension (FD) based feature for continuous valence level recognition with thresholds that allows recognizing more emotions defined in Valence-Arousal-Dominance model in real time with less training sessions. Fractal dimension reflects complexity of signals and is used to analyze the chaos of EEG signals. For example, FD can be used in EEG-based detection of the concentration level in real time [35]. In this paper, the hypothesis that fractal dimension value can be used as an important index of emotional state assessment is validated. The proposed valence level recognition algorithm is tested on the proposed and implemented EEG database and on the benchmark affective EEG database DEAP [16]. Both databases follow the Valence-Arousal-Dominance emotion model. The proposed algorithm is applied for recognition of 16 emotions defined by high/low arousal, high/low dominance and 4 levels of valence dimension as follows. First, 4 classes (combinations of high/low arousal and high/low dominance levels) are recognized by using fractal dimension and statistical features proposed in [22] and the Support Vector Machine (SVM) classifier. Second, 4 valence levels are recognized with the proposed valence levels recognition algorithm using thresholds. In [21], only fractal dimension based feature was used in valence levels recognition. In this paper, statistical features of EEG signals and powers features of different EEG bands are analyzed and compared as well.

In [31], discrete emotions labels were given for emotions defined by high/low arousal, high/low dominance and 8 levels of valence in Valence-Arousal-Dominance emotion model. We use just 4 levels of the valence scale, and we have 16 names of the emotions defined as follows. High arousal, high dominance, different valence (2 positive ones, from the lowest positive to highest positive) correspond to activated/elated and joyful/happy emotions. High arousal, high dominance, different valence (2 negative ones, from the lowest negative to highest negative) correspond to contempt/hostile and angry/frustrated. High arousal, low dominance, different valence (2 positive ones, from the lowest positive to highest positive) correspond to anxious/surprised and fascinated/loved. High arousal, low dominance, different valence (2 negative one, from the lowest negative to highest negative) correspond to sinful/displeased and embarrassed/fearful. Low arousal, high dominance, different valence (2 positive ones, from the lowest positive to highest positive) correspond to nonchalant/leisurely and relaxed/secure. Low arousal, high dominance, different valence (2 negative ones, from the lowest negative to highest negative) correspond to mildly annoyed/disdainful and selfish/dissatisfied. Low arousal, low dominance, different valence (2 positive ones, from the lowest positive to highest positive) correspond to solemn/quiet and humble/protected. Low arousal, low dominance, different valence (2 negative ones, from the lowest negative to highest negative) correspond to fatigued/sad and bored/depressed.

The proposed algorithm is also applied for recognition of up to 9 levels of valence with controlled dominance (high and low). In some applications, it is important to know if the subject is feeling more positive or less positive. Knowing the current emotion label may not be needed in such cases.

In Section 2, the peer work including review on emotion classification models and on EEG-based emotion recognition algorithms is given. Statistical features, fractal dimension algorithm used as a feature extraction method and benchmark affective EEG database DEAP are introduced as well. In Section 3, the designed and implemented experiment is described. The proposed real-time valence level recognition algorithm and its application in recognition of 16 emotions are given in Section 4. Finally, Section 5 concludes the paper.

2 Background

2.1 Peer Work

In order to get a comprehensive description of emotions, Mehrabian and Russell proposed 3-dimensional Pleasure-Arousal-Dominance (PAD) model in [24]. In this model, "pleasure-displeasure" (valence) dimension evaluates the pleasure level of the emotion. "Arousal-non-arousal" (arousal) dimension refers to the alertness of an emotion. "Dominance-submissiveness" which is also named as control dimension of emotions [24,25], ranges from a feeling of being in control during the emotional experience to the feeling of being controlled by the emotion [23].

The EEG-based emotion recognition algorithms could be either subject-dependent or subject-independent. The advantage of subject-dependent recognition is that higher accuracy could be achieved since the classification is catered to each individual, but the disadvantage is that every time a new classifier is needed for a new subject.

In [15], a subject-dependent algorithm was proposed. Power Spectral Density and Common Spatial Patterns approaches were used to extract features, and Support Vector Machine (SVM) was selected as the classifier. The best accuracy obtained was 76% for two levels valence dimension recognition, and 67% for two levels arousal dimension recognition with 32 electrodes. In [37], two levels of valence were recognized, and the accuracy obtained was 73% with 2 electrodes. Despite the works using dimensional emotion model, there are also subject-dependent algorithms that use emotion labels. For example, in [18], four emotions - happy, angry, sad, and pleasant were recognized with 24 electrodes by using power differences at the symmetric electrodes pairs and SVM as a classifier. In [19], 6 emotions - pleasant, satisfied, happy, sad, frustrated, and fear were recognized with 3 electrodes. In work [20], high and low dominance were recognized by using beta/alpha ratio from 2 electrodes as features and SVM as the classifier with the best accuracy of 87.5%.

In [32], a subject-independent algorithm was proposed and implemented. Power spectral features were extracted and SVM was used to classify the data. Finally, an accuracy of 57% was obtained for 3 levels valence dimension recognition, and 52.4% for 3 levels arousal dimension recognition with 32 electrodes. In [8] and [34] subject-independent algorithms were described. In [8], 3 emotional states were detected by using the power values of 6 EEG frequency bands from 34 electrodes as features, and the maximum accuracy of 56% was achieved. In [34], the accuracy 66.7% was obtained by using the statistical features from 3 electrodes and SVM to recognize three emotions.

In [28], both subject-dependent and subject-independent algorithms were proposed and 4 electrodes were used. An accuracy of 69.51% was achieved to differentiate two levels of valence dimension when the algorithm was subject-independent. Accuracies ranging from 70% to 100% were achieved when the algorithm was subject-dependent.

Subject-dependent algorithms have generally higher accuracy than subject-independent ones. The number of the emotions that is possible to recognize is very important for algorithms comparison as well. In this paper, our main objective is to propose an algorithm allowing recognizing more than two levels of valence with short training session and performing with higher accuracy in real-time applications.

2.2   Statistical Featrures

Six statistical features were described in work [29] and applied in emotion recognition from EEG in works [34] and [27] as follows:

1. The means of the raw signals

$$\mu_X = \frac{1}{N} \sum_{n=1}^{N} X(n). \tag{1}$$

2. The standard deviations of the raw signals

$$\sigma_X = \sqrt{\frac{1}{N} \sum_{n=1}^{N} (X(n) - \mu_X)^2}.$$ (2)

3. The means of the absolute values of the first differences of the raw signals

$$\delta_X = \frac{1}{N-1} \sum_{n=1}^{N-1} |X(n+1) - X(n)|.$$ (3)

4. The means of the absolute values of the first differences of the normalized signals

$$\overline{\delta_X} = \frac{1}{N-1} \sum_{n=1}^{N-1} |\overline{X}(n+1) - \overline{X}(n)| = \frac{\delta_X}{\sigma_X}.$$ (4)

5. The means of the absolute values of the second differences of the raw signals

$$\gamma_X = \frac{1}{N-2} \sum_{n=1}^{N-2} |X(n+2) - X(n)|.$$ (5)

6. The means of the absolute values of the second differences of the normalized signals

$$\overline{\gamma_X} = \frac{1}{N-2} \sum_{n=1}^{N-2} |\overline{X}(n+2) - \overline{X}(n)| = \frac{\gamma_X}{\sigma_X}.$$ (6)

where n, N are sampling number and the total number of samples respectively, and $\overline{X}(n)$ refers to the normalized signals (zero mean, unit variance)

$$\overline{X}(n) = \frac{X(n) - \mu_X}{\sigma_X}.$$ (7)

2.3   Fractal Dimension Feature Extraction

In our work, we used Higuchi algorithm [11] for fractal dimension values calculation. The algorithm gave better accuracy than other fractal dimension algorithms as it was shown in [36]. The implemented algorithms were evaluated using Brownian and Weierstrass functions where theoretical FD values were known. The Higuchi algorithm is described as follows:

Let $X(1), X(2), \ldots, X(N)$ be a finite set of time series samples. Then, the newly constructed time series is

$$X_t^m : X(m), X(m+t), \ldots, X\left(m + \left[\frac{N-m}{t}\right] \cdot t\right).$$ (8)

where $m = 1, 2, \ldots, t$ is the initial time and t is the interval time [11].

t sets of $L_m(t)$ are calculated by

$$L_m(t) = \frac{\left\{\left(\sum_{i=1}^{\left[\frac{N-m}{t}\right]} |X(m+it) - X(m+(i-1)\cdot t)|\right) \frac{N-1}{\left[\frac{N-m}{t}\right]\cdot t}\right\}}{t}. \quad (9)$$

$\langle L(t)\rangle$ denotes the average value of $L_m(t)$, and one relationship exists

$$\langle L(t)\rangle \propto t^{-dim_H}. \quad (10)$$

Then, the fractal dimension dim_H could be obtained by logarithmic plotting between different t(ranging from 1 to t_{max}) and its associated $\langle L(t)\rangle$ [11].

$$dim_H = \frac{\ln\langle L(t)\rangle}{-\ln t}. \quad (11)$$

2.4   Benchmark Affective EEG Database

Recently, the DEAP database based on Valence-Arousal-Dominance emotion model was published in [16]. It has a relatively large amount of subjects (32 subjects) who participated in the data collection. The stimuli to elicit emotions used in the experiment were one-minute long music videos, which are considered as combined stimuli (visual and audio). 40 music videos were used. In the DEAP database, 32 EEG channels of the Biosemi ActiveTwo device [4] were used in the data recording.

There are different datasets available in DEAP database, for example, the EEG dataset and the videos dataset with the recorded subjects' facial expressions. Here, we used the dataset of the preprocessed EEG data [17]. The sampling rate of the original recorded data is 512 Hz, and the set of preprocessed data is down sampled to 128 Hz. As suggested by the developers of DEAP, this dataset is well-suited for testing new algorithms. Thus, in our work, we use the dataset to validate the proposed algorithm. More details about the DEAP database could be found in [16] and [17].

3   Experimental

Besides the affective EEG database DEAP, we also design and carry out an Experiment (Exp. 1) based on Valence-Arousal-Dominance emotion model to collect EEG data with labeled emotions.

Sound clips selected from the International Affective Digitized Sounds (IADS) [6] database which also follows the Valence-Arousal-Dominance emotion model are used to induce emotions. The experiment consists of 16 sessions. The choice of sound clips is based on their Valence, Arousal and Dominance level rating in the IADS database. The sound clips with the corresponding numbers in IADS for each session are as follows. Session 1: 262, 602, 698. Session 2: 113, 221, 225, 361, 400. Session 3: 107, 111, 224, 364, 403. Session 4: 360, 363, 378, 415, 610. Session 5: 171, 172, 377, 809, 812. Session 6: 132, 230, 724, 725, 726. Session

7: 109, 254, 351, 601, 820. Session 8: 311, 352, 367, 815, 817. Session 9: 243, 245, 250, 251, 252. Session 10: 105, 106, 291, 380, 502. Session 11: 115, 282, 284, 420, 624. Session 12: 275, 279, 286, 424, 712. Session 13: 700, 701, 702, 720, 728. Session 14: 246, 358, 376, 382, 627. Session 15: 104, 320, 702, 706, 722. Session 16: 410, 729. In Session 1 and Session 16, since only 3 and 2 clips are chosen, the clips are repeated to make the duration the same with the other sessions.

There are a total of 12 (3 female and 9 male) subjects participating in the experiment. All of them are university students whose age ranged from 18 to 27 years old and they are without auditory deficit or any history of mental illness.

After a participant was invited to a project room, the experiment protocol and the usage of a self-assessment questionnaire were explained to him/her. The subjects needed to complete the questionnaire after the exposure to the audio stimuli. The Self-Assessment Manikin (SAM) technique [5] was employed which used the 3D model with valence, arousal and dominance dimensions and nine levels indicating the intensity level in each dimensions. In the questionnaire, the subjects were also asked to describe their feelings in any words including the emotions like relaxed, happy, or any other emotions they feel. The experiments were done with one subject at each time. The participants had to avoid making any movements when the sound clips were played.

The construction of each experimental session is as follows. The experimental design complies with the standard EEG-based affective experiment protocol [15,18,37]. 1. A beep tone to indicate the beginning of sound clip (1 second). 2. A silent period for the participant to calm down (15 seconds). 3. The sound stimulus (30 seconds). 4. Silent period (2 seconds). 5. A beep tone to indicate the ending of the sound clip (1 second). In summary, each session lasted 49 seconds plus the self-assessment time.

In the Exp. 1, we use Emotiv [1] device with 14 electrodes locating at AF3, F7, F3, FC5, T7, P7, O1, O2, P8, T8, FC6, F4, F8, AF4 standardized by the American Electroencephalographic Society [3] (plus CMS/DRL as references) for the experiment. The technical parameters of the device are given as follows: bandwidth - 0.2-45Hz, digital notch filters at 50Hz and 60Hz; A/D converter with 16 bits resolution and sampling rate of 128Hz. The data are transferred via wireless receiver. Recently, the Emotiv device became more used in the research area [26,30]. The reliability and validity of the EEG data collected by Emotiv device was done in [33]. EEG data recorded from standard EEG device and Emotiv were compared, and the results showed that the Emotiv device could be used as the standard EEG device in real-time applications where fewer electrodes were needed.

4   Emotion Recognition

According to [10], there are individual differences when recognizing emotions from EEG for each subject. We propose a novel subject-dependent valence level recognition algorithm and apply it to recognize up to 16 emotions where 4 levels of valence are identified with each of the four arousal-dominance combinations, and to recognize up to 9 levels of valence states with controlled dominance level (high or low). In the proposed emotions recognition algorithm, first, four classes of combinations of high/low dominance and high/low arousal levels or two classes of high/low dominance are recognized according to the algorithm proposed in [22]. Fractal dimension and statistical features are extracted with sliding window, and Support Vector Machine (SVM) is used as a classifier. Then, the targeted number of valence levels is recognized with the proposed threshold-based algorithm. For example, for 16 emotions recognition, first, 4 classes (combinations of high/low dominance and high/low arousal levels) are recognized, and then 4 levels of valence dimension are recognized.

4.1   Analysis of Self-assessment Questionnaire

Although the chosen sound clips targeted at the special emotional states, we found out from the self-report questionnaire records that some emotions were not confirmed by the subjects. Our analysis was based on the questionnaire which gave us the recorded participants' feelings. Since we have EEG data labeled with 9 levels rating of dominance dimension and arousal dimension, we considered dominance or arousal level rating>5 as high dominance or arousal level, and dominance or arousal level rating<5 as low dominance or arousal level.

For the 4 levels of valence recognition (with Arousal-Dominance combinations), we divide the valence ratings into 4 levels. The re-grouped valence levels are defined as follows, Valence Level 1 includes valence rating 1 and 2, Valence Level 2 includes valence rating 3 and 4, Valence Level 3 includes valence rating 5 and 6, and Valence Level 4 includes valence rating 7 to 9. For the 9 levels of valence recognition (with high and low dominance), the entirely available different valence ratings are used in the processing. For example, if a set of data are labeled with low dominance and its valence ratings are 2, 5, 6, 8, 9, then the data are considered to have 5 out of 9 levels of valence.

4.2   Channel Selection

For both Arousal-Dominance and high and low dominance recognition, all channels are used to improve the algorithm accuracy. For valence level recognition, 2 channels (one from the left hemisphere, the other from the right hemisphere) are used from all channels and the channel choice is subject-dependent to improve the algorithm accuracy.

4.3   Feature Extraction

Based on our previous work [22], the combination of 6 statistical and FD features is used in the recognition of 4 Arousal-Dominance combinations or high and low dominance states since it has reduced feature size and obtains high accuracy.

Then, the statistical features in (1)-(6) $(\mu_X, \sigma_X, \delta_X, \overline{\delta_X}, \gamma_X, \overline{\gamma_X})$, FD features in (11) (dim_H), and powers of delta, alpha, beta, theta, gamma EEG bands $(P_{delta}, P_{alpha}, P_{beta}, P_{theta}, P_{gamma})$ are used as the feature F for valence level recognition to analyze and choose the best feature for the algorithm. The way to extract F is as follows. First, the data are filtered by the bandpass filter which is 2-42 Hz. The sliding window size is 512, and each time it shifts by 1 new sample to compute a new values of F, where F can be dim_H, μ_X, σ_X, δ_X, $\overline{\delta_X}$, γ_X, $\overline{\gamma_X}$, P_{delta}, P_{alpha}, P_{beta}, P_{theta}, P_{gamma}. In works [14] and [7], it was found for valence level recognition that left hemisphere was more active during positive emotion, and right hemisphere was more active during negative emotion. Thus, we compute ΔF which is the difference of the features computed from right and left hemisphere channels as follows:

$$\Delta F = (F_{left})_m - (F_{right})_n. \tag{12}$$

where $(F_{left})_m$ denotes the statistical features, FD or the power features computed from the left hemisphere and $(F_{right})_n$ denotes the statistical features, FD or the power features computed from the right hemisphere. In DEAP database, the recording device has 32 channels, 14 from the left hemisphere and 14 from the right hemisphere, thus, in (12), $m=1,2,\ldots,14$ denotes channels from the left hemisphere, $n=1,2,\ldots,14$ denotes channels from the right hemisphere. In total, 196 different channel pairs can be obtained to compute the difference of two features (ΔF), e.g. channel pairs (AF3-AF4), (AF3-F8), (AF3-F4), (AF3-FC6), (AF3-T8), (AF3-P8) and (AF3-O2). ΔF can be the FD-based feature Δdim_H, statistical-based features $\Delta\mu_X$, $\Delta\sigma_X$, $\Delta\delta_X$, $\Delta\overline{\delta_X}$, $\Delta\gamma_X$, $\Delta\overline{\gamma_X}$, or power-based features ΔP_{delta}, ΔP_{alpha}, ΔP_{beta}, ΔP_{theta}, ΔP_{gamma}. Next, the obtained ΔF values are averaged every 128 samples to get the averaged differences feature $(\overline{\Delta F})$, and it is used as the feature for valence level recognition.

4.4   Classification

For the classification of Arousal-Dominance combinations or high and low dominance states, the Support Vector Machine classifier with polynomial kernel implemented by LIBSVM [9] is used. The corresponding parameter setting includes the following: the value of *gamma* was set to 1, *coef* was set to 1, order d was set to 5, and the cost was set to 1 based on the grid search results for parameter selection [22].

To set the thresholds for different valence levels recognition, EEG data labeled with positive and negative states are considered as the input. As mentioned in Section 4.3, there is a lateralization pattern for valence recognition. However, individual difference may affect the processing of emotion by brain [10] and we also found that individual difference exists for different subjects [19] as follows. Most of the subjects had more activities in the left hemisphere during positive emotion, but few others had the right hemisphere more active during positive emotion. Thus, we need to figure out this pattern for the current user first. The output is the optimal thresholds and the lateralization pattern for valence levels detection. The thresholds selection algorithm for valence recognition is the same for HA/HD, HA/LD, LA/HD, LA/LD combinations, thus the one with HA/HD is described as follows.

Firstly, ΔF in (12) is computed from all the possible channel pairs from right and left hemispheres. The sliding window with size of 512 and moving by 1 new sample each time is used to get one new ΔF. Secondly, $\overline{\Delta F}$ is computed by averaging every 128 samples of ΔF. The lateralization pattern is figured out by comparing the mean $\overline{\Delta F}$ values for data labeled with negative and for data labeled with positive valence levels. If the mean $\overline{\Delta F}$ for the negative valence level is larger than the mean $\overline{\Delta F}$ for the positive valence level, the lateralization pattern label is assigned to 0. Otherwise, the lateralization pattern label is assigned to 1. After finding out the lateralization pattern, the maximum $\overline{\Delta F}_{Max}$ and $\overline{\Delta F}_{Min}$ are assigned according to the pattern label (0 or 1), which means if the label is 0, the $\overline{\Delta F}_{Max}$ equals to the maximum value of $\overline{\Delta F}$ computed from the data labeled with negative valence level, and $\overline{\Delta F}_{Min}$ equals to the minimum value of $\overline{\Delta F}$ computed from the data labeled with positive valence level; if the label is 1, the $\overline{\Delta F}_{Max}$ equals to maximum value of $\overline{\Delta F}$ from the data labeled with positive valence level, and $\overline{\Delta F}_{Min}$ equals to the minimum value of $\overline{\Delta F}$ computed from the data labeled with negative valence level. Finally, the thresholds for the different valence levels are set by dividing the inbetween area of $\overline{\Delta F}_{Max}$ and $\overline{\Delta F}_{Min}$ based on the targeted number of valence levels to be recognized. For example, if n valence levels are targeted to be recognized, then $n-1$ thresholds are needed and they are set up as follows.

$$T_1 = \overline{\Delta F}_{Max} - (\overline{\Delta F}_{Max} - \overline{\Delta F}_{Min})/n,$$
$$T_2 = T_1 - (\overline{\Delta F}_{Max} - \overline{\Delta F}_{Min})/n,$$
$$T_3 = T_2 - (\overline{\Delta F}_{Max} - \overline{\Delta F}_{Min})/n,$$
$$\dots$$
$$T_{n-1} = T_{n-2} - (\overline{\Delta F}_{Max} - \overline{\Delta F}_{Min})/n$$

The thresholds obtained from the proposed algorithm are with descending or ascending orders based on the valence pattern labels (0 or 1), e.g. $T_1 > T_2 \cdots > T_{n-1}$. In real-time recognition, the values of $\overline{\Delta F}$ are compared with these thresholds and the current valence state of the subject is identified consequently. For example, if one $\overline{\Delta F}$ is larger than T_2 and smaller than T_1, then the sample is considered to belong to valence level 2.

4.5   Results

Four   Levels   Valence   Recognition   with   Arousal-Dominance Combinations. The proposed algorithm is tested to recognize 16 emotions as follows. First, we classified data into 4 arousal-dominance combinations which include high arousal/high dominance, high arousal/low dominance, low arousal/high dominance, and low arousal/low dominance. Next, we recognized 4 valence levels in each class using the threshold algorithm.

With SVM classifier, the 5-fold cross validation was done: first, the raw data were partitioned into 5 sets without overlapping, and then statistical and FD features were extracted from each set as it was proposed in [22]. During the classification phase, 4 sets were used as training sets, and 1 set was used as validation data for testing. The training and testing sets were separated. The process was run 5 times, and every set was used as the testing data for once. The mean accuracy of the classification in 5 runs was computed as the final estimation of the classification accuracy. The cross-validation allows us to avoid the problem of over fitting [12].

With the thresholds, 90% of the data with the most negative rating and the most positive rating available within each arousal-dominance combination from one subject are used as the training data to set the thresholds for that subject, and then, the testing data are composed by the other 10% of the data with the most negative and positive rating which were not used in the training sessions and the data labeled with other valence levels. The best accuracy obtained from the channel pairs is selected and averaged across four arousal-dominance combinations.

Based on the analysis of self-assessment questionnaire, 11 subjects' data from DEAP database are used to analyze the algorithm performance. The resulting accuracy using SVM for four arousal-dominance combinations is shown in Table 1. As we can see from the table, the best accuracy obtained in recognition of four arousal-dominance combinations is 80.50% for Subject 13, while the averaged accuracy across all subjects is 63.04%.

With valence level recognition, the box plots of the $\overline{\Delta dim_H}$ values for Subject 5, 10 and 14 for different valence levels ranging from most negative (Valence Level 1), negative (Valence Level 2) to positive (Valence Level 3), most positive (Valence Level 4) are shown in Fig. 1. The cross in the box plots denotes the mean value of $\overline{\Delta dim_H}$. It shows that the values of $\overline{\Delta dim_H}$ and different levels of valence have a linear dependency, which supports the use of thresholds in the continuous recognition of different levels of valence. For example, as shown in Fig. 1a, the values of $\overline{\Delta dim_H}$ for Subject 5 decrease when the valence level changes from the most negative one to the most positive one. In Fig. 1b, the values of $\overline{\Delta dim_H}$ for Subject 10 increase when the valence level changes from the most negative one to the most positive one. In Fig. 1c, the values of $\overline{\Delta dim_H}$ for Subject 14 increase when the valence level changes from the most negative one to the most positive one. From Fig. 1, we can also see that the valence pattern for different subjects may not be the same. For example, Subject 10 and 14 have the same pattern – the values of $\overline{\Delta dim_H}$ are positive linear to the valence level when it changes from negative to positive. Subject 5 has the opposite pattern - the values of $\overline{\Delta dim_H}$ are negative linear to the valence level when it changes from negative to positive.

The resulting accuracy using thresholds for four levels of valence recognition is shown in Table 2. The valence recognition accuracy presents the mean accuracy across the 4 levels of valence recognitions from each case of the arousal-dominance combinations. For example, the valence level recognition accuracy for a subject is computed as the mean accuracy of 4 levels of valence recognition with high arousal/high dominance, and low arousal/low dominance. The

Table 1. Arousal-Dominance recognition accuracy (%) of data from DEAP database

Subject ID	Arousal-Dominance Recognition
S01	63.25
S05	53.08
S07	74.17
S10	65.21
S13	80.50
S14	46.67
S16	67.12
S19	67.29
S20	58.41
S22	49.72
Avg.	63.04

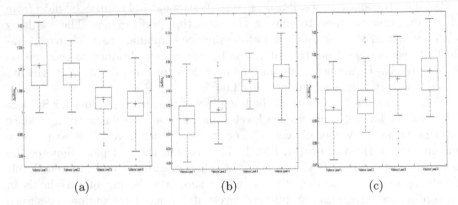

(a)   (b)   (c)

Fig. 1. The box plots of $\overline{\Delta dim_H}$ with different valence levels for 3 subjects: (a) Subject 5; (b) Subject 10; (c) Subject 14

best accuracy of 65.32% is obtained for Subject 10 using the FD-based feature ($\overline{\Delta dim_H}$). The best averaged accuracy of 51.49% across different subjects is also obtained by using the FD-based feature $\overline{\Delta dim_H}$, followed by the means of the absolute values of the first differences of the normalized signals-based feature $\overline{\Delta \bar{\delta}_X}$ (51.01%) and the means of the absolute values of the second differences of the normalized signals-based feature $\overline{\Delta \bar{\gamma}_X}$ (50.56%). From Table 2, we can see that FD-based feature ($\overline{\Delta dim_H}$) outperforms all the power-based features by 3.51% ($\overline{\Delta P_{delta}}$) to 5.52% ($\overline{\Delta P_{alpha}}$). The accuracy results show that all 3 features: FD-based feature $\overline{\Delta dim_H}$, the statistical-based features $\overline{\Delta \bar{\delta}_X}$ and $\overline{\Delta \bar{\gamma}_X}$ could be used in the valence recognition, but the FD-based feature has the best linearity associated with the valence levels since it gives the best classification accuracy.

Table 2. Valence recognition accuracy (%) of data from DEAP database with controlled arousal-dominance

Subject ID	$\Delta\mu_X$	$\Delta\sigma_X$	$\Delta\delta_X$	$\Delta\overline{\delta}_X$	$\Delta\gamma_X$	$\Delta\overline{\gamma}_X$	Δdim_H	ΔP_{delta}	ΔP_{theta}	ΔP_{alpha}	ΔP_{beta}	ΔP_{gamma}
S01	50.00	45.16	63.71	53.23	55.65	50.81	45.16	45.16	45.16	49.19	61.29	61.29
S05	38.31	46.77	57.66	64.92	50.40	56.85	48.79	41.94	41.53	45.56	60.89	62.10
S07	49.19	58.06	50.00	47.58	45.97	50.81	56.45	48.39	51.61	44.35	58.06	48.39
S10	50.00	51.61	55.65	54.84	54.03	45.97	65.32	51.61	47.58	50.81	43.55	50.81
S13	42.74	35.48	50.00	42.74	53.23	47.58	34.68	47.58	37.90	35.48	50.00	39.52
S14	42.74	47.58	40.32	54.03	44.35	57.26	54.03	48.39	51.61	48.39	41.94	38.71
S16	48.39	47.58	37.10	52.42	42.74	49.19	54.84	47.58	50.81	38.71	36.29	41.94
S19	48.39	54.84	55.65	51.61	50.40	54.44	50.00	50.00	52.82	54.44	52.82	60.48
S20	41.94	43.55	46.77	41.13	45.97	44.35	52.42	48.39	48.39	36.29	43.55	46.77
S22	49.19	49.19	27.42	47.58	28.23	48.39	53.23	50.81	48.39	56.45	25.00	29.03
Avg.	46.09	47.98	48.43	51.01	47.10	50.56	51.49	47.98	47.58	45.97	47.34	47.90

Up to Nine Levels Valence Recognition with High and Low Dominance.

For dominance dimension recognition, the data from Exp. 1 and DEAP database are first separated into two classes labeled with high and low dominance based on the analysis of self-assessment questionnaires. In the high and low dominance datasets, there could be more than one session having the same valence rating and one of the sessions with the same valence rating was used. The corresponding classification accuracy is shown in Table 3 for DEAP database using the combined features (6 statistical and FD features) and SVM as the classifier. The best accuracy of 89.72% is obtained for Subject 15. The averaged accuracy across all subjects is 73.64%. In Table 4, the corresponding classification accuracy is shown for Exp. 1. The best accuracy of 93.52% is obtained from the data of Subject 11, and the averaged accuracy across all subjects is 70.07%. The results from DEAP database and Exp. 1 database are comparable. It confirms the hypothesis that our proposed algorithm can be used with any devices and can recognize emotions evoked by different stimuli.

For valence levels recognition, first, we test our algorithm on the DEAP database. 32 subjects' data labeled with high/low dominance and different valence levels are used. In Table 2, it was shown that the best accuracy in valence level recognition can be achieved when fractal dimension based feature $\overline{\Delta dim_H}$ is used. Thus, the best accuracy among different channel pairs is given in Table 5 for $\overline{\Delta dim_H}$. "X" in the table means that data of different valence levels with low dominance are not available for Subject 17, 27, 32. From Table 5 , we can see that for 9 levels of valence recognition, the best accuracy is 23.02% which is obtained from data of Subject 27 with high dominance; for 8 levels of valence recognition, the best accuracy is 21.84% which is obtained from data of Subject 24 with high dominance; for 7 levels of valence recognition, the best accuracy is 31.16% which is obtained from data of Subject 29 with high dominance; for 6 levels of valence recognition, the best accuracy is 37.29% which is obtained from data of Subject 16 and 28 with low dominance; for 5 levels of valence recognition, the best accuracy is 49.44% which is obtained from data of Subject 7 with high dominance and Subject 10 with low dominance; for 4 levels of valence recognition, the best accuracy is 60.48% which is obtained from data of Subject 9 with

Table 3. Dominance level classification accuracy (%) of DEAP

Subject ID	Accuracy	Subject ID	Accuracy
S1	66.82	S17	X
S2	76.25	S18	88.13
S3	76.14	S19	73.27
S4	63.39	S20	73.04
S5	73.21	S21	66.88
S6	71.14	S22	75.45
S7	86.25	S23	86.75
S9	69	S25	88.86
S10	65.36	S26	67.71
S11	85.63	S27	X
S12	66.75	S28	74.5
S13	73.28	S29	78.85
S14	73.28	S30	75.28
S15	89.72	S31	67.69
S16	74.77	S32	X

Table 4. Dominance level classification accuracy (%) of Exp. 1 database

Subject ID	Accuracy	Subject ID	Accuracy
S1	51.19	S7	67.5
S2	55	S8	x
S3	80.56	S9	79.76
S4	75	S10	77.5
S5	63.89	S11	93.52
S6	59.17	S12	67.71

low dominance; for 3 levels of valence recognition, the best accuracy is 86.76% which is obtained from data of Subject 22 with low dominance; for 2 levels of valence recognition, the best accuracy is 91.67% which is obtained from data of Subject 25 with low dominance. The data collected in Exp. 1 were also used to test the valence level recognition algorithm with controlled dominance level. 12 subjects' data labeled with high/low dominance and different valence levels are used. The best accuracy obtained from all the channel pairs using $\overline{\Delta dim_H}$ are shown in the Table 6. Here, "X" in the table means data of different valence levels with low dominance are not available for Subject 8. For 7 levels of valence recognition, the best accuracy is 28.68% which is obtained from data of Subject 11 with high dominance, for 6 levels of valence recognition, the best accuracy is 50.91% which is obtained from data of Subject 2 with high dominance; for 5 levels of valence recognition, the best accuracy is 53.57% which is obtained from data of Subject 5 with low dominance; for 4 levels of valence recognition, the best accuracy is 62.07% which is obtained from data of Subject 4 with high dominance; for 3 levels of valence recognition, the best accuracy is 75% which

Table 5. Valence levels classification accuracy (%) from DEAP database using $\overline{\Delta dim_H}$

Subject ID	High Dominance	Low Dominance	Subject ID	High Dominance	Low Dominance
S1	7 levels	4 levels	S17	5 levels	X
	26.03%	55.65%		38.33%	X
S2	8 levels	4 levels	S18	5 levels	3 levels
	19.54%	56.45%		41.67%	82.35%
S3	5 levels	6 levels	S19	7 levels	6 levels
	41.67%	30.08%		29.79%	33.47%
S4	7 levels	7 levels	S20	7 levels	7 levels
	23.63%	24.66%		29.11%	28.42%
S5	8 levels	6 levels	S21	7 levels	5 levels
	21.26%	34.32%		29.79%	48.89%
S6	5 levels	6 levels	S22	8 levels	3 levels
	31.67%	36.02%		20.69%	86.76%
S7	5 levels	5 levels	S23	7 levels	3 levels
	49.44%	46.11%		30.14%	80.88%
S8	7 levels	5 levels	S24	8 levels	4 levels
	23.63%	31.11%		21.84%	57.26%
S9	6 levels	4 levels	S25	9 levels	2 levels
	35.59%	60.48%		19.80%	91.67%
S10	9 levels	5 levels	S26	7 levels	5 levels
	19.55%	49.44%		28.77%	37.22%
S11	7 levels	5 levels	S27	9 levels	X
	27.74%	40.00%		23.02%	X
S12	5 levels	5 levels	S28	9 levels	6 levels
	33.33%	36.11%		20.79%	37.29%
S13	7 levels	9 levels	S29	7 levels	6 levels
	24.32%	22.28%		31.16%	33.90%
S14	6 levels	7 levels	S30	6 levels	3 levels
	32.63%	26.37%		34.32%	75.00%
S15	5 levels	4 levels	S31	6 levels	7 levels
	42.22%	51.61%		22.03%	26.03%
S16	5 levels	6 levels	S32	7 levels	X
	42.22%	37.29%		24.66%	X

is obtained from data of Subject 9 with low dominance; for 2 levels of valence recognition, the best accuracy is 100% which is obtained from data of Subject 8 with high dominance and Subject 11 with low dominance.

As it is seen from Table 5 and 6, the results from Exp. 1 are comparable with results from the benchmark database DEAP. The mean accuracy decreases when the number of valence levels increases as illustrated in Fig. 2 for Exp. 1 and DEAP dataset. The proposed algorithm can be adapted to the targeted number of valence levels.

Table 6. Valence levels classification accuracy (%) of data from Exp. 1 database

Subject ID	High Dominance	Low Dominance	Subject ID	High Dominance	Low Dominance
S1	5 levels 36.90%	2 levels 83.33%	S7	5 levels 50.00%	5 levels 31.82%
S2	6 levels 50.91%	4 levels 50.00%	S8	2 levels 100.00%	X X
S3	6 levels 23.64%	3 levels 56.25%	S9	4 levels 50.00%	3 levels 75.00%
S4	4 levels 62.07%	5 levels 35.71%	S10	3 levels 68.75%	7 levels 21.32%
S5	4 levels 58.62%	5 levels 53.57%	S11	7 levels 28.68%	2 levels 100.00%
S6	4 levels 40.48%	6 levels 41.67%	S12	4 levels 44.83%	4 levels 60.34%

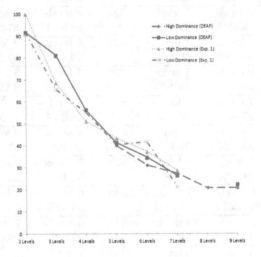

Fig. 2. Mean accuracy across all the data from two EEG databases

Fig. 3. Real-time emotion-enabled application

When comparing the proposed algorithm with other emotion recognition algorithms such as [15] and [37], which can recognize two levels valence with an accuracy of 76% and 73% respectively, our algorithm can recognize up to nine valence levels, and if only two levels of valence are targeted, the accuracy can be up to 100% (e.g. Table 6, Subject 8).

5 Conculsion

Classification of valence dimension levels ranging from most negative to most positive is very important in applications such as games, E-learning systems, and neuromarketing. For example, the difficulty levels of games could be adjusted according to the users' current emotional states.

In this work, we designed and carried out one experiment on emotion induction with audio stimuli using Valence-Arousal-Dominance emotion model. The EEG database labeled with different valence levels, and high/low dominance and high/low arousal levels was established. Based on the data analysis results, we proposed a novel subject-dependent valence level recognition algorithm using the difference of FD values computed from the left and right hemispheres as features and setting thresholds to identify different valence levels. Fewer training sessions are required in the proposed algorithm. Up to 16 emotions can be recognized by using SVM to classify the arousal-dominance combinations (high arousal/high dominance, low arousal/high dominance, high arousal/low dominance, and low arousal/low dominance) and thresholds to classify the 4 levels of valence within each arousal-dominance combination. The algorithm can be applied in real time with fewer training sessions. For example, only 8 training sessions are needed to recognize 16 emotions. The best accuracy of 80.50% is obtained for the recognition of four arousal-dominance combinations. The best accuracy of 65.32% and the averaged accuracy of 51.49% are obtained for the 4 levels valence recognition using the FD-based feature ($\overline{\Delta dim_H}$). This algorithm can be used in many applications such as adaptive games where the recognition of different levels of valence dimension and more emotions are needed.

The proposed algorithm can also recognize up to 9 levels valence with controlled dominance (high and low). The high and low dominance are recognized using the SVM classifier while the valence levels are recognized using thresholds. For the dominance level recognition, the best accuracy of 93.52% is obtained. For the valence level recognition, the best accuracy is 23.02% for 9 levels recognition, 21.84% for 8 levels recognition, 31.16% for 7 levels recognition, 50.91% for 6 levels recognition, 53.57% for 5 levels recognition, 62.07% for 4 levels recognition, 86.76% for 3 levels recognition, and 100% for 2 levels recognition.

The real-time EEG-based emotion recognition algorithm could be used in adaptive games, E-learning systems, etc. In Fig. 3, the user with Emotiv device is interacting with the emotion-enabled application Haptek [2]. The user's emotions recognized in real time from EEG are visualized on the user's avatar [19]. Videos of the implemented real-time EEG-enabled applications such as emotional avatar and emotional music players are presented in [13].

Acknowledgments. This research was done in School of EEE and in Fraunhofer IDM@NTU, which is funded by the National Research Foundation (NRF) and managed through the multi-agency Interactive & Digital Media Programme Office (IDMPO) hosted by the Media Development Authority of Singapore (MDA).

References

1. Emotiv, http://www.emotiv.com
2. Haptek, http://www.haptek.com
3. American electroencephalographic society guidelines for standard electrode position nomenclature. Journal of Clinical Neurophysiology 8(2), 200–202 (1991)
4. Biosemi, http://www.biosemi.com
5. Bradley, M.M.: Measuring emotion: The self-assessment manikin and the semantic differential. Journal of Behavior Therapy and Experimental Psychiatry 25(1), 49–59 (1994)
6. Bradley, M.M., Lang, P.J.: The international affective digitized sounds (2nd edition; IADS-2): Affective ratings of sounds and instruction manual. Tech. Rep., University of Florida, Gainesville (2007)
7. Canli, T., Desmond, J.E., Zhao, Z., Glover, G., Gabrieli, J.D.E.: Hemispheric asymmetry for emotional stimuli detected with fMRI. NeuroReport 9(14), 3233–3239 (1998)
8. Chanel, G., Rebetez, C., Betrancourt, M., Pun, T.: Emotion assessment from physiological signals for adaptation of game difficulty. IEEE Transactions on Systems, Man, and Cybernetics Part A: Systems and Humans 41(6), 1052–1063 (2011)
9. Chang, C.C., Lin, C.J.: LIBSVM: a library for support vector machines (2001), http://www.csie.ntu.edu.tw/~cjlin/libsvm
10. Hamann, S., Canli, T.: Individual differences in emotion processing. Current Opinion in Neurobiology 14(2), 233–238 (2004)
11. Higuchi, T.: Approach to an irregular time series on the basis of the fractal theory. Physica D: Nonlinear Phenomena 31(2), 277–283 (1988)
12. Hsu, C.W., Chang, C.C., Lin, C.J.: A practical guide to support vector classication. Tech. Rep., National Taiwan University, Taipei (2003), http://www.csie.ntu.edu.tw/cjlin/libsvm
13. IDM-Project: Emotion-based personalized digital media experience in co-spaces (2008), http://www3.ntu.edu.sg/home/eosourina/CHCILab/projects.html
14. Jones, N.A., Fox, N.A.: Electroencephalogram asymmetry during emotionally evocative films and its relation to positive and negative affectivity. Brain and Cognition 20(2), 280–299 (1992)
15. Koelstra, S., Yazdani, A., Soleymani, M., Mhl, C., Lee, J.S., Nijholt, A., Pun, T., Ebrahimi, T., Patras, I.: Single trial classification of EEG and peripheral physiological signals for recognition of emotions induced by music videos (2010)
16. Koelstra, S., Muhl, C., Soleymani, M., Lee, J.S., Yazdani, A., Ebrahimi, T., Pun, T., Nijholt, A., Patras, I.: DEAP: A database for emotion analysis;using physiological signals. IEEE Transactions on Affective Computing 3(1), 18–31 (2012)

17. Koelstra, S., Muhl, C., Soleymani, M., Lee, J.S., Yazdani, A., Ebrahimi, T., Pun, T., Nijholt, A., Patras, I.: DEAP dataset (2012), http://www.eecs.qmul.ac.uk/mmv/datasets/deap

18. Lin, Y.P., Wang, C.H., Wu, T.L., Jeng, S.K., Chen, J.H.: EEG-based emotion recognition in music listening: A comparison of schemes for multiclass support vector machine. In: ICASSP, IEEE International Conference on Acoustics, Speech and Signal Processing - Proceedings, Taipei, pp. 489–492 (2009)

19. Liu, Y., Sourina, O., Nguyen, M.K.: Real-time EEG-based emotion recognition and its applications. In: Gavrilova, M.L., Tan, C.J.K., Sourin, A., Sourina, O. (eds.) Transactions on Computational Science XII. LNCS, vol. 6670, pp. 256–277. Springer, Heidelberg (2011)

20. Liu, Y., Sourina, O.: EEG-based dominance level recognition for emotion-enabled interaction. In: The IEEE International Conference on Multimedia & Expo, ICME, pp. 1039–1044 (2012)

21. Liu, Y., Sourina, O.: EEG-based valence level recognition for real-time applications. In: Proc. 2012 Int. Conf. on Cyberworlds, Germany, pp. 53–60 (2012)

22. Liu, Y., Sourina, O., Nguyen, M.K.: Real-time EEG-based emotion recognition algorithm for adaptive games. IEEE Transactions on Computational Intelligence and AI in Games (2012) (under revision)

23. Mauss, I.B., Robinson, M.D.: Measures of emotion: A review. Cognition and Emotion 23(2), 209–237 (2009)

24. Mehrabian, A.: Framework for a comprehensive description and measurement of emotional states. Genetic, Social, and General Psychology Monographs 121(3), 339–361 (1995)

25. Mehrabian, A.: Pleasure-arousal-dominance: A general framework for describing and measuring individual differences in temperament. Current Psychology 14(4), 261–292 (1996)

26. O'Regan, S., Faul, S., Marnane, W.: Automatic detection of EEG artefacts arising from head movements. In: 2010 Annual International Conference of the IEEE Engineering in Medicine and Biology Society, EMBC, pp. 6353–6356 (2010)

27. Petrantonakis, P.C., Hadjileontiadis, L.J.: Emotion recognition from EEG using higher order crossings. IEEE Transactions on Information Technology in Biomedicine 14(2), 186–197 (2010)

28. Petrantonakis, P.C., Hadjileontiadis, L.J.: Adaptive emotional information retrieval from EEG signals in the time-frequency domain. IEEE Transactions on Signal Processing 60(5), 2604–2616 (2012)

29. Picard, R.W., Vyzas, E., Healey, J.: Toward machine emotional intelligence: Analysis of affective physiological state. IEEE Transactions on Pattern Analysis and Machine Intelligence 23(10), 1175–1191 (2001)

30. Ranky, G.N., Adamovich, S.: Analysis of a commercial EEG device for the control of a robot arm. In: Proceedings of the 2010 IEEE 36th Annual Northeast Bioengineering Conference, pp. 1–2 (2010)

31. Russell, J.A., Mehrabian, A.: Evidence for a three-factor theory of emotions. Journal of Research in Personality 11(3), 273–294 (1977)

32. Soleymani, M., Lichtenauer, J., Pun, T., Pantic, M.: A multimodal database for affect recognition and implicit tagging. IEEE Transactions on Affective Computing 3(1), 42–55 (2012)

33. Stytsenko, K., Jablonskis, E., Prahm, C.: Evaluation of consumer EEG device emotiv epoc. Poster Session Presented at MEi: Cog. Sci. Conference 2011, Ljubljana (2011)

34. Takahashi, K.: Remarks on emotion recognition from multi-modal bio-potential signals. In: 2004 IEEE International Conference on Industrial Technology, vol. 3, pp. 1138–1143 (2004)
35. Wang, Q., Sourina, O., Nguyen, M.K.: Fractal dimension based algorithm for neurofeedback games. In: Proc. CGI 2010, Singapore, p. SP25 (2010)
36. Wang, Q., Sourina, O., Nguyen, M.: Fractal dimension based neurofeedback in serious games. The Visual Computer 27(4), 299–309 (2011)
37. Zhang, Q., Lee, M.: Analysis of positive and negative emotions in natural scene using brain activity and gist. Neurocomputing 72(4-6), 1302–1306 (2009)

Towards Multi-hazard Resilience as a New Engineering Paradigm for Safety and Security Provision of Built Environment

Igor Kirillov[1], Sergei Metcherin[2], and Stanislav Klimenko[3]

[1] National Research Centre "Kurchatov Institute", Moscow, Russia
kirillov.igor@gmail.com
[2] Moscow Institute of Physics and Technology, Dolgoprudny, Russia
sergey.metcherin@gmail.com
[3] Institute of Computing for Physics and Technology, Protvino, Russia
stanislav.klimenko@gmail.com

Abstract. A new engineering paradigm of integrated safety and security provision for built environment is proposed. Evolution and limits of former safety paradigms are described. Definition of building/structure resilience is introduced. Differentiation of building/structure resilience from community resilience and organizational resilience are delineated. Main hypotheses for multi-hazard resilience paradigm development are introduced.

Keywords: built environment, multi-hazard resilience, integrated safety and security, paradigm.

1 Introduction

Permanent increasing of losses from natural and man-made disasters in recent decades dictates a necessity both to develop new technologies for disaster prevention and response and also to reconsider the cornerstone concepts for disaster analysis, management and engineering.

In this paper a new engineering paradigm of integrated safety and security provision for built environment is proposed. At first, a motivation for searching of the new paradigm is described. It is made via brief synopsis of evolution and appropriate limits of the former safety concepts — reliability-based and risk-informed ones. Attention is focused on two specific features of current situation world-wide — necessity to react or pro-act on multi-hazard threats and inability to protect (to provide guarantee for un-interruptible functioning and full scale performance) all assets at risk. Then, a working definition of building/structure resilience is introduced and differentiation of building/structure resilience from community resilience and organizational resilience are delineated. In conclusion, a set of the hypotheses, which are important for systematic development and operationalization of multi-hazard resilience paradigm, are introduced.

M.L. Gavrilova et al. (Eds.): Trans. on Comput. Sci. XVIII, LNCS 7848, pp. 121–136, 2013.

2   Societal Need: Level of Protection of People Inside Built Environment against a Variety of Hazards Should Be Drastically Enhanced

Building was, is and will be an ultimate protection layer for peoples. Civil built environment (human-made systems — like buildings, structures — bridges and other constructions for civil applications) provides the vital settings for human life and social activities. From the ancient times, peoples believed that "My home is my castle". However, this belief should, at least, be checked and justified now. Fragility of our real, comfortable and safe world is enormous. Ageing of built environment and vital infrastructure, increasing of a frequency and scale of damages due to instantiation of the different emergency situations, permanent shortage of the available resources for timely maintenance, response and recovery are, unfortunately, attributes of current life.

Properly functioning (under normal conditions), robust and readily bouncing off of threats of built-up environment (in case of malevolent action, accident or natural catastrophe) is of vital importance to the well-being of people, society and states worldwide.

The entire built environment (hereafter - BE) in our urban areas, including essentially every constructed facility, which can be used for shelter, food, transportation, business, health care, power supply, telecommunications, water supply, and waste disposal is highly vulnerable to natural and human-induced hazards. Moreover, frequency and intensity of the natural disasters, technological calamities or terrorist attacks (in terms of the losses) seems to be continually rising. These trends in the evolution of threats as well as drastic changes in structure of the built environment by high-rise residential buildings, densely populated multi-functional business, trading and entertainment centres, large inter-transport hubs, etc. are posing a set of the new challenges to safety and security of the inhabitants. This is exacerbated by permanent growth of cities, formation of the megapolisys and even megalopolises, complication of their internal structure and functions, and concentration of critically important infrastructure in smaller areas (volumes).

On the other hand, all previous history shows, that with appropriate research and development, vulnerability of BE to extreme hazards can be appreciably diminished. Built environment systems and their components can be designed, constructed or retrofitted to exhibit the necessary resilience not only to survive extreme events, but make it in such a way, that it is possible to bounce back to normal state with as high as possible speed and without, if it is possible, significant disruption to society and natural environment.

3   Long-Term Trends in Natural and Man-Made Disaster Occurence

During last decades, a permanent growth of frequency and intensity of emergencies and an increase in damages/losses scale were recorded by insurance community and disaster relief organizations (see Fig.1 below). At the same time, large resources (both human and financial) were spent world-wide in attempts to provide an acceptable level of safety and security via hardening of the buildings/structures, development of the new protective technologies, materials, technical standards, and organizational procedures.

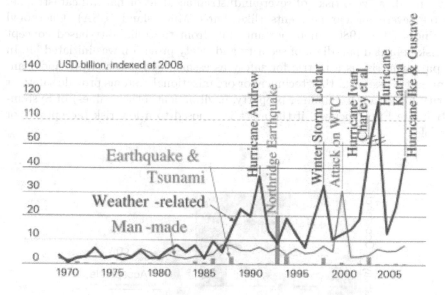

Fig. 1. Long-term trends in natural and man-made disaster losses [1]

Analysis of disaster-related statistical data results in assumption — it looks like, that our built environment is loosing its fundamental ability to protect its inhabitants against accidental natural and malevolent man-made disasters. In other words, safety and security of peoples inside of built environment is challenged by multiple threats. It should also be admitted, that total protection (as well as a "zero risk" of mishap events) is, probably, impossible. Both natural disasters, technological calamities and terrorist attacks of recent decades unambiguously demonstrated, that currently dominating paradigm - prevention (of the mishap events) and protection (rescue, live saving, restoration) of the elements under risk — human lives, built environment, nearby natural environment — by means of the currently available special forces (intelligence services, police, civil guards, emergency, ambulance, etc.), tools (dams, protection layers) or mechanisms (insurance) can not, in fact, prevent the mishaps nor provide level of safety and security, which are expected by citizens today.

So, it is critically important today to develop more effective paradigms of integrated safety and security provision for built environment.

4   Evolution of Prior Art Safety/Security Paradigms

Before major industrial accidents (Bhopal (India), Seveso (Italy) [2]) in 1970th, rational versions of crisis or disaster management paradigm were based on reliability theory. A protective system was considered as safe or secure if it was reliable. Reliability was a scale (indicator or index) of safety or security. Harmful consequences of a hypothetical accident were not considered. At that time, crisis management analysts believed that reliability of protective systems could provide a "zero risk" of severe industrial accident or natural catastrophe.

After severe nuclear accidents (like Three Mile Island (USA), Chernobyl (Ukraine) in the 1980s an important shift from the reliability-based concept to a risk-informed paradigm of security and safety provision was initiated [3]. In this paradigm risk is a metric for safety assessment. In risk analysis and management it is assumed, that technical or organizational systems provide safety or security for an asset (humans, property, environment, other values) of System-at-Risk (see Fig. 2 below), if the asset is exposed to a low risk (acceptable or tolerable).

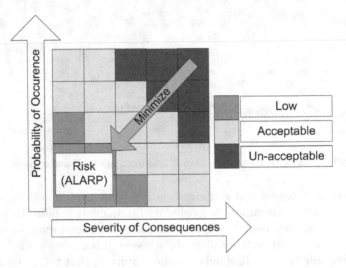

Fig. 2. Risk management strategy — minimize risk (ALARP is As Low As Reasonably Practicable)

Now, a risk-informed paradigm is dominant in practically all application domains, where safety and security are of utmost importance - nuclear energy [4], decision making in homeland security [5], transportation security [6] and in many other practical disciplines — from space exploration to treatment of patients in medicine.

However, two calamities of recent decade — the terrorist attack in New-York (09/11/2001) and the nuclear disaster in Fukushima (03/2011) unambiguously testify, that the risk-informed paradigm has certain inherent limits and weaknesses. It should evolve into a new one.

In both mentioned cases authorities and owners have large resources, ample experience and different mechanisms for risk reduction and calamity prevention. However, they could not utilize available capabilities in an effective way due to the absence of appropriate paradigm.

Common features of other calamities can be illustrated by the 9/11 case:

- absence of shared situation awareness between different supporters. Police and fire brigade had different communication lines, but the absence of Common Operational Picture (in fact — a unified standard for disaster communication and management) prevented timely coordination of the command centers of police, fire brigade and the mayor of New York,
- absence of on-line monitoring of structural health and water supply in building,
- weaknesses existing at the moment of the terrorist attack — i.e. low fire resistance of protective elements of steel structural elements after recent repairs, low productivity of the fire hydrants, - were not revealed. At that time, engineering methodologies for vulnerability assessment of the critically important components of building were absent and even the necessity to perform vulnerability analysis was not acknowledged,
- adaptive capacities of the building (structural robustness, productivity of fire hydrants, performance of evacuation routes) and adaptive capacities of the nearest environment (topology and productivity of the water supply at the World Trade Center site, etc.) did not have sufficient reserves.

In other words, despite a high technological level of New York infrastructure and reasonably high capabilities of the first responders (fire brigade, ambulance, police), the consequences of the 9/11 calamity were not minimized due to insufficient resilience of the built environment of World Trade Center.

5   Limitations of Prior Art Safety/Security Paradigms

5.1   How Protect against Multi-hazards?

Traditional tools of safety provision, used in civil engineering, good quality of the construction works, mechanical stability and durability of the bearing constructions of the building, reliability of whole construction and its constituents — are permanently improving. However, is it enough to protect its inhabitants from the contemporary threats of different nature: natural, technological, terroristic? Especially, if these threats will be realized in combination: in immediate sequence or in parallel?

Two largest calamities of the recent decade: WTC collapse in USA (impact – explosion – fire sequence) and Fukushima disaster in Japan (earthquake – tsunami – and following severe accident at nuclear power plant) provide firm evidence, that in case of a multiplicity of hazards even a high robustness of construction (WTC case) and multiple layers of protection (Fukushima case) are not sufficient to minimize number of victims and time to recover (bounce back) to normal state.

Although significant improvements have been achieved in correcting identified deficiencies following the terrorist attacks of September 2001 (e.g., in public policy, threat and risk assessment, preparation for such disasters, emergency response, etc.), it is clear that no coherent approach (neither at empirical level

— by politicians, communities, competent authorities (fire brigade, ambulance, etc.) nor at scientific or technological level — by academic or engineering communities) has been developed to address realistic societal vulnerabilities to extreme multi-hazard events. Scientific and engineering communities must embark urgently in developing a feasible approach to remedy this situation.

5.2   Necessity to Shift from "Mono-" to "Multi-hazard" Approach in Integrated Safety/Security Provision

Security and safety of the civil inhabitants of the modern cities is subjected to the multiple hazards of different nature. Devastating hurricanes in US, terrorist explosions in trains in Spain or metro in U.K., flooding in Central Europe are just some of the mostly known examples during the last years. Mentioned challenges have caused specific reactions, such as enhanced security at transport junctions or planning of global monitoring networks. This "mono-hazard" approach is not enough to cope with the modern challenges, especially taking into account a growing terrorist threat. Current trends require a more comprehensive, holistic approach for disaster prediction and prevention.

The 9/11 tragedy in New York demonstrates clearly that high rise buildings are vulnerable specifically to combined hazards. A blend of perilous effects — mechanical impact, short-duration explosion and long-lasting fire resulted in progressive collapse of the building. The WTC towers had enough structural resistance to cope with the primary mechanical impacts and the subsequent fuel-air explosive combustion. However, their integral resistance was not enough to survive under the loading by post-impact fires.

Due to absence of knowledge on synergetic (joint) action of the combined hazards, nobody — neither fire protection experts, nor explosion experts or civil structure engineers were able to predict the mode of building collapse and the remaining time till collapse. At the same time, the duration of the pre-collapse period was vitally important for occupant behaviour, egress and implementation of the emergency operations of the first responders. Different types of combined hazards can also threaten the other key structures of the built environment, such as the multi-floor transport junctions/hubs, bridges, tunnels, multiple-use public sites, etc..

The problem of the multi-hazards for the built environment has a timeless nature. In the past, people were concerned not only with earthquake consequences but also with the subsequent large-scale fires. Today, mechanical impact, subsequent BLEVE and fuel-air explosion and long-lasting fire can be a threat to people in different urban structures as a result of a transport accident or malevolent terrorist attack. In the future, it will be highly un-probable, that complexity, high energy-loading and strong interdependence of the different sub-systems of structures, energy supply and communication of modern cities will diminish. It means, that the necessity in understanding and prediction of the consequences of the combined hazardous effects (multi-hazards) will be going to stay in the list of research priorities. The 9/11 case just accentuates with utmost intensity a topical need in understanding, modelling and prediction of high-consequence events, where a combination of multiple hazards can take place.

5.3   How to Provide Means to Sufficiently Quick and Resource-Saving Bounce Back to Normal State?

After each calamity peoples restore their built-up environment. However, required resources (human, material, financial, time) for restoration are permanently increasing. Restoration of the vital functions of the key elements of the built environment (so called critical infrastructure) should be made in first instance in order to provide the right conditions for other elements of the built environment to get restored. Question is, how to perform the recovery of BE with utmost speed and minimal cost? How to compile a priority list of topical actions? What metrics and criteria can be used for recovering planning and execution? Today, this set of questions does not arise during the design and erection stages of the life-cycle of built environment. This complex, multi-scale, inter-disciplinary work is making up to this moment in ad hoc, mainly empiric manner, without a solid scientific or engineering basis, focused particularly on the behaviour of BE during accident and recovering.

A new paradigm for integrated safety and security provisions for people inside built environment is necessary.

6   Multi-hazard Resilience of Built Environment as Innovative Paradigm for Integrated Safety and Security Provision

Resilience of the built environment (from viewpoints, at least, of personal security and safety, structural safety, physical and cyber-physical protection of events) should become a goal and standard for provision of integrated safety and security of government assets both for homeland and overseas.

A good resilience of the "hardware" part of built environment (the site, buildings and their components), i.e. its capacity to withstand different hazardous effects (wind, earthquake, flooding, fire, blast or others), also when the strength and nature of the disturbance is unexpected, is an important prerequisite for the modern cities.

The necessity to shift to an innovative holistic paradigm for provision of safety and security for people inside of built environment was articulated by the different authors [7–9] during the recent decade.

Some aspects of the mentioned global problem were addressed by the paradigms of the "resilient city" and "resilient community", proposed and elaborated by social sciences communities (non-traditional forms of governance, community, regional and land use planning, social and individual psychology), mainly, in North America (The Resilient City project (2003-2005), Community Resiliency, Transition and Recovery project (2004-2006)) and by environmental scientists [10–12].

The concept of "resilience" appeared at first and demonstrated already its effectiveness in

- ecology [13, 14]
- social-ecological systems [15, 16]
- business continuity [17, 18]

Now, the concept of "resilience" is an emerging research and development topic in

- counter-terrorism strategy in UK [19, 20]
- protection of physical and social infrastructure in USA [21, 22].

The idea of using the "multi-hazard resilience of built environment" as a new comprehensive engineering paradigm for security and safety provision just at specific scale of building and for nearby surroundings appeared as a result of the following research, development and dissemination activities:

- June 2002 – June 2004: Russian-Dutch research project "Hazard and Risk Analysis of Aircraft Collision with High-Rise Building" (11 Russian research establishments, TNO and TU Delft from Dutch side) [23],
- 10-12 June 2004: "Results of the Aircraft-Building-Crash project" Dissemination day for the Dutch Royal Fire Brigades and Russian Ministry of Emergency,
- 16-18 July, 2007: NATO Advanced Research Workshop "Resilience of Building against Combined Threats", 17 invited participants from NATO countries, 32 participants from Russia [24],
- 2008: "Resilience of Cities to Terrorist and Threats: learning from 9/11 and further research issues" [25].

The mentioned research and development activities highlighted the following conclusions:

- Enhancing the resilience of the built environment is the key option for the protection of society from multi-hazard incidents.
- Current empirically-based building regulations and risk assessment technologies cannot cope with 1) multi-hazard threats (e.g., combinations of impact, explosion, fire, storm, seismic movements, toxic dispersion, etc.), 2) and are not suitable for risk assessment at the scale of a building (only for regional or national scales).
- A comprehensive and cost-effective methodology is urgently needed to remedy this deficiency. Such a methodology must enable society to both assess the risk and prepare for, and to efficiently respond to such incidents
- Addressing issues with multi-hazard resilience of built environment will have a profound effect on national and international peace, prosperity, and security. Essential work must be conducted in several important areas that include natural science and engineering topics, as well as socio-economics and public policy.

Following to [11, 26] the next working definition of the resilience of built environment can be proposed.

Resilience is a capability of buildings/structure to maintain their functions and structure in the face of internal and external change and to degrade gracefully, that provides opportunities to reasonably avoid intolerable (or un-acceptable) harm to peoples or losses to the building, associated with potential dangerous direct effects or in-direct consequences of a multi-hazard accident.

The proposed working definition is, in first turn, intended to reach a consensus between stakeholders with different backgrounds. It speaks to the issues of human safety, construction damage, but gives no specific guidance on how one should be protected during, or recovered after, an accident. So, associated functional definitions are needed.

In order to be operational, the above mentioned general definition can be articulated as a set of the functional requirements or technical goals for design or maintenance of a building/construction, considered as a system, comprising structural, engineering and safety/security components (Fig. 3 below):

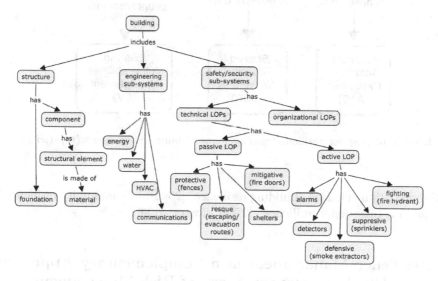

Fig. 3. Key safety- and security-related components of building [26]

Resilience is the ability of:

- structural sub-systems of a building (load-bearing structure, internal architectural design, external adjacent site) to resist, absorb, and recover from or adapt to an adverse occurrence that may harm people and damage the building,
- engineering sub-systems of a building (electricity-, water supply, heating, ventilation and air conditioning) to react expeditiously in accordance with

the severity of the hazard during accident, and to "bounce back" to enhanced functioning under post-accident conditions,
— information and communication sub-systems of building (network-enabled sensors and video surveillance, communication channels) are to provide "as Complete As Reasonably Possible a Common Operational Picture" shared between people inside the building and rescue/ambulance/ emergency teams/ systems outside the building, subjected to multi-hazard risks.

From the mentioned functional definitions of the resilience of a building, follows the following top-tier concept of resilience management (see Fig. 4 below):

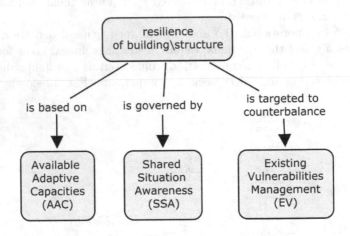

Fig. 4. Concept map for resilience management of built environment (top-tier representation)

Differentiation of notion "building resilience" [26] from "community resilience" [11] and "organizational resilience" [27] is illustrated at Fig. 5.

7   Resilience Management as a Complementary Approach to and an Evolutionary Stage of Risk Management

Today integrated safety and security of the built environment is, mainly, provided by using a widely accepted paradigm of risk management [28]. This paradigm has a proven track record in military and disaster/emergency applications, in high technology - nuclear energy, aerospace, off-shore platforms - and many other civil applications. However, in spite of a long list of successful applications of risk management, and a scientific and engineering maturity of this approach, there are still many problems and issues, which cannot be solved within the framework of the currently available technologies and techniques of risk analysis and management.

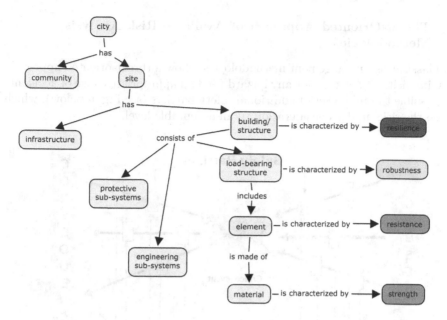

Fig. 5. Differentiation between notions "building resilience", "community resilience" and "organizational resilience"

7.1 Treatment of Multiple Risks in Contemporary Methodologies

In the past decade, an understanding emerged that during a major accident or large-scale calamity the risks from multiple (sometimes concurrent) hazards or threats should be taken into account. For example, in the detailed engineering investigation [29] it was revealed that during the tragic events of 9/11 in New York, the load-bearing structures of the twin-towers of the World Trade Centre were robust enough to withstand the initial mechanical impact from an aircraft-building collision and the subsequent explosion of the jet fuel-air mixture. However, overall resilience of these high rise buildings was insufficient to cope with the combination of the different, but closely related hazardous effects (impact-explosion-fire) and to prevent a collapse of building.

Available risk assessment technologies are not fit for application specifically to buildings and cannot treat the multi-hazard risks in a unified, systematic manner.

Available or proposed multi-risk methodologies focused mainly on spatial planning against natural hazards [30–32], such as earthquakes, volcanic eruptions, landslides, tsunamis, wildfires, winter storms. They are still at an immature stage. Most importantly, they cannot be applied for multi-risk analyses of the built environment, specifically to governmental assets. The mentioned methodologies were targeted on medium $(1 - 10^1$ km) scale of cities and regions or large $(10^2 - 10^3)$ scale areas (country, continent) and do not have tools for fine $(100 - 1000$ m) scale analysis of a building/structure.

7.2   Threat-Oriented Approach of Available Risk Analysis Methodologies

The classical risk management methodologies follow a threat-oriented approach. They implicitly infer, that for any hazard (and an appropriate cause of accident) it is possible to build a set of additional safety barriers (see Fig. 6 below), which reduce the risks under consideration to an acceptable level.

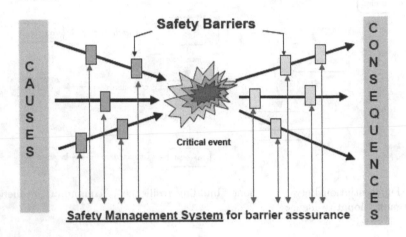

Fig. 6. Bow-tie diagram: influence of safety barriers (layers of protection) on consequences of accident [33]

In the threat-oriented approach, a sensitivity of the assets to the harmful effects assumed a priori as insufficient to cope with threat by themselves. It means, that the intrinsic capabilities of the assets to resist, absorb, and recover from or adapt to an accident that may cause damage or destruction are not taken into account.

In the threat-oriented approach — own capacities of the asset to withstand harmful effects are considered negligible.

In fact, the resilience of existing buildings and constructions is sizable and can be enhanced. So, the threat-oriented approach should be exchanged against a resource-based approach.

Resource-oriented approach the own capacities of an asset to withstand harmful effects are considered as capable to "bounce back".

8   Main Hypotheses for Development of Multi-hazard Resilience Paradigm

1. The built environment is and will be exposed to risks of different nature. Resilience of the civil built environment is an ultimate means for protecting human lives, private or public assets and the biogeocenosis environment

during a natural catastrophe, major industrial accident or terrorist calamity. Resiliency is the capability of a buildings construction to maintain its functions and structure in the face of internal and external change and to degrade gracefully, that provides opportunities to reasonably avoid intolerable (or un-acceptable) harm to people or losses to the building, associated with potential dangerous direct effects or in-direct consequences of a multi-hazard accident.

2. Managing multiple risks requires resilience of the built environment - the ability to survive, adapt and gracefully evolve even under disastrous conditions. Resilience is required along with the other key performance indexes of a building: strength, stability, safety in fire, durability, reliability, robustness and sustainability.

3. During a whole life-cycle of a built environment both construction industry (contractors, designers, civil engineers), technical regulatory bodies (standardization establishments, auditors) safety concerned communities (emergency managers, safety/security experts, ambulance, rescue, etc.) and authorities (land use planners, political and social decision-makers) need to supplement traditional risk management techniques with the concept of building resilience that is better designed to cope with extreme complexities and unpredictable events and threats.

4. Multi-hazard resilience of the built environment can be assessed in term of three key dimensions:
   (a) vulnerabilities
   (b) adaptive capacities of building, and
   (c) network-enabled shared situation awareness, which permits the peoples inside buildings,
   responders/emergency managers outside the building and monitoring systems of the building itself to interact effectively and, most importantly, coherently.

5. Without conceptualization, including ontology of the application area (standardized definitions of terms and their relations); measurable (or accessible) variables, metrics and criteria, accepted by the professional communities; verified and validated measurement tools, risk-informed methodologies of the built environment vulnerabilities and adaptive capabilities assessment, resilience of a building is just another speculative idea. Resilience of a building (hereafter RB) should be implemented in a decision-making and managerial processes as Building Resilience Assessment, Management and Engineering (BRAME) technology.

6. The main difference of the proposed "resilience management" paradigm from the well-known "risk management" paradigm is related to a choice of a strategic governing parameter. In case of risk management, it is a reduction of risk. Key governing principle here — ALARP — is to make risk "As Low as Reasonably Practicable". In case of resilience management, a key governing principle (see below) — AOARP — is to make resilience of built object "As Optimal (or Balanced) as Reasonably Practicable".

9 Conclusions

1. The resilience of the built environment is, probably, the only available now, under-estimated resource and systemic factor, which can really reduce multi-hazard risks in the near future.
2. Resilience of the built environment should become a goal and standard for provision of integrated safety and security of modern cities.
3. The proposed paradigm of "multi-hazard resilience management" is a natural evolution and extension of the risk management paradigm.
4. Management of resilience of the built environment should include at least three components:
   (a) network-enabled management of Shared Situational Awareness,
   (b) multi-hazard risk-informed management of Existing Vulnerabilities,
   (c) multi-hazard risk-informed management of Available Adaptive Capabilities.
5. The attaining of this formidable goal can permit to transform the implementation of BE to resist specific hazard combinations and thus enhance the quality of life, economic prosperity, safety, and security. A transformational engineering approach, which will be developed, permitting to enable society to build more resilient and robust civil constructions and systems. Whereas the new research will not create new infrastructures per se (that would take billions of dollars), new engineering design approaches and tools will emerge from this vital effort in multi-hazard research that will enable safer, more economical, and more secure BE.

Acknowledgment. Authors are grateful to the Russian Foundation of Basic Research for support of the grants, targeted on the development of the risk-informed technologies (11-07-00329-) and advanced visualization systems (11-07-13166-ofi--2011_RZD) for crisis management.

References

1. Carpenter, G.: Reinsurance Market Review 2010. Guy Capenter & Company (2010)
2. EU SEVESO II Directive, EU (1982)
3. Rasmussen, N.: The Reactor Safety Study WASH-1400. Nuclear Regulatory Commission (1975)
4. A Framework for an Integrated Risk Informed Decision Making Process, Insag-25. International Atomic Energy Agency, Vienna (2011)
5. Risk-Informed Decisionmaking for Science and Technology, Center for Technology and National Security Policy National Defense University, USA (2010)
6. Transportation security, Comprehensive Risk Assessments and Stronger Internal Controls Needed to Help Inform TSA Resource Allocation, GAO, USA (2009)
7. Kröger, W.: Critical infrastructures at risk: A need for a new conceptual approach and extended analytical tools. In: Reliability Engineering & System Safety, vol. 93(12), pp. 1781–1787 (2008)

8. Bosher, L. (ed.): Hazards and the Built Environment: Attaining Built-in Resilience. Taylor and Francis, Loughborough University (2008)
9. Vale, L.J., Campanella, T.J.: The Resilient City: How Modern Cities Recover from Disaster. Oxford University Press (2005)
10. Burby, R.J., Deyle, R.E., Godschalk, D.R., Olshansky, R.B.: Creating Hazard Resilient Communities through Land-Use Planning. Natural Hazards Review 1(2) (2000)
11. Allenby, B., Fink, J.: Toward Inherently Secure and Resilient Societies. Science 309, 1034–1036 (2005)
12. Allenby, B.: Environmental Threats and National Security: An International Challenge to Science and Technology. Lawrence Livermore National Laboratory (1999)
13. Holling, C.S.: Resilience and Stability of Ecosystems. Annual Review of Ecology and Systematics 4, 1–23 (1973)
14. Bodin, P., Wiman, B.: Resilience and other stability concepts in ecology: notes on their origin, validity and usefulness. ESS Bulletin 2(2), 33–43 (2004)
15. Resilience Alliance (1999), http://www.resalliance.org/
16. Stockholm Resilience Centre (2007), http://www.stockholmresilience.org/
17. Business continuity in Europe (2007), http://www.eurofound.europa.eu/emcc/content/source/eu04021a.htm?p1=reports&p2=null
18. Standard on business continuity (2012), http://www.bsigroup.com/en-GB/iso-22301-business-continuity/
19. Domestic Security: Civil Contingencies and Resilience in the United Kingdom. Chatham House, UK (2007)
20. UK government counter-terrorism strategy (2011), https://www.mi5.gov.uk/home/news/news-by-category/government/new-government-counter-terrorism-strategy-published.html
21. National Inrastructure Advisory Council: Critical Infrastructure Resilience (2009), http://www.dhs.gov/xlibrary/assets/niac/niac_critical_infrastructure_resilience.pdf
22. The Homeland Security Blog: DHS Reorienting around Resilience (2010), http://www.thehomelandsecurityblog.com/2010/04/23/dhs-reorienting-around-resilience/
23. Hazard and Risk Analysis of Aircraft Collision with High-Rise Building, Russian-Dutch research project, suported by NWO (NL) and RFBR (RU) (2002-2004)
24. Nato scientific publications (2012), http://www.nato.int/science/2012/scientific_publications.pdf
25. Pasman, H., Kirillov, I.: Resilience of Cities to Terrorist and Threats: learning from 9/11 and further research issues. NATO Science for Peace and Security Series C, Environmental Security. Springer (2008)
26. Kirillov, I.A., Klimenko, S.V.: Platos Atlantis Revisited: Risk-informed, Multi-Hazard Resilience of Built Environment via Cyber Worlds Sharing. In: 2010 International Conference on Cyberworlds (CW), Singapore, October 20-22, pp. 445–450 (2010), 10.1109/CW.2010.38
27. Wybo, J.L.: Mastering risks of damage and risks of crisis: the role of organisational learning. International Journal of Emergency Management 2(1/2) (2004)
28. Commission Staff Working Paper, Risk Assessment and Mapping Guidelines for Disaster Management, Brussels, 1626 final (2010)
29. NIST and the World Trade Center (2011), http://wtc.nist.gov/

30. ARMONIA: Assessing and Mapping Multiple Risks for Spatial Planning - project (2007), http://ec.europa.eu/research/environment/pdf/publications/fp6/natural_hazards//armonia.pdf
31. MATRIX: New Multi-Hazard and Multi-Risk Assessment Methods for Europe (2010), http://matrix.gpi.kit.edu/downloads/Fact-sheet-matrix-general.pdf
32. SMARTeST: Smart Resilience Technology, Systems and Tools (2009), http://www.citg.tudelft.nl/fileadmin/Faculteit/CiTG/Over_de_faculteit/Afdelingen/Afdeling_Waterbouwkunde/sectie_waterbouwkunde/people/personal/gelder/doc/SMARTest.pdf
33. Delvosalle, C., Fievez, C., Pipart, A., Londiche, H., Debray, B.: Effect of Safety Systems on the Definition of Reference Accident Scenarios in Seveso Establishments. In: WP 1, ARAMIS Project (2004), http://mahb.jrc.it/fileadmin/ARAMIS/downloads/wp1/WP1_LP_04.pdf

Recognizing Avatar Faces Using Wavelet-Based Adaptive Local Binary Patterns with Directional Statistical Features

Abdallah A. Mohamed[1,3], Marina L. Gavrilova[2], and Roman V. Yampolskiy[1]

[1] Computer Engineering and Computer Science,
University of Louisville, Louisville, KY, 40292, USA
[2] Department of Computer Science, University of Calgary,
Calgary, Alberta, T2N1N4, Canada
[3] Department of Mathematics, Menoufia University,
Shebin El-Koom, Menoufia, 32511, Egypt
{aamoha04,roman.yampolskiy}@louisville.edu,
marina@cpsc.ucalgary.ca

Abstract. In this paper, a novel face recognition technique based on discrete wavelet transform and Adaptive Local Binary Pattern (ALBP) with directional statistical features is proposed. The proposed technique consists of three stages: preprocessing, feature extraction and recognition. In preprocessing and feature extraction stages, wavelet decomposition is used to enhance the common features of the same subject of images and the ALBP is used to extract representative features from each facial image. Then, the mean and the standard deviation of the local absolute difference between each pixel and its neighbors are used within ALBP and the nearest neighbor classifier to improve the classification accuracy of the LBP. Experiments conducted on two virtual world avatar face image datasets show that our technique performs better than LBP, PCA, multi-scale Local Binary Pattern, ALBP and ALBP with directional statistical features (ALBPF) in terms of accuracy and the time required to classify each facial image to its subject.

Keywords: Face recognition, avatar, Adaptive Local Binary Pattern (ALBP), wavelet transform, LBPF.

1   Introduction

Biometrics research investigates methods and techniques for recognizing humans based on their behavioral and physical characteristics or traits [1]. Face recognition is something that people usually perform effortlessly and routinely in their everyday life and it is the process of identifying individuals from their faces' intrinsic characteristics. Automated face recognition has become one of the main targets of investigation for researchers in biometrics, pattern recognition, computer vision, and machine learning communities. This interest is driven by a wide range of commercial and law enforcement practical applications that require the use of face recognition

M.L. Gavrilova et al. (Eds.): Trans. on Comput. Sci. XVIII, LNCS 7848, pp. 137–154, 2013.

technologies [2]. These applications include access control, automated crowd surveillance, face reconstruction, mugshot identification, human-computer interaction and multimedia communication.

Face recognition is not limited only to recognizing human faces but it should also work for recognizing faces of non-biological entities such as avatars from virtual worlds. Virtual worlds are populated by millions of avatars. These avatars have the ability to do a lot of good and bad things. These bad and destructive purposes include traditional crimes like identity theft, fraud, tax evasion and terrorist activities [3].

Second Life is one of the virtual worlds that are populated by numerous terrorist organizations associated with Al-Qaeda who can train in such environments similar to the real ones. These criminal activities emerged the interest of the law enforcement experts in accurate and automatic tracking of users and their avatars [3]. To address the need for a decentralized, affordable, automatic, fast, secure, reliable, and accurate means of identity authentication for avatars, the concept of Artimetrics has emerged [4, 5, 6]. Artimetrics is a new area of study concerned with visual and behavioral recognition and identity verification of intelligent software agents, domestic and industrial robots, virtual world avatars and other non-biological entities [4, 5, 6]. People often complain about the insufficient security system in the Second Life which motivates our research on security in virtual worlds [4, 6].

Many algorithms were proposed to recognize human faces, such as Principal Component Analysis (PCA) [7], Linear Discriminant Analysis (LDA) [8] and Local Binary Pattern (LBP) [9-12], however recognizing virtual worlds' avatar faces is still very limited. There were some attempts to recognize avatar faces. For example, Boukhris et al. [13] used Daubechies wavelet transform with Support Vector Machines (SVM). Mohamed and Yampolskiy [14] applied the first and the second levels of decomposition with LBP. Mohamed et al. [3] applied hierarchical multi-scale LBP with wavelet transform. Mohamed and Yampolskiy [2] applied different levels of Daubechies wavelet transform on multiscale adaptive LBP with directional features to recognize avatar faces from two different virtual worlds.

In this paper, we propose a new face recognition technique to recognize avatar faces from different virtual worlds. In our technique, we apply different wavelet families on two datasets of avatar faces from two virtual worlds rather than just apply one wavelet family as Mohamed and Yampolskiy applied in [2]. Therefore, we have to select the wavelet family that best describe each dataset. We applied these wavelet families with different numbers of training and testing images. Also, our technique computes the mean and the standard deviation of the local absolute difference between each pixel and its neighbors (in a specific block of pixels) within the Adaptive Local Binary Pattern (ALBP) operator and the nearest neighbor classifier to improve the accuracy rate. We have to note that during our experiments avatar faces are chosen for training randomly to increase the confidence in our technique. The efficacy of our proposed method is demonstrated by performing experiments on two different avatar datasets from Second Life and Entropia Universe virtual worlds.

The rest of this paper is organized as follows; Section 2 introduces a background about virtual worlds, avatars and the insecurity of virtual worlds. Section 3 provides an introduction to wavelet decomposition. In Section 4, an overview of LBP with directional statistical features is presented. Section 5, presents the proposed method, Wavelet Adaptive LBP with directional statistical features (WALBPF). In Section 6, experimental results are presented followed by conclusions in Section 7.

2   Background

2.1   Virtual Worlds

Becoming an indispensable part of today's modern life, the internet has added new contexts for daily activities. Specifically, one of the major breakthroughs of the World Wide Web is that it facilitates the creation of interactive web pages that can be accessed worldwide [15]. The roles these web pages play range from facilitating simple communications (e.g., emails, chat, etc.) to more complex ways of communicating including video conferencing and banking. One of the most recent and fast growing applications of these interactive web pages is what has been called three-dimensional virtual worlds. In these virtual worlds (Virtual Reality), computer graphics are manipulated to render simultaneous, interactive, and three-dimensional environments, which mimics real world environments [16]. Designed this way, virtual worlds look realistic to the user to a great extent. This virtual reality thus provides the user with a personal digital space where he or she can perform real world activities. Individuals as well as groups sharing common interests and activities can communicate across the world easily [17]. Accessing these worlds is becoming easier and easier with technology advancement. The presence of virtual worlds and their being easily accessed may lead to transformation of the operation of whole societies. With advancement in building Massively Multiplayer Online Games (MMOG), virtual worlds became even more accessible and popular [15].

At the present time, there are several well-known virtual world online applications such as Second Life [18], Entropia Universe [19], Active Worlds [20] and Sims Online [21]. Second Life for instance is a multi-user online three-dimensional virtual world, which includes up to 20 million registered users. It facilitates education, socializing, shopping, starting small businesses and enterprises as well as making money [18]. The diversity of interests that can exist in a virtual world is clearly shown in the activities that are facilitated by second life as well as other worlds. Thus, real businesses can exist and actually flourish in virtual worlds. Realizing how popular these sites are becoming, well know companies, TV and radio channels as well as prestigious schools are using them. Reuters for instance has built a virtual headquarters in second life so that it would be able to broadcast news not only in the real world but to the virtual one as well. News broadcast sessions have been broadcast by the National Public Radio through second life as well. IBM arranged for a gathering of its employees also in Second Life. Universities are building islands in virtual worlds where classes can be offered. For instance, Harvard Law School offers a CyberOne course partly on Berkman Island in Second Life [22]. Indiana University's Kelly school of business has established a presence also in Second Life virtual world [13, 23]. Companies like Dell, Cisco, Xerox and Nissan have stores within Second Life. Virtual worlds thus host and offer different activities for its residents. They have been used as environments for games and adventure. For example in Everquest and World of Craft which are examples of Massively Multiplayer Online Role Playing Games (MMORPGs) the main activity that the virtual world establishes is the creation of an entertaining virtual world for games. Unlike games, adventure based virtual worlds, offer computer mediated environment so that the residents would interact free of a dictated plot or a specific story or adventure line. Music Television (aka MTV) established a virtual world (i.e., MTV's Virtual Laguna Beach) where users can have access to the MTV Laguna Beach television and can interact live with family and friends. MTV future plans include holding virtual music concerts as well [24].

(a)   (b)

Fig. 1. a) Harvard Law School lecture in Second Life [22] b) and Indiana University Kelly School of business in second Life [23]

2.2   Avatars

Originally, the word avatar comes from a religious Hindu expression meaning the appearance or the manifestation of a god in human or super human form [25]. An avatar is simply a digital identity of a user. An avatar is a representation of the user that enables interaction in 3D or in 2D contexts. Users usually prefer to have social presence in these worlds by creating distinct and different avatars. The created avatars sometimes refer to user's own personality or to a made-up identity. Although the avatar is a representation of a user identity, it is still not authentic. Users have the choice of how they would look like as well as how they can express themselves via such chosen appearance. Some users might make decisions to disclose facts about themselves with their choice of the appearance of an avatar. Others might use a popular image as their avatar. The same avatar can be used by a user in different online sessions. Some of the avatars mirror a user's role in virtual world which is reflected by an outfit or a specific appearance. Some users avatars are given a realistic look that resembles a human being. Users who tend to make such realistic choice of avatar appearance believe this would help them create a closer connection with their avatars. Some online websites restrict avatar identities to one per a single user. This requirement would avoid problems of trust, as a user will not be able to use alternative identities. Avatars have different aspects that include animations, emotions, gestures, speech, and voice. Virtual world service providers require that a user gives up his or her rights of the avatar they created or chose to the providers.

Subsequently, this agreement makes ownership of an avatar a debatable issue. Virtual world service providers also have the right to terminate an avatar as well as its user's account [26].

The figures below (Fig. 2) show examples of avatars from Second Life and Entropia Universe. There is a relationship between how an avatar would look like and how the user would behave within virtual worlds. For instance, users who create attractive avatars usually reveal more information to strangers more than users with unattractive avatars. Also, tall avatars correspond to a confident user especially during tasks requiring decision making. Realistic looking avatars show a great deal of positive social interactions.

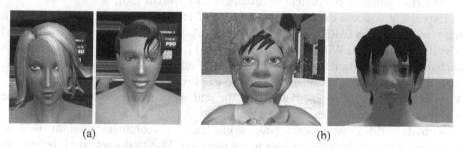

(a)   (b)

Fig. 2. Examples of avatar images from: a) Enrtopia Universe virtual world [19], b) Second Life virtual world [18]

It has been noticed that users would treat avatars warmly if the avatar looks similar to them [27]. Within virtual worlds, an avatar has the ability to move within its 3D or 2D environment to execute a task. Important characteristics of this society is sharing and trading which maintain and increase the unity within avatar groups. Communication is a very essential characteristic of an avatar as it maintains interactions with other users in the virtual world. Communication can take different forms. It could be 1) Verbal, 2) non-Verbal, 3) Asynchronous, 4) Synchronous, 5) direct and 6) indirect. Users can communicate using instant messages, message boards, emails, Voice over Internet Protocol (VoIP) as well as text chat.

2.3   The Lack of Security of Virtual Worlds

Because of their becoming part of our society, determining the identity of avatars is indispensable. Determining the identity of these artificial entities is as important as authenticating human beings. Mostly, an avatar would bear resemblance to its real life owner. There is a high demand for an affordable, fast, reliable means to authenticate avatars [4].

Terrorist activities as well as cybercrimes are increasing in virtual worlds. For instance, it has been reported that terrorists recruit within virtual communities such as Second Life [28]. Authorities such as U.S. government's Intelligence Advanced Research Projects Activity (IARPA) believe that they may use virtual worlds for illegal activities. They issue the warning that "avatars" could be used to recruit new members online, transfer untraceable funds and engage in training exercises useful for real-world terrorist operations [28]. Several examples of terrorist activities have been reported within Second Life like flying a helicopter into Nissan Building or the bombing of ABC's headquarters. Another example is where armed militants forced their way into an American Apparel store and shot several customers and then plant a bomb outside a store [29].

Regrettably, these wrong doers cannot be prosecuted for their criminal behavior because these crimes were committed in a virtual world where laws do not exist. Anonymity as well as global access in an online virtual world where there are ease of access banking services that allow for transactions away from the normal routs has made virtual worlds a convenient environment for terrorists [30].

Expressing concern over the consequences of leaving virtual worlds in such as a state, researchers in IARPA note that "The virtual world is the next great frontier and is still a very much a Wild West environment [31]. It provides many opportunities to exchange messages in the clear without drawing unnecessary attention. Additionally, there are many private channels that can be employed to exchange secret messages". Virtual world has all the activities that the real world has and therefore, possible scenarios of these activities should be thought about [30].

Virtual world environments pose a challenge as communication as well as commercial service between avatars is not recorded. Due to the set-up of the system, companies cannot monitor the creation and use of virtual buildings as well as training centers. Although some of them have been protected by what is described as unbreakable passwords, there have been reports of fraud and other virtual crimes. The situation is getting gloomier as companies in other countries are starting to establish their own virtual worlds. This shows urgency in addressing the issue of the security of virtual worlds. For instance, the founders of the Chinese virtual world HiPiHi [32] which houses prestigious companies such as IBM and Intel aim to create ways to enable avatars to move freely from their virtual world and other virtual environments such as Second Life or Entropia. This in turn would make it difficult to identify avatar or real users behind avatars. The underground activities associated with real world criminals and terrorists will increase in these environments due to accessibility and secrecy they offer.

3   Decomposing an Image Using Wavelet Transform

Wavelet Transform (WT) or Discrete wavelet Transform (DWT) is a popular tool for analyzing images in a variety of signal and image processing applications including multi-resolution analysis, computer vision and graphics. It provides multi-resolution representation of the image which can analyze image variation at different scales. Many articles have discussed its mathematical background and advantages [2, 33]. WT can be applied in image decomposition for many reasons [2, 33]: WT reduces the computational complexity of the system, reduces the computational overhead of the system and supports both spatial and frequency characteristics of images.

WT decomposes facial images into approximate, horizontal, vertical and diagonal coefficients. Approximate coefficient of one level is repeatedly decomposed into the four coefficients of the next level of decomposition. The process goes on until you find the best level of decomposition describing the dataset of images that we have.

Decomposing an image with the first level of WT provides four sub-bands LL_1, HL_1, HL_1 and HH_1. The sub-band LL represents the approximation coefficient of the wavelet decomposition and it has the low frequency information of the face image [34]. This information includes the common features of the same class. The other sub-bands represent the detailed coefficients of the wavelet decomposition and they have most of the high frequency information of the face image. This information includes local changes of face image such as illumination and facial expression. To improve recognition performance we have to enhance the common features of the same class and remove changes. So, during our experiments we considered only the approximation images. Decomposing an image with two scales will give us seven sub-bands [33]: LL_2, HL_2, LH_2, HH_2, HL_1, LH_1 and HH_1 as in Fig. 3.

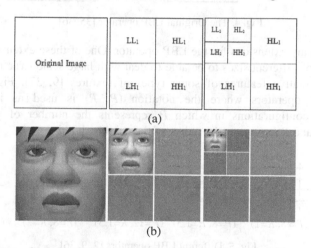

Fig. 3. a) Structure of one-level and two-level wavelet decomposition [34] b) An example of decomposing an image using one-level and two-level wavelet decomposition

4 Local Binary Pattern (LBP) with Directional Statistical Features

4.1 LBP Operator

The local binary pattern (LBP) is a very simple and efficient descriptor proposed by Ojala et al. [35] to describe local textural patterns. LBP has gained a wide range of popularity in describing images' texture [36]. It labels each pixel in an image by thresholding its neighbors with the central pixel value of that neighborhood, multiplied by powers of two and then added together to form the new value (label) for the center pixel (see Fig. 4) by using [11]:

$$LBP(x_c, y_c) = \sum_{i=0}^{7} 2^i S(g_i - g_c) \tag{1}$$

where g_c denotes the gray value of the center pixel (x_c, y_c), g_i ($i = 0,1,2,..,7$) are the gray values of its surrounding 8 pixels and the decision function $S(g_i - g_c)$ can be defined as follows:

$$S(g_i - g_c) = \begin{cases} 1, & g_i \geq g_c \\ 0, & otherwise \end{cases} \tag{2}$$

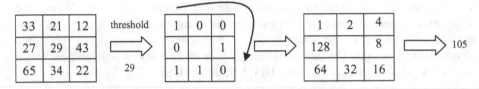

Fig. 4. The Original LBP operator [35, 36]

There are many extensions for the LBP operator. One of these extensions is to use neighborhood of different sizes to be able to deal with large scale structures that may be the representative features of some types of textures [9, 37]. Fig. 5 displays different LBP operators where the notation (P, R) is used as indication of neighborhood configurations in which P represents the number of pixels in the neighborhood and R represents the radius of the neighborhood.

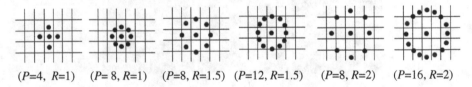

$(P=4, R=1)$ $(P= 8, R=1)$ $(P=8, R=1.5)$ $(P=12, R=1.5)$ $(P=8, R=2)$ $(P=16, R=2)$

Fig. 5. Different LBP operators [2, 9, 36]

LBP operator can also be extended to other definitions and patterns. One of the most important extensions to the basic LBP operator is called uniform LBP (ULBP). An LBP is called uniform if the binary pattern representation contains at most two different conversions from 0 to 1 or 1 to 0 when the binary string is viewed as a circular bit string [9]. For example, 10000001, 10111111 and 10000011 are uniform patterns. The results of statistical analysis indicated that most of patterns in images are uniform patterns. Ojala reported that with (8, 1) neighborhood, uniform patterns account for a little less than 90% of all patterns and with (16, 2) neighborhood, uniform patterns account for around 70% of all patterns [35].

4.2   LBP Histogram

After labeling an image with the LBP the histogram of the labeled image can be defined as follows [35]:

$$H_i = \sum_{x,y} I(f(x, y) = i), i = 0,1,.., n-1 \tag{3}$$

where '$n=2^P$' is the number of different labels produced by the LBP operator, $f(x, y)$ is the labeled image and $I(A)$ is a decision function with value 1 if the event A is true and 0 otherwise.

To form the LBP histogram, the image has to be divided into sub-regions. Then, the LBP histogram for each sub-region has to be computed and then all sub-regions histograms have to be combined to form the feature histogram of the whole image [12].

4.3 LBP with Directional Statistical Features

For any given image of size N x M, let g_c is its central pixel and g_p is its circular neighbors, where $p = 0,1,...,P-1$. The local difference $|g_c - g_p|$ has the mean (μ_p) and the standard deviation (σ_p) that can be computed using:

$$\mu_p = \sum_{i=1}^{N} \sum_{j=1}^{M} |g_c(i, j) - g_p(i, j)| / (M * N) \tag{4}$$

$$\sigma_p = \sqrt{\sum_{i=1}^{N} \sum_{j=1}^{M} (|g_c(i, j) - g_p(i, j)| - \mu_p)^2 / (M * N)} \tag{5}$$

where μ_p and σ_p represent the first-order and the second-order directional statistics of the local difference $|g_c - g_p|$ along orientation $2\pi p/P$ [38]. The vector $\vec{\mu} = [\mu_0, \mu_1,..., \mu_{P-1}]$ refers to the mean vector and $\vec{\sigma} = [\sigma_0, \sigma_1,..., \sigma_{P-1}]$ refers to the standard deviation (*std*) vector.

The two vectors represent the directional statistical features of the local difference $|g_c - g_p|$ and they carry useful information for image discrimination that can be used to define the weighted LBP dissimilarity. Let $\vec{\mu}_X$ and $\vec{\sigma}_X$ refer to the directional statistical feature vectors for a sample test image X while $\vec{\mu}_Y$ and $\vec{\sigma}_Y$ refer to the two vectors for a class model Y then the normalized distances between $\vec{\mu}_X$ and $\vec{\mu}_Y$, and $\vec{\sigma}_X$ and $\vec{\sigma}_Y$ can be defined as:

$$d_\mu = \sum_{p=0}^{P-1} |\vec{\mu}_X(p) - \vec{\mu}_Y(p)| / (P * e_\mu), \quad d_\sigma = \sum_{p=0}^{P-1} |\vec{\sigma}_X(p) - \vec{\sigma}_Y(p)| / (P * e_\sigma) \tag{6}$$

where e_μ and e_σ are the standard deviations of $\vec{\mu}$ and $\vec{\sigma}$ respectively from training samples images [38, 39].

So the weighted LBP dissimilarity with statistical features using d_μ and d_σ can be defined as:

$$D_{LBP}^F(X,Y) = D_{LBP}(X,Y) * (1 + c_1 - c_1 * \exp(-d_\mu / c_2)) * (1 + c_1 - c_1 * \exp(-d_\sigma / c_2)) \tag{7}$$

where $D_{LBP}(X, Y)$ is the LBP histogram dissimilarity, c_1 and c_2 are two control parameters for the weights[38].

5   Wavelet Adaptive LBP with Directional Statistical Features (WALBPF)

5.1   Preprocessing Datasets

For both types of datasets (Second Life dataset and Entropia Universe dataset) we have to get rid of the background of each image. The presence of the background of an image has an effect on identifying that image. To remove the background of an image we manually cropped this image so that that the new face only image contains two eyes, nose and mouth.

During our experiments we decomposed all facial images using different levels of decomposition and with different wavelet families to decide which will be the best family for the accuracy rate and inside this family which level of decomposition will be better for both accuracy rate and processing time.

5.2   Adaptive Local Binary Pattern (ALBP)

The directional statistical feature vectors can be used to improve the classification performance of an image by minimizing the variations of the mean and the *std* of the directional difference along different orientations. To this end a new version of the LBP was proposed by Guo et al., called Adaptive LBP (ALBP), to reduce the estimation error of local difference between each pixel and its neighbors [38]. A new parameter called weight (w_p) is defined in the LBP equation and so the new definition of the LBP equation will have the following form [38, 40]:

$$ALBP_{P,R} = \sum_{p=0}^{P-1} 2^p S(g_p * w_p - g_c) \qquad (8)$$

where the objective function to compute the weight w_p is as follows:

$$J = \sum_{i=1}^{N} \sum_{j=1}^{M} (g_c(i,j) - w.g_p(i,j))^2 \qquad (9)$$

The target of the objective function is to minimize the directional difference $|g_c - w_p * g_p|$. To this end we have to derive equation 9 with respect to w and assign the derivation to zero as follows:

$$\frac{\partial J}{\partial w} = -2\sum_{i=1}^{N} \sum_{j=1}^{M} (g_p(i,j)(g_c(i,j) - wg_p(i,j))) = 0 \qquad (10)$$

So we get:

$$w\sum_{i=1}^{N} \sum_{j=1}^{M} g_p(i,j)g_p(i,j) = \sum_{i=1}^{N} \sum_{j=1}^{M} g_p(i,j)g_c(i,j) \qquad (11)$$

$$w = \frac{\sum\limits_{i=1}^{N}\sum\limits_{j=1}^{M} g_p(i,j) g_c(i,j)}{\sum\limits_{i=1}^{N}\sum\limits_{j=1}^{M} g_p(i,j) g_p(i,j)} \qquad (12)$$

From equation 12 we get:

$$w_p = \vec{g}_p^T \vec{g}_c / (\vec{g}_p^T \vec{g}_p) \qquad (13)$$

where $\vec{g}_c = [g_c(1,1); g_c(1,2); \ldots; g_c(N,M)]$ is a column vector that contains all possible values of any pixel $g_c(i,j)$, $N \times M$ is the size of an image and $\vec{g}_p = [g_p(1,1); g_p(1,2); \ldots; g_p(N,M)]$ is the corresponding vector for all $g_p(i,j)$ pixels. Let $\vec{w} = [w_0, w_1, \ldots, w_{P-1}]$ refers to the ALBP weight vector. We have to note that each weight w_p is computed along one orientation $2\pi p/P$ for the whole image.

5.3   ALBP with Directional Statistical Features (ALBPF)

By using the ALBP weight the directional statistics equations (4) and (5) can be changed to [38]:

$$\mu_p = \sum\limits_{i=1}^{N}\sum\limits_{j=1}^{M} \left| g_c(i,j) - g_p(i,j) * w_p \right| / (M * N) \qquad (14)$$

$$\sigma_p = \sqrt{\sum\limits_{i=1}^{N}\sum\limits_{j=1}^{M} \left(\left| g_c(i,j) - g_p(i,j) * w_p \right| - \mu_p \right)^2 / (M * N)} \qquad (15)$$

Based on the ALBP weight w_p, we have three vectors $\vec{\mu}$, $\vec{\sigma}$ and $\vec{w}$. Similar to the normalized distance between $\vec{\mu}_X$ and $\vec{\mu}_Y$, and $\vec{\sigma}_X$ and $\vec{\sigma}_Y$ we can define the normalized distance between $\vec{w}_X$ and $\vec{w}_Y$ as:

$$d_w = \sum\limits_{p=0}^{P-1} \left| \vec{w}_X(p) - \vec{w}_Y(p) \right| / (P * e_w) \qquad (16)$$

where e_w is the standard deviation of $\vec{w}$ from training samples images [38, 39].

The weighted ALBP dissimilarity with statistical features using d_μ, d_σ and d_w can be defined as:

$$D_{ALBP}^F(X,Y) = D_{ALBP}(X,Y) * (1 + c_1 - c_1 * \exp(-d_\mu / c_2))$$
$$* (1 + c_1 - c_1 * \exp(-d_\sigma / c_2)) * (1 + c_1 - c_1 * \exp(-d_w / c_2)) \qquad (17)$$

where $D_{ALBP}(X, Y)$ is the ALBP histogram dissimilarity [38].

6   Experiments

In this section, we verify the performance of the proposed algorithm on two different types of datasets: the first type is the Second Life data set and the second is the

Entropia Universe dataset. Fig. 6 displays an example of two subjects from each dataset. The proposed method is compared with PCA [7], which is one of the most well-known methods in face recognition, single scale LBP, traditional multi-scale LBP, ALBP and ALBP with directional statistical features (ALBPF).

6.1   Experimental Setup

To evaluate the robustness of our proposed technique, we have to apply our system on different datasets of virtual characters and then compare the performance of our technique with others. During these experiments we collected two different datasets of avatars.

The first dataset was collected from the Second Life (SL) virtual world [18]. This dataset contains 581 gray scale images with size 1280 x 1024 pixels each to represent 83 different avatars. Each avatar subject has 7 different images for the same avatar with different frontal pose angle (front, far left, mid left, far right, mid right, top and bottom) and facial expression.

The second dataset was collected from Entropia Universe (ENT) virtual world [19]. ENT dataset contains 490 gray scale images with size 407 x 549 pixels. These images were organized in 98 subjects (avatars). Each subject has different 5 images for the same avatar with different frontal angle and facial details (wearing a mask or no).

The facial part of each image in SL and ENT datasets was manually cropped from the original images based on the location of the two eyes, mouth and the nose. The new size of each facial image in SL dataset is 260 x 260 pixels while in ENT dataset each facial image was resized to the size of 180 x 180 pixels. After applying the first level of wavelet decomposition the resolution of each facial image in the SL dataset will be reduced to be 130 x 130 and to 90 x 90 for ENT dataset.

Each one of the two datasets is divided into two independent groups, one for training and the second for testing. The training group images for each dataset are chosen randomly while the rest of images are used for testing. The size of each group differs from one experiment to another as we will explain in sections 6.2 and 6.3.

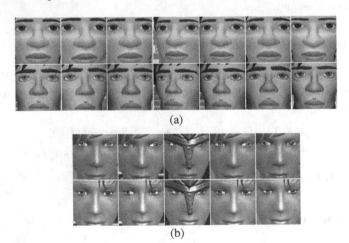

(a)

(b)

Fig. 6. Samples of two subjects of facial images from: a) Second Life dataset [18] b) Entropia Universe dataset [19]

6.2   Tests

We performed many tests in order to retain the best mother wavelet family to deal with our datasets and to decide the most efficient decomposition level within this wavelet family describing our datasets. The tests are performed under the condition of randomly selecting 4 images from each SL subject for training (3 images from each subject for testing) and 3 facial images from each ENT subject for training (2 images from each subject for testing). The results obtained from these tests are summarized in table 1.

The results obtained after applying different discrete wavelet families on SL and ENT datasets showed that the recognition rates are alike (ranged between 91.97% and 95.18% for SL dataset and between 91.33% and 95.92% for ENT dataset). The best recognition rate recorded for the SL dataset by two different wavelet families: "Symlet5" and "Db9" and its value is 95.18% while the best recognition rate recorded for ENT dataset by the wavelet family "Symlet9" and its value is 95.92. Once we determined the best wavelet family and its index we have to decide the best level of decomposition of this family. Table 2 summarizes the recognition rates obtained by applying different decomposition levels of the wavelet family "Symlet5" on SL dataset and the obtained recognition rates after applying different decomposition levels of "Symlet9" on ENT dataset.

Table 1. Recognition rate for SL and ENT datasets using tested wavelet families

Wavelet Family		Recognition Rate for SL	Recognition Rate for ENT
Haar		93.98%	93.37%
BiorSplines	Bior1.1	92.37%	92.35%
	Bior2.2	93.17%	94.39%
	Bio3.3	92.77%	91.84%
	Bior5.5	94.38%	91.33%
Daubechies	Db2	93.17%	93.37%
	Db5	94.38%	94.39%
	Db7	94.78%	94.90%
	Db9	**95.18%**	93.88%
	Db13	94.78%	92.35%
Coiflets	Coif1	93.98%	91.33%
	Coif3	94.38%	91.84%
	Coif5	93.17%	93.37%
Symlet	Sym2	94.38%	94.38%
	Sym5	**95.18%**	94.90%
	Sym9	93.57%	**95.92%**
	Sym13	93.17%	94.39%
ReverseBior	Rbio1.1	91.97%	93.37%
	Rbio2.6	93.17%	93.88%
	Rbio3.9	93.57%	94.39%
	Rbio5.5	92.77%	93.37%

Table 2. Recognition rates of the retained wavelet families with different decomposition levels

Decomposition Level	SL Recognition rate	ENT Recognition Rate
Level 1	92.37%	93.37%
Level 2	93.57%	93.88%
Level 3	**95.58%**	94.39%
Level 4	94.38%	95.41%
Level 5	94.38%	95.41%
Level 6	93.57%	**95.92%**
Level 7	93.17%	94.90%

6.3   Experimental Results

In order to gain better understanding on whether using wavelet transform with ALBPF is advantageous or not we compared WALBPF with ALBPF and ALBP. First we got the performance of WALBPF, ALBPF and ALBP with different LBP operator values (see Fig. 7) over the SL and ENT datasets.

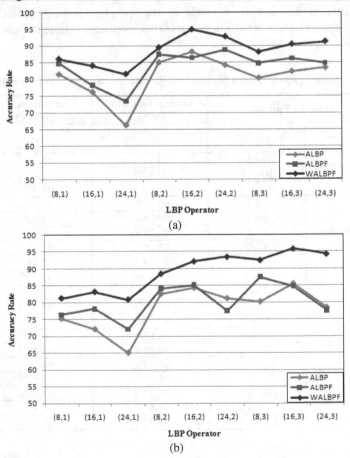

Fig. 7. Recognition rate using ALBP, ALBPF and WALBPF for: a) SL dataset b) ENT dataset

In this experiment the training sets were built by randomly selecting 4 images from each class of the SL dataset and 3 images from each class in ENT dataset. The results showed that the recognition rates obtained by WALBPF are better than those obtained by the other two methods with almost all LBP operators and with all datasets. The recognition rate on average obtained by WALBPF is greater than that of its closest competitor, which is ALBPF for both SL and ENT datasets by about 4% with SL dataset where the greatest accuracy is about 95% when LBP operator is (16, 2) and by about 9% with ENT dataset where the greatest accuracy is about 96% when the LBP operator is (16, 3).

The results showed also that not only the recognition rate of using WALBPF is better than that of the other two methods but also the time required to classify each input facial image to its class in case of applying WALBPF is less than that in the other two methods with different LBP operators (see table 3 to recognize the time required for processing the SL dataset). This is an expected result since one of the main reasons of using wavelet decomposition in face recognition systems is that it reduces the computational complexity and overhead of the system and so the system can run faster.

Table 3. Time in seconds required by different algorithms

Algorithm	LBP operator		
	(8, 1)	(16, 2)	(24, 3)
ALBP	5.34	11.34	178.34
ALBPF	5.55	11.73	179.45
WALBPF	2.12	4.29	166.78

We also compared the performance of our method, WALBPF, with some well-known face recognition algorithms such as PCA, LBP and multi-scale LBP using SL and ENT datasets and based on different number of training and testing images.

For both SL and ENT datasets we performed three experiments: for SL dataset, we selected one, three and five images from each class for training while the rest is for testing. For ENT dataset we selected one, two and three images from each class for training while the rest is for testing. All training images are selected randomly. We summarize the recognition rates in tables 4 and 5.

Table 4. Accuracy rates for SL dataset obtained by different algorithms

Algorithm	Number of training images		
	1	3	5
PCA	74.70% [14]	79.52%	84.34%
LBP	75.31% [14]	80.96%	89.16%
Multi-scale LBP	77.51%	82.41%	92.17%
WALBPF	80.12%	86.75%	93.98%

Table 5. Accuracy rates for ENT dataset obtained by different algorithms

Algorithm	Number of training images		
	1	2	3
PCA	61.22%	69.73%	85.20%
LBP	65.82% [3]	72.11%	88.27%
Multi-scale LBP	69.39%	75.51%	90.82%
WALBPF	72.19%	79.25%	96.43%

It is very clear from Fig. 7, tables 3, 4 and 5 that our proposed method can achieve better result than the other algorithms in terms of accuracy and classifying time.

7   Conclusion and Future Works

This paper describes a new face feature recognition approach based on applying different discrete wavelet transform families and an adaptive LBP descriptor with directional statistical features on avatar face datasets from different virtual worlds. Selecting the best wavelet family describing each avatar face dataset and deciding the proper level of decomposition within this family has a great effect on the performance of our technique. To evaluate the performance of our technique, we performed many comparisons between our technique and other techniques. Compared with ALBPF and ALBP and with different LBP operators, our proposed technique improved the recognition rate of the SL and ENT datasets by about 4% and 9% respectively. Also the time required by our technique to classify each input facial image to its class is less than the time in case of other methods. Compared with traditional well-known face recognition techniques (PCA, LBP and multi-scale LBP), our technique improved the recognition rate of faces based on different number of training and testing images from each class of the datasets used in the experiments. Applying different classifiers may lead to differentiate between avatar face images and other avatar face images and between avatar face images and human face images and this is what we intend to attempt in the future.

References

1. Zhenhua, G., Lei, D., Zhang, X.M.: Hierarchical multiscale LBP for face and palmprint recognition. In: Proc. IEEE International Conference on Image Processing, Hong Kong, pp. 4521–4524 (2010)
2. Mohamed, A.A., Yampolskiy, R.V.: Wavelet-Based Multiscale Adaptive LBP with Directional Statistical Features for Recognizing Artificial Faces. ISRN Machine Vision 2012 (2012)
3. Mohamed, A.A., D'Souza, D., Baili, N., Yampolskiy, R.V.: Avatar Face Recognition using Wavelet Transform and Hierarchical Multi-scale LBP. In: Proc. 10th IEEE International Conference on Machine Learning and Applications, Honolulu, Hawaii, pp. 194–199 (2011)

4. Gavrilova, M.L., Yampolskiy, R.: Applying biometric principles to avatar recognition. In: Gavrilova, M.L., Tan, C.J.K., Sourin, A., Sourina, O. (eds.) Transactions on Computational Science XII. LNCS, vol. 6670, pp. 140–158. Springer, Heidelberg (2011)
5. Oursler, J.N., Price, M., Yampolskiy, R.V.: Parameterized generation of avatar face dataset. In: Proc. 14th International Conference on Computer Games: AI, Animation, Mobile, Interactive Multimedia, Educational & Serious Games, Louisville, KY, pp. 17–22 (2009)
6. Gavrilova, M.L., Yampolskiy, R.V.: Applying biometric principles to avatar recognition. Transactions on Computational Sciences 12, 140–158 (2011)
7. Turk, M., Pentland, A.: Face recognition using Eigenfaces. In: Proc. IEEE Conference on Computer Vision and Pattern Recognition, Maui, HI, pp. 586–591 (1991)
8. Lu, L., Plataniotis, K.N., Venetsanopoulos, A.N.: Face recognition using LDA based algorithms. IEEE Trans. Neural networks 14(1), 195–200 (2003)
9. Ahonen, T., Hadid, A., Pietikäinen, M.: Face description with local binary patterns: Application to Face Recognition. IEEE Trans. Pattern Anal. Mach. Intell. 28(12), 2037–2041 (2006)
10. Chen, L., Wang, Y.-H., Wang, Y.-D., Huang, D.: Face recognition with statistical local binary patterns. In: Proc. 8th International Conference on Machine Learning and Cybernetics, Baoding, pp. 2433–2438 (2009)
11. Meng, J., Gao, Y., Wang, X., Lin, T., Zhang, J.: Face recognition based on local binary patterns with threshold. In: IEEE International Conference on Granular Computing, San Jose, CA, pp. 352–356 (2010)
12. Yang, H., Wang, Y.D.: A LBP-based face recognition method with hamming distance constraint. In: Proc. 4th International Conference on Image and Graphics, pp. 645–649 (2009)
13. Boukhris, M., Mohamed, A.A., D'Souza, D., Beck, M., Ben Amara, N.E., Yampolskiy, R.V.: Artificial human face recognition via Daubechies wavelet transform and SVM. In: Proc. 16th International Conference on Computer Games: AI, Animation, Mobile, Interactive Multimedia, Educational & Serious Games, Louisville, KY, pp. 18–25 (2011)
14. Mohamed, A.A., Yampolskiy, R.V.: An improved LBP algorithm for avatar face recognition. In: 23th International Symposium on Information, Communication and Automation Technologies, Sarajevo, Bosnia & Herzegovina, pp. 1–5 (2011)
15. Thompson, C.W.: Next-generation virtual worlds: architecture, status, and directions. IEEE Internet Computing 15(1), 60–65 (2011)
16. Dyck, M., Winbeck, M., Leiberg, S., Chen, Y., Gur, R.C., Mathiak, K.: Recognition profile of emotions in natural and virtual faces. PLoS ONE 3(11), e3628 (2008)
17. Trewin, S., Laff, M., Hanson, V., Cavender, A.: Exploring visual and motor accessibility in navigating virtual world. ACM Trans. Accessible Computing 2(2), 1–35 (2009)
18. Second Life, http://www.secondlife.com
19. Entropia Universe, http://www.entropiauniverse.com
20. Active Worlds, http://www.activeworlds.com
21. Sims Online, http://www.thesims.ea.com
22. Harvard Extension Class on Virtual Law Offers Lectures in Second Life, http://virtuallyblind.com/2007/11/17/harvard-extension-second-life/
23. Kelly School of Business, its executive education program to unveil virtual campus in Second Life, http://info.kelley.iu.edu/news/page/normal/8773.html

24. Bray, D.A., Konsynski, B.R.: Virtual worlds: multi-disciplinary research opportunities. SIGMIS Database 38(4), 17–25 (2007)
25. The Free Dictionary, http://www.thefreedictionary.com/avatar
26. Boberg, M., Piippo, P., Ollila, E.: Designing avatars. In: Proc. 3rd International Conference on Digital Interactive Media in Entertainment and Arts, Athens, Greece, pp. 232–239 (2008)
27. Neustaedter, C., Fedorovskaya, E.: Presenting identity in a virtual world through avatar appearances. In: Graphics Interface, Kelowna, British Colombia, Canada, pp. 183–190 (2009)
28. Cole, J.: Osama Bin Laden's "Second Life", Salon, http://www.salon.com/2008/02/25/avatars_2/
29. O'Brien, N.: Spies watch rise of virtual terrorists, http://www.news.com.au/top-stories/spies-watch-rise-of-virtual-terrorists/story-e6frfkp9-1111114075761
30. O'Harrow, R.: Spies Battleground Turns Virtual. The Washington Post, (2008), http://www.washingtonpost.com/wp-dyn/content/article/2008/02/05/AR2008020503144.html
31. Intelligence Advanced Research Projects Activity, http://www.iarpa.gov/
32. HiPiHi, http://www.hipihi.com/en/
33. Mazloom, M., Ayat, S.: Combinational method for face recognition: wavelet, PCA and ANN. In: International Conference on Digital Image Computing: Techniques and Applications, Canberra, pp. 90–95 (2008)
34. Garcia, C., Zikos, G., Tziritas, G.: A wavelet-based framework for face recognition. In: Proc. 5th European Conference on Computer Vision, Freiburg, Allemagne, pp. 84–92 (1998)
35. Ojala, T., Pietikäinen, M., Harwood, D.: A comparative study of texture measures with classification based on feature distributions. Pattern Recognition 29(1), 51–59 (1996)
36. Ojala, T., Pietikäinen, M., Mäenpää, T.: Multiresolution gray-scale and rotation invariant texture classification with local binary patterns. IEEE Trans. Pattern Anal. Mach. Intell. 24(7), 971–987 (2002)
37. Wang, W., Chang, F., Zhao, J., Chen, Z.: Automatic facial expression recognition using local binary pattern. In: 8th World Congress on Intelligent Control and Automation, Jinan, China, pp. 6375–6378 (2010)
38. Guo, Z., Zhang, L., Zhang, D., Zhang, S.: Rotation Invariant Texture Classification Using Adaptive LBP with Directional Statistical Features. In: 17th IEEE International Conference on Image Processing, Hong Kong, pp. 285–288 (2010)
39. Manjunath, B.S., Ma, W.Y.: Texture features for browsing and retrieval of image data. IEEE Trans. Pattern Anal. Mach. Intell. 18(8), 837–842 (1996)
40. Mohamed, A.A., Yampolskiy, R.V.: Face recognition based wavelet transform and adaptive local binary pattern. In: 4th International Conference on Digital Forensics & Cyber Crime, Lafayette, Indiana, USA (2012)

Real-Time Reactive Biped Characters
Staying Upright and Balanced

Ben Kenwright

School of Computer Science
Newcastle University
United Kingdom
b.kenwright@ncl.ac.uk

Abstract. In this paper, we present a real-time technique of generating reactive balancing biped character motions for used in time critical systems, such as games. Our method uses a low-dimensional physics-based model to provide key information, such as foot placement and postural location, to control the movement of a fully articulated virtual skeleton. Furthermore, our technique uses numerous approximation techniques, such as comfort reasoning and foot support area, to mimic real-world humans in real-time that can respond to disturbances, such as pushes or pulls. We demonstrate the straightforwardness and robustness of our technique by means of a numerous of simulation examples.

Keywords: real-time, biped, reactive, animation, balancing, inverse kinematics, in-verted pendulum, foot placement, stepping.

1   Introduction

1.1   Motivation, Interest, and Importance

Generating, adapting, and identifying realistic, life-like virtual 3D biped character movements in real-time is challenging, important, and interesting [1][2][3]. Moreover, for interactive environments, such as games, there is the added complexity of adapting the final motions, so they engage and accommodate unforeseen circumstances, such as pushes, trips, and falls, while being controllable and natural looking. What is more, since virtual characters possess a huge number of degrees of freedom, they can create a vast and diverse set of distinct actions with emotions, such as sad, tired, and happy. These actions in real-life are usually unique, since people have different characteristics (e.g., strength, size, age, and mood). Consequently, a flexible dynamic physics-based solution can solve the majority of the problems and create unique, non-repetitive, and interactive virtual character movements that are believable, both on their own or as part of a crowd situation [1][4].

A key biped character action that is fundamental for any virtual environment is upright balancing (i.e., the ability to remain upright during either standing or during locomotion). Consequently, this paper focuses specifically on creating upright balancing motions without key-frame data. Whereby, we use simplified physics-based

M.L. Gavrilova et al. (Eds.): Trans. on Comput. Sci. XVIII, LNCS 7848, pp. 155–171, 2013.

approximation methods and intelligent stepping logic to generate the final motions. We focus in particular on the dynamic and adaptable nature of upright biped characters and the creation of interactive and responsive animations that are controllable and physically realistic (i.e., less Spiderman like). We approach the problem using a KISS (keep it simple and straightforward) methodology by means of simplified estimations that allow us to create solutions that are computationally fast, robust, and practical, and can be used in time critical environments, such as games.

We demonstrate our approach using numerous simulation situations (e.g., being pushed, holding objects of varying weight, following paths) to show the potential, dynamic nature, and robustness of using our method for creating a more engaging and interactive character solution. Our results show how a character can generate physically realistic motions for balancing and stepping that can recover from force disturbances, such as hits. While our approach is limited to upright motions and focuses purely on balancing and stepping logic, we believe that our method can easily be combined with other techniques (e.g., motion capture data, or random coherent motions [5][6]) to produce a hybrid solution. This hybrid solution would present a more complete character system with a large repertoire of actions that is both physically accurate and interactive while possessing highly realistic human characteristics.

Making human-like characters react convincingly and in a physically plausible way to disturbances is difficult due to characters possessing a high degree of complexity and flexibility. While approaches that use purely inverse kinematic methods in conjunction with key-framed data to emulate responsive character movements can produce realistic movement in real-time they can fail to generate realistically interactive results [7][8]. Moreover, while pre-canned animations can produce very life-like and realistic character movements, they can also be repetitive, predictable, and unresponsive [5][6] (i.e., lack the ability to adapt to unforeseen circumstances in real-time realistically).

The inverted pendulum (IP) has long been a popular solution for providing dynamic and responsive physics-based information for character systems [9][10] that we also employ in this paper. The IP method is a low-dimensional mechanism for approximating dynamic characteristics of a biped. We use this model in place of the complex articulated character structure. The IP model gives us a computationally fast and robust way to generate reliable dynamic information for balancing. However, the IP basic model does not provide any decisive data about the feet (e.g., how they transition, or how they handle constraint conditions). Nevertheless, we use the basic IP model and extend it to include additional foot information to produce a more stable and physical accurate biped character stepping model (e.g., include foot orientation, foot torque, position transition paths). Hence, our approach builds on development a robust and efficient foot placement controller that can generator or correct character motions so are more natural and responsive.

1.2   Contribution

The contributions of this paper are numerous approximation techniques for creating a practical, computationally efficient, and robust balancing biped character system that can produce physically realistic, responsive, character motions. The novel approach focuses around simplifying the biped foot support region (e.g., using spheres and capsules) to produce approximate foot placement and balancing information (e.g., position, orientation, path trajectories) in conjunction with an intelligent physics-based model to generate interactive character movements that we can use to control a fully articulated skeleton body.

1.3   Roadmap

The roadmap for the rest of the paper is as follows. Section 2 gives a broad overview of the related research; Section 3 presents a system overview of the interconnected components and our approach. Then Sections 4 to Section 6 describe the individual components and their workings. Section 7 presents our results. Section 8 and 9 discusses limitation and performance factors. Finally, we conclude with Section 10 that discusses further work and conclusions.

2   Related Work

Creating stable, responsive, balancing biped characters by means of physics-based techniques has been investigated across numerous fields (e.g., computer graphics and robotics). Hence, we briefly review some of the most recent and interesting developments over the past few years that have contributed to creating more dynamic and reactive character solutions.

2.1   Computer Graphics

One of the biggest challenges in 3D character development, and probably one of the most rewarding and interesting, is mimicking the dynamic interactive properties of actual real-world human characters. Hence, it has been a hot topic of research in the graphics industry for a number of years. Firstly, Komura [11] simulated reactive motions for running and walking of human figures, while Zordan [12] simulated characters that responded automatically to impacts and smoothly returned to tracking, and later [13] presented work for combining existing motion capture data from humans to produce physics-based responsive motion segments that reacted to varying force disturbances (demonstrated using a martial art test bed).

Shiratori [14] developed a novel controller that could generate responsive balancing actions; while Tang [15] modified interactive character motions for falling with realistic responses to unexpected forces.

McCann [16] presented that blending between various motion capture segments to produce responsive character motions. Additionally, Arikan [17] did similar work on generating how people respond to being pushed around.

In the same way, a method similar to the one we presented in this research paper was also offered by Singh [2] who focused on a simplified footstep model for simulating crowds by means of circle foot approximations and local pelvis space to generate foot position and orientation information. Wu [18] presented a method for controlling animated characters by modifying their foot placement information so that it was physically correct.

The work in the paper follows on from Kenwright [1] who focused on foot placement approximations to produce responsive biped characters for real-time environments. We similarly embrace the same low-dimensional physics-based model in combination with a foot support area to create a fast, robust, and straightforward method of generating reactive character motions that can automatically compensate for disturbances, such as pushes. However, we incorporate a physics-based rigid body skeleton on top of the inverse kinematic solution (i.e., joint angles) and joint torques to produce more fluid and less rigid movement.

2.2   Robotics

Emphasising some of the relevant work in the field of robotics that contributed to the development of responsive biped controllers, we outline a few interesting and important papers. Shih [19] developed a straightforward model for enabling characters to respond to small disturbances. While Stephens [20] and Pratt [21] developed controllers that could generate motions to recover from a range of push disturbances.

3   System Overview

In our approach, we use a low-dimensional base controller for estimating key information for highly complex articulated characters that enable us to determine intelligent foot place information to remain balanced and upright. The low-dimensional controller calculates information on where to place the characters foot to produce the desired upright motion. The controller can be iteratively updated to give corrective feedback information to ensure the resulting motion is achieved (e.g., due to minor force disturbances and numerical inaccuracies).

We take the basic inverted pendulum model and incorporate additional information to gain greater control through feedback approximations from the feet. However, while this paper primarily focuses on the feet to gain additional control, alternative research has been done to extend other areas of the inverted pendulum. For example, Kenwright [22] extended the inverted pendulum model to include an elongated 3D rigid body to produce additional postural information in collaboration with further control possibilities.

The inverted pendulum model presents an ideal method for emulating a character's leg since the human muscle is mechanically analogous to a spring-damper system; consequently, stiffness and damping factors can be calculated to mimic a person's limbs and how they would respond (see Figure 1).

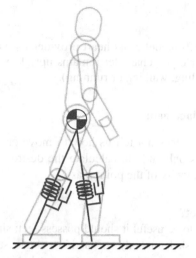

Fig. 1. Illustration of how the inverted pendulum can represent a character's overall centre-of-mass and legs

The system produces physically realistic responsive character motions, which have the added advantage of being computationally simple and robust.

Each foot's support area is represented by a circle that is projected onto the ground. When both feet are in contact with the ground the support area changes to a capsule shape. Projecting the Centre-of-Mass (CoM) onto the ground, we can use these simplified support regions to give us essential balancing information. Hence, as the inverted pendulum changes between the single and the double support phase over time we can gather additional information to give corrective balancing and control feedback values (see Figure 3).

Furthermore, since we add a support region to the feet of the inverted pendulum this allows us to induce an ankle torque to correct small disturbances without needing to take a corrective footstep. Moreover, this ankle torque provides a means of correcting minor disturbances due to any approximation errors (e.g., ankle torque can introduce corrective balancing and steering parameters).

The logic is managed using a finite state machine. The state machine examines the information from the inverted pendulum model to determine the next state of action that needs to be performed (e.g., apply ankle torque, take corrective step, or continue walking). The state machine has three primary logic components shown in Figure 6.

The inverted pendulum on its own is a very minimalistic physics-based controller that has little overhead and is capable of producing practical, robust, and reliable data for balancing and locomotion; hence, it is ideal for time critical systems (e.g., games). Furthermore, the inverted pendulum is able to handle uneven terrain (e.g., stairs and slopes). Finally, by altering the placement of the foot position and the urgency that the foot reaches its target position, we can produce numerous styles of walking (e.g., relaxed, urgent).

4   Pose Tracking

The inverted pendulum (IP) model at its heart provides us with crucial balancing information that ensures our biped character remains upright while performing various actions (e.g., such as standing, walking or running).

4.1   Intelligent Foot Placement

The fundamental IP model does not tell us how to move or orientate the feet during foot transitions, since it is only able to calculate the desired final foot position from the current position and velocity of the point mass.

4.1.1   Do We Need Feet?

In essence, for a character to be useful it should possess feet; since, it is impossible for a passive platform, such as a skeleton body, to stand in a single, stable position, if only two points are supporting it. However, a dynamic system can balance on two points like stilts if the supporting points are allowed to move and are controlled by a sufficiently sophisticated control system. *The stiff-legged stilt character must remain in a continual state of motion to maintain balance* (see Sias [23] for further details on why we need feet).

4.1.2   Determining the Support Polygon

The support polygon represents the support area for the feet used to keep the character balancing and upright. Without the support polygon, the character would constantly need to move to remain balanced. Exact approaches of exist for calculating the feet contact area. These exact methods use complex contact polygon constructions or simplified rectangles. Our method uses a simplified approximation of circles to represent each foot's support region and a capsule when both feet are in contact with the ground. The circle-capsule method of calculating the support region is a computationally simple approach of generating valid foot approximation information (see Yin [24] for detailed explanation of support regions and more exact methods).

4.1.3   Feet Location Comfort Factor

The dynamic model determines the necessary foot placement information to remedy any force disturbances and remain upright. However, the resulting foot placement movement can result in the character's feet being left in an uncomfortable and unnatural looking pose. To remedy this, we include an additional logic step to determine if the character has reached a stable state and needs to take a corrective step to return the feet to positions that are more comfortable.

4.1.4   Foot Placement Constraints

The final calculated foot position and orientation had limiting constraints imposed upon them. This ensured they never stepped on another foot or in an undesired location.

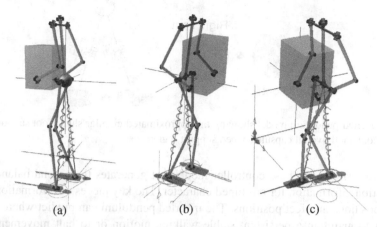

Fig. 2. Uncomfortable poses can arise during stepping, which are physically accurate and balancing yet look awkward and unnatural. For example, (a) and (b) show the character cross-legged and (c) shows the character with one foot in front of the other.

For example, if we wanted to avoid the foot being placed in a hole, we would select the next closest point. The corrective step would then go ahead using the alternative position. However, if the corrective step were not able to balance the model, then the state logic would again repeat the corrective step calculation based upon the new position of the body and feet. This process is automatic and repeats until it reaches a stable balancing state.

4.2 Body Orientation

The feet and centre-of-mass are moving around to keep the character upright and balanced. Nevertheless, the body stores the desired direction from which all other orientations are calculated (see Figure 4). The feet will always use the parent body as the reference location to determine the final orientation of the foot. Moreover, as the character's main body turns and rotates the ideal resting location for each foot is modified so that the feet have to take corrective steps to match the desired orientation of the pelvis.

5 Base Controller

The base controller for determining where to place the characters foot to achieve walking or halt motion is based on the spring loaded inverted pendulum (SLIP) [1]. The SLIP model approximation represents the mass properties of the character as a single-particle point mass. This single-point mass is balanced upon mass-less spring-damper sticks that mimic the legs and muscles of a human.

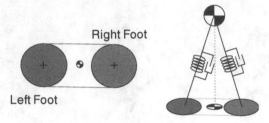

Fig. 3. Inverted pendulum model showing the approximated circular shape foot support regions and the combined overall capsule shaped support region

Figure 3 shows the base controller model that generates the crucial balancing and locomotion information for our biped character. The key pieces of information are the pelvis positions and feet positions. The inverted pendulum can predict where to move the feet to maintain a persistent stable walking motion or to halt movement in any direction.

Initially, it positions the centre-of-mass above the centre-of-pressure (CoP), from there on, then it lifts its front body up, while compensating with the lower body to maintain the CoM above the foot position. Due to the dynamic feedback of the model, any disturbances that might arise (e.g., pushes, trips, un-even terrain), will be fed back into the base-controller, which will attempt to compensate for them in further steps.

5.1 Controller Constraints

We impose a number of additional constraints on the base-controller to achieve a reliable upright posture. It must be possible for the controller to place its centre-of-mass above its foot position. Since the inverted pendulum model has massless legs it means we can move the leg and hence the final foot position to its target destination instantly to achieve the desired task (e.g., walking, stopping falling). Hence, the path taken or movement of the leg does not affect the default motion and in practice, we interpolated the final foot movement along a trajectory spline path over a specific time to mimic human-like stepping more closely.

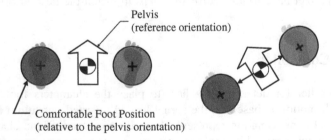

Fig. 4. Illustrating the comfortable positions the feet will return to after a disturbance or when idling

5.2   Foot Swing

When we have calculated the desired position and orientation for the foot we will move, it is necessary to generate a path that the foot must travel to reach its target. While initially, an elliptical arc was used based on an uncomplicated Bezier curve, it produced an unnatural looking stepping action. Hence, when we analyzing the walking motion of a human character, we was found that the foot trajectory path would shoot up and exponentially decays towards the target location, which is due to the toe and heal (see Figure 5).

The trajectory path was modified to mimic human stepping motions to present a more life-like and realistic effect. The trajectory was calculated using a Bezier curve approximation with the peak curve shifted towards the beginning to matching the path shown in Figure 5.

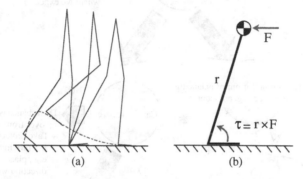

Fig. 5. (a) Common foot swing trajectory for a human casually walking. (b) Ankle torque can provide minor steering and control abilities for the upper body.

5.3   Foot Logic

We iteratively update the decision logic for our model based on the current state of the system (e.g., position of the CoM, foot location, comfort reasoning). A state-machine logic analysis the current state of the biped and decides upon the necessary corrective actions (see Figure 6). The foot logic is recursive in nature because it might take a number of corrective steps to remedy a disturbance push and regain stable balancing control. Furthermore, when taking foot placement steps to gain a more desirable and comfortable posture it can again in certain situations can take a number of steps to accomplish this. This constantly correcting recursive nature is highly desirable, for example, if we impose constraints on where the foot can be placed due to terrain holes or objects being in its way, we can calculate the next closes target and have our model try again the next time around.

The centre-of-mass is projected onto the simplified support region to provide information on how the character should proceed at each step as shown in Figure 7. The three main balancing choices are: firstly, through ankle torque; secondly, through corrective stepping; and, finally, identification of unrecoverable loss of balance.

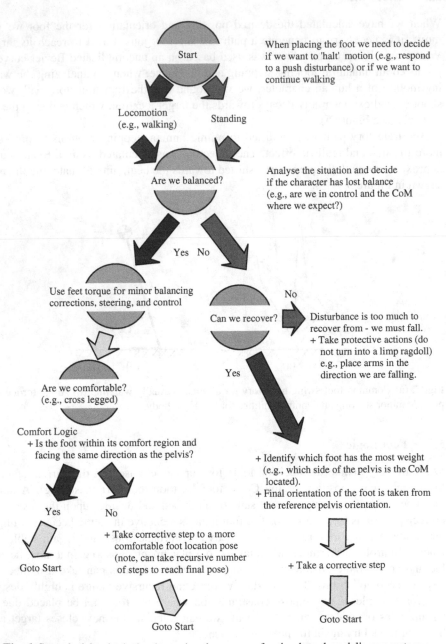

When placing the foot we need to decide
if we want to 'halt' motion (e.g., respond
to a push disturbance) or if we want to
continue walking

Analyse the situation and decide
if the character has lost balance
(e.g., are we in control and the CoM
where we expect?)

Use feet torque for minor balancing
corrections, steering, and control

Disturbance is too much to
recover from - we must fall.
+ Take protective actions (do
  not turn into a limp ragdoll)
  e.g., place arms in the
  direction we are falling.

Comfort Logic
+ Is the foot within its comfort region and
  facing the same direction as the pelvis?

+ Identify which foot has the most weight
  (e.g., which side of the pelvis is the CoM
  located).
+ Final orientation of the foot is taken from
  the reference pelvis orientation.

+ Take corrective step to a more
  comfortable foot location pose
  (note, can take recursive number
  of steps to reach final pose)

+ Take a corrective step

Fig. 6. State decision logic for determine the course of action based model's parameters

6   Inverse Kinematics

The inverse kinematics (IK) solver takes the key information from the low-dimensional model to create the final articulated character poses (e.g., including the knee joints, pelvis, and arms) as shown in Figure 11. The IK solver generates the joint angles for the character model. Furthermore, it imposes constraints to ensure we always produce legal human poses. The key information from the controller guarantees the character remains balanced and upright. We pass the feet and body information (i.e., positions and orientations) along to the IK solver to generate the final pose. We use a real-time Jacobian inverse matrix method to solve IK problem [25][26].

There is a large amount of ambiguity between the initial low-dimensional model and the highly articulated character mode. This ambiguity comes largely comes from a lack of information for describing the arms, neck, and posture. However, this additional redundancy means that behaviors, such as waving, looking around, can be added from additional sources (e.g., stored key framed animation) and combined with the final solution to incorporate human feeling into the movement.

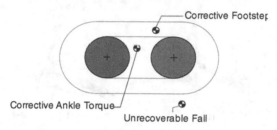

Fig. 7. Response decision

6.1   Biped Model

The mechanical functioning of the biped is modeled as a series of multiple rigid segments (or links) connected by joints. This series will also be called a kinematic chain. As shown in Figure 9(b), the body is represented by 16 segments and is connected using 16 links. The character gives us 36 degrees of freedom (DOF). Joints such as the shoulder have three DOF corresponding to abduction/adduction, flexion/extension and internal/external rotation (e.g., rotation around the x, y and z-axis).

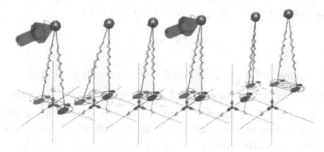

Fig. 8. Illustrate the basic model standing before being pushed twice and having to take corrective steps before returning to a relaxed stance

It is convenient to note that a joint with n DOF is equivalent to n joints of 1 DOF connected by n-1 links of length zero. Thus, the shoulder joint can be described as a sequence of 3 joints. Each separate joint has 1 DOF and 2 of the joints are connected with zero length links.

Figure 11 shows the skeleton pose and Figure 9(b) shows the model combined with the inverse pendulum model. The foot was set as the root of the IK solver. The IK system had five end-effectors (i.e., head, pelvis, right-hand, left-hand and left-foot). The base controller would feed information to the feet and pelvis.

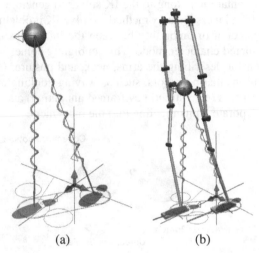

(a)   (b)

Fig. 9. Simple spring loaded inverted pendulum and full skeleton model used for testing

6.2   Articulated Rigid Body Control

The inverse kinematic solver provides joint angles that we use to calculate joint torques to control the articulated rigid body skeleton structure. The approach is analogous to a puppet on strings since the rigid body structure emulates the inverse kinematic solution through angular springs (i.e., proportional derivative servos). However, since the final motions were generated using an articulated rigid body structure the movements were smoother while still possessing their responsive and interactive properties. The joint torques for the articulated character were generated using a proportional derivative (PD) controller, shown in Equation (1)

$$\tau = k_p(\theta_d - \theta) - k_d\theta' \tag{1}$$

where θ_d is the desired joint angle, θ *and* θ' is the current joint angle and joint angular velocity, and k_p *and* k_d is the gain and damping constants. The gain and damping constants are crucial for the character's motions to appear responsive and fluid; however, calculating reliable, robust coefficients that result in the pose reaching its desired target within a specific time reliably and safely is difficult due to the highly dynamic model. Hence, it was necessary to hand-tune the coefficients to achieve pleasing results.

7   Results

The controller generates essential information for the biped character to remain upright. This information is passed to the IK solver end-effector to produce the full character biped motion. Furthermore, an additional step is used to make the final motions more fluid by applying the generated full body movement to an articulated rigid body skeleton.

It is difficult to produce interactive and dynamic motions in real-time for purely inverse kinematic and data-driven solutions. While data-driven approaches can produce life-like results that can engage the environment using inverse kinematics they usually fail realistically emulate responsive balancing motions of the real world. Furthermore, for a physics-based solution, we can accommodate physical changes (e.g., size, strength, and weight) and reflect them in the final character animations.

The preliminary work shows promising results and great potential for simulating crowds of characters. The model is minimalistic and computationally efficient. The largest computational overhead was generating the inverse kinematic skeleton pose from the end-effectors information generated by our inverse pendulum model and foot logic algorithm (see Figure 9, Figure 8, and Figure 12 for simulation screenshots).

Figure 12(a) shows the uncomplicated inverted pendulum model being pushed to illustrate its responsive balancing nature that provides us with computationally fast model for generating crucial stepping information for remaining upright even during disturbances, such as being pushed (however, with just needle-like points for the feet the model constantly needs to keep stepping). Then Figure 12(b) extends the uncomplicated inverted pendulum to include a minimalistic foot support region using a circle-capsule approximation. This foot support region enables us to inject upper steering forces for additional balancing and steering control. Following on, Figure 12(c) goes on to show comfort logic to prevent the character being left in an uncomfortable and unnatural looking pose (e.g., cross-legged). Finally, Figure 12(d) integrates the low-dimensional inverted pendulum model with a fully articulated skeleton.

Due to the dynamic nature of our balancing biped model, it automatically compensates for changes. For example, in Figure 11 we have our biped character hold a box that adds to the overall weight of our character. Furthermore, as we increase the weight of the box our character remains balanced but shows the strain of the extra weight by bending his legs.

Fig. 10. Biped character holding a box that is gradually increases in weight (left to right) while maintaining balance

8   Performance

We performed our simulation tests on a desktop computer (3.4 GHz, Intel i7-2600 CPU, 16 GB ram, Windows 7 64-bit). Due to the minimalistic nature of our mode and its computational efficiency, we were effortlessly able to run at real-time speeds. The physical simulation frame-rate was set at 100 fps. The inverse kinematic solver consumed the majority of the frame-rate time, while the stepping model and logic consumed very little due to its simplicity.

9   Limitations

Our model focused on upright biped characters with an emphasis on foot placement information. Hence, we would need a larger repertoire of actions to make our method a viable option for virtual gaming environments (e.g., getup, climb, fight, and dance).

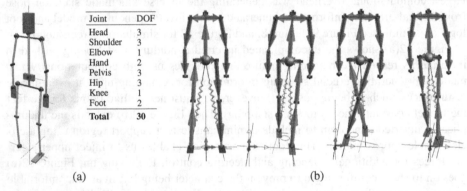

Joint	DOF
Head	3
Shoulder	3
Elbow	1
Hand	2
Pelvis	3
Hip	3
Knee	1
Foot	2
Total	**30**

(a)   (b)

Fig. 11. (a) The joint configuration with the support foot set as the root of the IK (i.e., right foot in the figure); (b) the IK root swapping between left and right foot during stepping

10   Discussion

In this paper, we present a real-time biped character model for generating autonomous responsive balancing motions. We exploited numerous approximation techniques to create a straightforward, robust, and computationally efficient model that could be used in either, real-time environments, such as games, or in offline tools (e.g., for editing and correcting existing animations so they possess dynamic interactive qualities). Additionally, by controlling an articulated rigid-body skeleton by means of the generated inverse kinematic joint angles allowed us to produce more fluid and life-like full body movements.

The dynamic nature of our model means that it has the ability to recover from a variety of different disturbances, such as, dynamic or uneven terrain (e.g., bridges, stairs, obstacle avoidance), and foot placement constraints (e.g., does not have to be the desired foot placement target). It solves a number of problems for creating dynamic biped motions with intelligent foot placement logic that can be adapted to various types of virtual environments. Finally, since the feet provide crucial information for a biped character to remain upright and balanced it shows potential for further study in extending the model for greater realism (e.g., adding in heal-toe shifting during landing, better steering control).

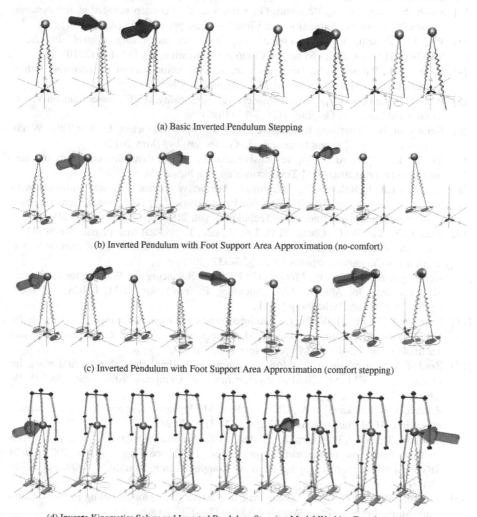

(a) Basic Inverted Pendulum Stepping

(b) Inverted Pendulum with Foot Support Area Approximation (no-comfort)

(c) Inverted Pendulum with Foot Support Area Approximation (comfort stepping)

(d) Inverse Kinematics Solver and Inverted Pendulum Stepping Model Working Together

Fig. 12. Simulation screenshots of the basic uncomplicated inverted pendulum model as shown in (a) through to the extended version with a support area (b)-(c), and finally integrating it with a fully articulated character to generate full body postural information

Acknowledgments. We wish to thank the reviewers for taking time out of their busy schedules and for providing valuable constructive comments and suggestions.

References

[1] Kenwright, B.: Responsive Biped Character Stepping: When Push Comes to Shove. In: 2012 International Conference on Cyberworlds, pp. 151–156 (September 2012)

[2] Singh, S., Kapadia, M., Reinman, G., Faloutsos, P.: Footstep navigation for dynamic crowds. In: Computer Animation and Virtual Worlds, pp. 151–158 (April 2011)

[3] Wu, C., Zordan, V.: Goal-directed stepping with momentum control. In: ACM SIGGRAPH/Eurographics Symp. on Computer Animation, pp. 113–118 (2010)

[4] Badler, N.I., Palmer, M.S., Bindiganavale, R.: Animation control for real-time virtual humans. Communications of the ACM 42(8), 64–73 (1999)

[5] Perlin, K.: Real time responsive animation with personality. IEEE Transactions on Visualization and Computer Graphics 1(1), 5–15 (1995)

[6] Kenwright, B.: Generating Responsive Life-Like Biped Characters. In: The Third Workshop on Procedural Content Generation in Games, pp. 1–8 (May 2012)

[7] Ye, Y., Liu, C.K.: Animating responsive characters with dynamic constraints in near-unactuated coordinates. ACM Transactions on Graphics 27(5), 1 (2008)

[8] Lee, J., Chai, J., Reitsma, P., Hodgins, J.: Interactive control of avatars animated with human motion data. In: SIGGRAPH 2002 Proceedings of the 29th Annual Conference on Computer Graphics and Interactive Techniques, vol. 21(3), pp. 491–500 (July 2002)

[9] Tsai, Y.-Y., Lin, W.-C., Cheng, K.B., Lee, J., Lee, T.-Y.: Real-time physics-based 3D biped character animation using an inverted pendulum model. IEEE Transactions on Visualization and Computer Graphics 16(2), 325–337 (2010)

[10] Kenwright, B., Davison, R., Morgan, G.: Dynamic Balancing and Walking for Real-Time 3D Characters. In: Allbeck, J.M., Faloutsos, P. (eds.) MIG 2011. LNCS, vol. 7060, pp. 63–73. Springer, Heidelberg (2011)

[11] Komura, T., Leung, H., Kuffner, J.: Animating reactive motions for biped locomotion. In: VRST 2004: Proceedings of the ACM Symposium on Virtual Reality Software and Technology, pp. 32–40. ACM Press, New York (2004)

[12] Zordan, V.B., Hodgins, J.K.: Motion capture-driven simulations that hit and react. In: Proceedings ACM SIGGRAPH Symposium on Computer Animation, pp. 89–96 (July 2002)

[13] Zordan, V.B., Majkowska, A., Chiu, B., Fast, M.: Dynamic response for motion capture animation. ACM Transactions on Graphics 24(3), 697 (2005)

[14] Shiratori, T., Coley, B., Cham, R., Hodgins, J.K.: Simulating balance recovery responses to trips based on biomechanical principles. In: Proceedings of the 2009 ACM SIGGRAPH/Eurographics Symposium on Computer Animation, SCA 2009, pp. 37–46 (2009)

[15] Tang, B., Pan, Z., Zheng, L., Zhang, M.: Interactive generation of falling motions. Computer Animation and Virtual Worlds 17(3-4), 271–279 (2006)

[16] McCann, J., Pollard, N.: Responsive characters from motion fragments. ACM Transactions on Graphics 26(3), 6:1–6:7 (2007)

[17] Arikan, O., Forsyth, D.A., O'Brien, J.F.: Pushing people around. In: Proceedings of the 2005 ACM SIGGRAPH/Eurographics Symposium on Computer Animation, pp. 59–66 (July 2005)

[18] Wu, C.-C., Medina, J., Zordan, V.B.: Simple steps for simply stepping. In: Bebis, G., Boyle, R., Parvin, B., Koracin, D., Remagnino, P., Porikli, F., Peters, J., Klosowski, J., Arns, L., Chun, Y.K., Rhyne, T.-M., Monroe, L. (eds.) ISVC 2008, Part I. LNCS, vol. 5358, pp. 97–106. Springer, Heidelberg (2008)

[19] Shih, C.L., Gruver, W.A., Lee, T.T.: Inverse Kinematics and Inverse Dynamics for Control of a Biped Walking Machine. Journal of Robotic Systems 10(4), 531–555 (1993)

[20] Stephens, B.: Humanoid push recovery. In: 2007 7th IEEE-RAS International Conference on Humanoid Robots, pp. 589–595 (November 2007)

[21] Pratt, J., Carff, J., Drakunov, S., Goswami, A.: Capture point: A step toward humanoid push recovery. In: 2006 6th IEEE-RAS International Conference on Humanoid Robots, pp. 200–207 (2006)

[22] Kenwright, B., Davison, R., Morgan, G.: Dynamic balancing and walking for real-time 3D characters. In: Allbeck, J.M., Faloutsos, P. (eds.) MIG 2011. LNCS, vol. 7060, pp. 63–73. Springer, Heidelberg (2011)

[23] Sias, F.R., Zheng, Y.F.: How many degrees-of-freedom does a biped need? In: IEEE International Workshop on Intelligent Robots and Systems, Towards a New Frontier of Applications, vol. 1, pp. 297–302 (1990)

[24] Yin, C., Zhu, J., Xu, H.: Walking Gait Planning And Stability Control. Power Engineering

[25] Kenwright, B.: Real-Time Character Inverse Kinematics using the Gauss-Seidel Iterative Approximation Method. In: International Conference on Creative Content Technologies, vol. (4), pp. 63–68 (2012)

[26] Meredith, M., Maddock, S.: Real-time inverse kinematics: The return of the Jacobian. Tech. Rep. CS-04-06, Dept. of Computer Science, Univ. of Sheffield, pp. 1–15 (2004)

Using Head Tracking Data for Robust Short Term Path Prediction of Human Locomotion

Thomas Nescher and Andreas Kunz

Innovation Center Virtual Reality (ICVR)
Institute of Machine Tools and Manufacturing
ETH Zurich, Switzerland
{nescher,kunz}@iwf.mavt.ethz.ch

Abstract. Modern interactive environments like virtual reality simulators or augmented reality systems often require reliable information
about a user's future intention in order to increase their immersion and
usefulness. For many of such systems, where human locomotion is an
essential way of interaction, knowing a user's future walking direction
provides relevant information.

This paper explains how head tracking data can be used to retrieve a
person's intended direction of walking. The goal is to provide a reliable
and stable path prediction of human locomotion that holds for a few seconds. Using 6 degrees of freedom head tracking data, the head orientation
and the head's movement direction can be derived. Within a user study
it is shown that such raw tracking data provides poor prediction results
mainly due to noise from gait oscillations. Hence, smoothing filters have
to be applied to the data to increase the reliability and robustness of a
predictor.

Results of the user study show that double exponential smoothing of
a person's walking direction data in combination with an initialization
using the head orientation provides a reliable short term path predictor
with high robustness.

Keywords: prediction, human path prediction, head tracking, walking
direction, facing direction, virtual reality, augmented reality, exponential
smoothing.

1 Introduction

Many research fields require a forecast about future actions, which can be
achieved by prediction. For this, mathematical models exist for a projection
into the future, which are fed by observations of past and current actions. Also
for the fields of virtual and augmented reality, it is beneficial to apply such
prediction for instance to human locomotion. This would allow calculating the
reaction of the computer generated environment not only based on the current
position and orientation of the user, but also his intended walking trajectory -
predicted from past observations - could be taken into account. By this, more

M.L. Gavrilova et al. (Eds.): Trans. on Comput. Sci. XVIII, LNCS 7848, pp. 172–191, 2013.
© Springer-Verlag Berlin Heidelberg 2013

time exists to prepare the system's adequate reaction on the most probable next action of the user.

Systems that rely on human locomotion could be significantly improved by prediction, not only regarding responsiveness, but also regarding the quality of the displayed environment. As an example, the system could output situation-specific information (e.g. a warning) before the user is in this situation. Moreover, location-based information systems could be improved by displaying prediction-based information. Thus, the system could e.g. inform a user that the subway service is not running prior he goes down the stairs. Another example could be a virtual environment, which could pre-calculate objects that the user will most probably experience in the next moment.

For many years, navigating in virtual environment was only possible using a joystick or a spacemouse, which did not address the most intuitive way of human locomotion. Thus, more recent research projects [1] also address this human perception entity to increase immersion and to provide more natural information e.g. about objects' sizes and distances to each other, which also facilitates a better and more intuitive orientation. However, today's step-in-place solutions and treadmills cannot completely fulfill this requirement, and thus new systems should go far beyond this current experience. New systems should be even more immersive, non-obtrusive and should not hinder the user to perform his task in a virtual environment. In order to realize such systems, new tracking systems will be required that can measure the user's position more reliably and more precisely. Moreover, the measured position and orientation values will be used as observation to predict the user's future actions.

In order to predict a user's future plans of action when walking in a real or virtual environment, a predictor needs to be fed by tracking data. For detecting angular rate and acceleration, sensors with a very small form factor exist (e.g. [2,3]), which can be easily attached to the user, e.g. in the head-up display or attached to AR-glasses. If the sensor signals are combined by sensor fusion, it is possible to realize a continuous position and orientation tracking [4].

In order to realize real walking in a virtual environment, it is crucial to attach the sensors to the visual output device, e.g. to the head-mounted display (HMD), since this is the only position to track a user's head orientation (i.e. gaze direction).

If real walking in a virtual environment should be realized, the problem occurs that usually the virtual space is larger than the physical space that is equipped with a tracking system. Thus, it is crucial to realize a so-called redirected walking, which compresses an ideally unlimited virtual space into a physically limited real space. Such a compression can be achieved by guiding the user on a curved or scaled path [5–7]. Such a compression takes benefit from the human rules of cognition, which define that the visual perception overrides the haptic sensation of walking. Thus, the user will follow a visual goal, while not taking into account the placement and orientation of his feet anymore, resulting in the fact that he does not note any compression. However, the compression and redirection needs to be carefully adapted to the available physical room, which requires planning ahead any compression procedure. For doing so, a path prediction is inevitable.

The tracking data of a person, i.e. his position and orientation, are the prerequisite for realizing a feasible prediction about the user's future path. This is in particular challenging since the user could make decisions in the virtual environment regarding the path he wants to go. While many publications (e.g. [8]) predict pedestrians' movements from an exocentric point of view, this paper approaches the problem from egocentric perspective.

There are three different time intervals for which a path prediction could be done. The shortest prediction interval for human locomotion is in the range of milliseconds and is physically limited by the human's abilities of movement like e.g. maximum acceleration. Short term prediction as the next time interval is in the range of some seconds and is determined by human way finding abilities and the decided direction in which a human wants to walk. This short term prediction is not influenced by any environmental constraints like obstacles, but just depends on the intended walk direction of the user. The third time interval is the long term path prediction and ranges from seconds to minutes. Obviously, the long term path prediction has to take into account the environment, while it is also influenced by a person's cognitive map of the environment and the planned destination he wants to reach.

The focus of this paper is on the short term prediction of human locomotion and how navigation or direction decisions are related to head tracking data that can be acquired by an inside-out tracking system. It shows a user study, in which participants have to walk in a maze-like environment and make decisions for different walking directions. The walking trajectories are recorded and analyzed, and show the challenges when trying to make a robust short term walking prediction. For this prediction, different approaches are introduced and discussed, while the remainder of this paper gives an evaluation of these different approaches.

2   Background

If locomotion interfaces such as treadmills should be replaced by real walking, prediction becomes especially important. Such a real locomotion interface was e.g. introduced by Peck et al., by which users could experience a virtual environment that is larger as the available and tracked physical space [9]. The system benefits from the psychological effect that vision dominates the proprioceptive sensation of walking. Thus, it was possible to slowly rotate the virtual environment around the user without noticing this [10]. This results in an imperceptible redirection of user, which keeps him the physically limited real space. However, in order to plan this redirection properly, it is crucial to have knowledge about the user's future path.

A very similar locomotion interface was proposed by Nitzsche et al., but with two different path prediction approaches [6]. One approach does not base on any targets and derives the user's future walking direction simply from the head orientation, assuming that the user always walks in the direction he looks. However, if specific targets can be identified in a virtual environment, the approach from the above can be further detailed. Every target or potential goal in the virtual environment is provided with a so-called weight coefficient. If an object or a target is in the user's field of view, the weight factor will be increased as long as the user looks at it, otherwise the value will be decreased. Now, the predicted walking direction of the user is simply towards the target with the highest weighting coefficient.

Another approach for the user's future path was introduced by [11]. Here, the future walking direction is simply determined by a linear extrapolation of the user's previous path.

Another hybrid approach for predicting the user's future path was proposed by Interrante et al. [12]. They used the past n seconds of a person's locomotion and calculate the average direction in this time interval for a prediction. If person is not moving, the facing direction is used instead. The influence of the facing direction on the predicted direction is decreased when a user starts walking, while on the other hand the influence of the averaged walking direction becomes more significant for the prediction.

Walking and facing direction were also used in a hybrid approach by Steinicke et al. [7]. Here, the prediction bases on the walking direction, while the facing direction is used for verification. Steinicke et al. consider that walking and facing direction are not consistent all the time. The walking direction is only used as prediction, if the angle between walking and facing direction is smaller than 45 degrees. In all other cases, no reliable prediction is possible.

Although many different approaches exist for a short-term path prediction in virtual environments, so far no evaluation and comparison was done of the proposed methods.

Research results from psychology or neuroscience provide insights how gaze behavior is related to the walking direction. Grasso et al. studied how individuals make eye and head movements to align with their future walking trajectory during walking around corners [13]. Furthermore, Hollands et al. analyzed how human gaze behavior is associated with maintaining and changing the direction of locomotion [14].

Knowing a person's intended action by using motion prediction is of particular interest in the research field of human-robot interaction. In order to derive a human's intentional actions from the relative movements between human and robot, Koo et al. used machine learning algorithms [15]. However, the prediction is regarded from an exocentric perspective, as interactions between the human and the robot are analyzed by the robot's artificial intelligence software.

Urban planning and transportation is another research field, in which the movement patterns of pedestrians are analyzed, see e.g. [16]. These complex models also take into account the interactions among pedestrians e.g. for collision avoidance, and are typically used for large scale simulations of pedestrian flow. It is obvious that these models are more suited for a long-term path prediction.

For tracking users, various systems were proposed, as for example shoe-mounted inertial sensors [17] or ultrasound-aided systems [18]. The focus of these systems is on providing a stable and accurate determination of the user's position. For the estimation of a user's position, typically a Kalman Filter (KF) is used, which can also be seen as some kind of predictive tracking. Such a KF was e.g. used by Kiruluta et al. [19], who proposed a method for predictive head movement tracking. Double exponential smoothing was used by LaViola [20], while Rhijn [21] gives a comparison of different filtering and prediction methods.

Predictive tracking algorithms like those mentioned in the above typically provide prediction times of several milliseconds up to one second and are thus often used to compensate for system latencies. These predictive tracking algorithms typically use a movement and noise model that fits such very short prediction times, e.g. 100 ms in [20].

Unlike the approaches in the above, the goal of this paper is not to make a robust estimation of the head position, but reliably predict the *intended* walking direction. The goal is to realize a prediction for several seconds rather than the very short-term prediction in the range of milliseconds.

3   Formal Derivation of Short Term Path Prediction from Tracking Data

A portable tracking system that is carried by a user typically provides 6 DOF data, i.e. position and orientation, at discrete time steps. Given a known and constant update rate, an approximation of the derivative from the discrete time samples gives information about the current speed and acceleration.

In our test setup, we attached the camera of the inside-out tracking system to the user's head and applied a static coordinate transformation to achieve the center of the user's head. Having this, the facing direction can be determined as the axis from this head center to the nose tip. For predicting a user's future direction of movement, tracking data can be interpreted and extrapolated in different ways as presented in the following.

For normal walking in a virtual environment, the problem can be reduced to 3 DOF in the walking plane: 2 dimensions for position, while the orientation is a rotation around the normal of the walking plane. The position data at time t is referred to as x_t where x denotes the 2-dimensional position vector and t is the discrete time index starting at time 0.

3.1   Facing Direction

The facing direction can be expressed as a 2-dimensional direction vector (in the reference frame of the user's head), which can be calculated from the orientation data. The normalized facing vector is denoted as f.

It is assumed that a user's facing direction indicates his intended direction of movement and thus can be used for prediction. This is in particular relevant if the user stands still, i.e. the recorded position data is constant. In this case, the orientation data from the head tracker is the only relevant data that can be used for prediction.

If the virtual environment has known targets, $\boldsymbol{f}$ can be used for prediction. For doing so, this target at position $\boldsymbol{p}$ is chosen that has the smallest angular deviation from the current facing direction $\boldsymbol{f}_t$. Using the scalar product, the angle between a target and the facing direction can be calculated as:

$$\theta_t = arccos\left(\frac{\boldsymbol{f}_t \cdot (\boldsymbol{p} - \boldsymbol{x}_t)}{|\boldsymbol{f}_t||(\boldsymbol{p} - \boldsymbol{x}_t)|}\right) \tag{1}$$

However, the facing direction of a user does not necessarily correspond to his gaze direction, which could result in major problems when using the facing direction for the prediction. Humans often only move their eyes instead of their complete head, in particular if two targets are close to each other. This problem could only be solved, if an additional eye tracker would also be employed for the tracking system.

3.2 Walking Direction and Speed

A person's current and past movement can be derived from the change of the position $\boldsymbol{x}$ over time. This results in a displacement vector $\boldsymbol{w}_t$ that is defined as follows:

$$\boldsymbol{w}_t = \boldsymbol{x}_t - \boldsymbol{x}_{t-1} \tag{2}$$

The displacement vector gives the direction of movement between two time steps t-1 to t. If the data is acquired with a constant sampling interval τ, the user's current speed is given by $|\boldsymbol{w}_t|/\tau$.

Following the above definition of short term path prediction, the goal is to only predict the user's path for a short time horizon, and thus we assume to have no further information about the virtual environment. Hence, we can further assume that due to energy minimization the user will approach the target on a straight line. A user's future path can therefore be intuitively predicted from the current walking direction. This means in other words that we will use linear extrapolation of the current walking direction to predict a user's future path.

Like for the facing direction above, $\boldsymbol{w}$ can be used to determine the chosen target in a virtual environment using the angular deviation.

If a person is standing still, $\boldsymbol{w}$ equals zero and no prediction can be made. This means that the displacement vector could give significantly wrong results for the predictor in case of slow movements. This is in particular the case if $|\boldsymbol{w}|$ is of the same magnitude or even smaller than tracking system's noise. Thus, the lower limit for the displacement vector must be carefully chosen depending on the characteristics of the tracking system (update rate, noise, etc.).

3.3 Smoothing and Robustness

Since tracking data is typically noisy, some data smoothing is required to reduce the effect of noise on the path prediction. Too much noise will make the path prediction unstable and thus worthless. A further disturbing effect for prediction is that the movement of the body during walking is not necessarily aligned with the intended walking direction. A tracking system that is mounted on the user's head, will also measure movements to the side as well as up and down due to the mechanisms of the human gait [22, 23]. Thus, the effects of noise and gait oscillations have to be filtered out in order to achieve a reliable prediction of the intended walking direction.

In the following section, various approaches for data smoothing are presented. These smoothers could be applied to the f_t or the w_t vectors. However, it was shown in Sect. 5 that smoothing is in particular important for predicting the walking direction. Hence, the equations are presented for the w_t vectors. s_t denotes the smoothed path prediction at time t.

Unweighted Moving Average. The moving average method is one of the simplest methods to smooth data. It is given by:

$$s_t = \frac{1}{k} \sum_{i=0}^{k-1} w_{t-i} \tag{3}$$

Here, k is the time horizon over which the arithmetic mean is calculated. Thus, s_t is the average displacement of the past k time steps.

Latency is one of the major problems of the unweighted moving average, meaning that at least k samples must be recorded before a prediction can be made. Another problem is given by the fact that the w_t are displacement vectors. Thus, the moving average rewritten using (2), reduces to

$$s_t = \frac{1}{k} \sum_{i=0}^{k-1} (x_{t-i} - x_{t-i-1}) = \frac{1}{k}(x_t - x_{t-k}) \tag{4}$$

As a result, all position samples in the time interval between t-1 and t-k+1 are actually ignored by the smoother. Thus, the prediction will become unstable e.g. due to noise, if the time horizon is not chosen properly.

Exponential Smoothing. When using a simple moving average smoother, all k past measurements will have the same weight, which might not be feasible since older values are of less importance than newer ones. Thus, an exponential smoothing can be used which weighs past measurements with an exponentially decaying factor.

$$s_0 = w_0 \tag{5}$$

$$s_t = \alpha w_t + (1 - \alpha)s_{t-1} \tag{6}$$

s_t can be rewritten as

$$s_t = \alpha w_t + \alpha \sum_{i=1}^{t-1} (1 - \alpha)^i w_{t-i} + (1 - \alpha)^t w_0 \tag{7}$$

With exponential smoothing, all past measurements are included into the current prediction (infinite impulse response filter). The efficiency of the smoothing can be controlled with the factor $\alpha \in (0, 1)$. If α is chosen close to 1, there is only a little smoothing since new measurements are weighted higher. On the other hand, if α is chosen close to 0, there is a high level of smoothing.

Choosing the correct value of α for exponential smoothing is a delicate task. If α is chosen too high, the smoothing is low, and noise will influence the correct prediction. If α is chosen too low, the latency of the smoother increases and real changes in the walk direction might be detected too late. In order to set a mathematical basis for the correct adjustment of α, the following limit case can be regarded. It is assumed that the measurements were constant with the value v_o, while the smoothed value was stable at $s_o = v_o$. At the time t-k, the measurement abruptly changes to a new constant value v_n. Now, the question is how many time steps k it will take until s_t reaches the factor q of the new measurement value v_n. Hence s_t becomes

$$s_t = \alpha v_n + \alpha v_n \sum_{i=1}^{k} (1 - \alpha)^i + \alpha v_o \sum_{i=k+1}^{t-1} (1 - \alpha)^i + (1 - \alpha)^t v_o \qquad (8)$$

Now the factor of change from the old to the new measurement is given as

$$q = \frac{s_t - v_o}{v_n - v_o} \qquad (9)$$

$$= 1 - (1 - \alpha)^{k+1} \qquad (10)$$

$$\alpha = 1 - (1 - q)^{1/k+1} \qquad (11)$$

Using the equations for the summation of geometric series on (8) and inserting in (9) gives an equation for determining α. For instance, if the smoother is to follow a step function to 80% ($q = 0.8$) within the next $k = 180$ measuring time steps, α should be about 0.009.

Double Exponential Smoothing. Exponential smoothing can be improved if there is a trend in the data like the change of the walking direction. This so-called double exponential smoothing is given by

$$s_0 = w_0 \qquad (12)$$

$$s_t = \alpha w_t + (1 - \alpha)(s_{t-1} + b_{t-1}) \qquad (13)$$

$$b_t = \beta(s_t - s_{t-1}) + (1 - \beta)b_{t-1} \qquad (14)$$

The b_t vectors represent the current trend in the data. Like in the normal exponential smoothing, α is the data smoothing factor. $\beta \in (0, 1)$ is the so-called trend smoothing factor, which controls how much the current trend is influenced by the change in the smoothed prediction output over time. b_0 defines the initial trend in the data.

Following the definition of w_t in (2), it becomes obvious that w_0 is not defined by the data. In order to apply the smoothing methods, prediction thus either has to start at time t=1 or some initial value for w_0 is required. The following method is proposed for a path prediction with a double exponential smoothing. Under the assumption that a person starts moving at the time t=0, the facing direction at time 0 is used to set $w_0 = cf_0$. This approach is similar to the one proposed by [12], but is more explicitly formalized here. It is now further assumed that the initial facing direction is the most likely direction of movement, which allows setting the initial trend to $b_0 = (0,0)$. The magnitude of w_0 influences how much impact it has on the smoothed output. Therefore the constant c should be chosen so that it reflects a reasonable speed. As an example, c could be defined by taking into account the averaged speed of human walk $\bar{v}$ together with the given update rate r as $c = \bar{v}/r$.

4   User Study

Within the user study we conducted, participants had to walk inside a simple maze-like environment. There were different possible paths through this maze, all of them with the same complexity. Thus, the participants were forced to make a choice which way to go. During the study, users wore a head-mounted tracking system (inside-out system) in order to record to walking trajectory. The goal of the study was to measure head position and orientation while users had to make a choice, and how this choice of a direction relates to the recorded data. Using the set of recorded user paths, a comparison of different path prediction approaches and the adjustment of smoothing parameters was possible.

4.1   Experimental Setup

Movable walls were installed in 5m x 7m room to realize a T-shaped maze. The design and the dimensions of this shape are shown in Fig. 1. The maze had an obstacle in its center in order to force subjects to decide whether they want to go left or right, see Fig. 2. At both ends of the maze, for different calendar pictures were attached (see Fig. 1). In order to avoid any biasing, the maze was perfectly symmetric (left, right) and no distractions were present except for the calendar pictures. However, these pictures could not influence the user during his decision phase whether to move left or right, since they were not visible at the beginning. The participants started the user study in the center of the maze's lower end.

Paper markers for the the Intersense IS-1200 tracking system [24] were attached to the ceiling of the room, in which the T-maze was installed. The sensor of the IS-1200 tracking system (inside-out tracking system) can be easily attached to an HMD. It allows tracking 6 degrees of freedom, i.e. the user's position and orientation, at an update rate of 180 Hz. Since the user should not be irritated by any wire connections, a notebook for recording data was mounted in a backpack the user had to wear during the study. The tracking system was attached to a Triviso Scout HMD. Since we built a real maze, the HMD was only

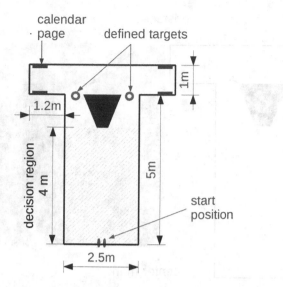

Fig. 1. Layout of the symmetric T-maze. Walls are in black and the four blue bars mark the position of the calendar pictures. The decision region and the targets (left, right) are only used for the analysis and are not visible for participants.

used to mount the tracking system properly on a subject's head, while we did not use the HMD's visualization capabilities. The maze environment and user wearing the notebook and the tracking system are shown in Fig. 2. As mentioned before, a static coordinate transformation was applied to the achieved tracking data in order to actually determine the approximate center of a participant's head.

In order to avoid any deficiencies of a virtual environment, a physical maze environment was constructed deliberately instead of a virtual environment. Thus, the HMD was not used even though the hardware would allow visiting a virtual environment. By this, we avoid any biasing due to the HMD's limited field of view (FOV) or due to simulator latencies.

4.2 Participants

In total, 11 participants took part in the experiment (7 male and 4 female, median age 31). The participants came from the institute and included students, senior researchers, as well as administrative staff. None of the participants was aware of the purpose of the user study.

4.3 Tasks and Conditions

In order to analyze if there is a difference regarding the walking direction, the facing direction or the whole user trajectory between a known and unknown environment, both cases were investigated. It might happen for instance that in

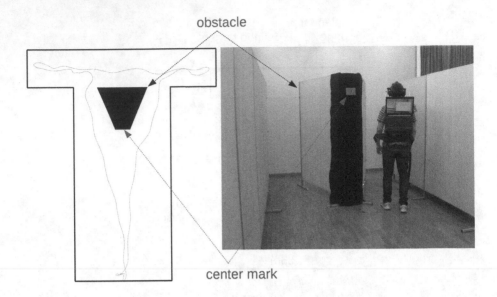

Fig. 2. Left: a typical walk path through the T-maze. Right: a subject during the user study. The subject wears the backpack with the notebook and the HMD with the tracking system. The obstacle forces participants to either walk left or right. The center mark is used for the initial calibration of the facing direction.

an unknown environment users will decide later whether they want to go left or right, or their facing direction might change more often due to orientation behavior.

Explore Condition (EX). Within the first task, the subjects were new to the environment and had no information about the maze. Their task was to walk through all corridors in the maze and to return to the starting point afterwards. The calendar pictures in the maze were of no relevance for this task.

Count Task Condition (CO). For the second task, the calendar pictures at the ends of the T-maze became relevant (see Fig. 1). Within this task, participants had to count the total number of Sundays on all 4 calendar pictures, and then had to return to their starting position. For this second condition, all participants were already familiar with the maze and knew where to find the targets.

4.4   Procedure

Prior to the study, all participants got oral explanations about the task and procedure. The participants were prepared in a separate room, where the HMD and the backpack were mounted. Then they were guided blindfolded to the starting position, so that they had no prior knowledge about the T-maze. After placing themselves properly at the start position, they were instructed to look at the center mark for 4 seconds for calibration before starting to walk (see Fig. 2). This initial calibration of the facing direction was performed to align the orientation of the tracking system with a participant's facing direction. Once a participant finished the first task (EX condition), the second task (CO condition) was explained to him.

5   Results and Discussion

The tasks of the user study were finished by 10 out of 11 participants. Although one participant did not properly finish the task in the EX condition, he could participate again in the CO condition. This results in 10 correct paths for the explore task (EX), and in 11 for the count task (CO).

In the following plots, the analysis of the tracking data is limited to the so-called decision region, which is within the first 4 m from the start position towards the obstacle. This direction is referred to as y-axis and the value y indicates the position in meters from 0 at the start position. Within this region, all participants had to decide whether they want to go left or right. Within the T-maze, two targets - i.e. the passage ways - were defined at a distance of $y = 5$ from the starting point. These targets were named 'left' and 'right' and are thus located in the centers of the possible paths around the obstacle, see Fig. 1.

As suggested in Sect. 3.1, the angular deviation of the prediction from the targets is used for the evaluation of the path prediction. Next, the hit rate $r \in [0,1]$ is calculated, which is the relative amount of time that a predictor predicts the correct target that a subject finally walked to. As shown in Fig. 3, all participants had already decided for a specific target until $y = 3$. Based on these results, the calculation of the hit rate is limited to the first 3 m ($y \in [0, 3]$), which is referred to as the evaluation area.

In Fig. 3, all paths that were recorded during the user study are shown. For most paths, the gait oscillations of the user's head are clearly visible. The paths also show that most of subjects decided very early, i.e. $y \leq 1$, for left or right. This is in particular the case for the CO condition, in which only one of 11 subjects changed the initially chosen direction after $y \approx 1.4$. During the EX condition, three to four of 10 subjects decided later at $y \approx 2.5$. This indicates that an early path prediction is more difficult if an environment is unknown to the user.

The average walk speed in the decision area for both conditions was 0.95 m/sec, with a standard deviation of 0.22 m/sec.

5.1   Facing Direction

Results. The angular deviation of the facing direction from the targets is shown in Fig. 4. Three different subjects are represented by three plots while they moved from $y = 0$ to $y = 4$.

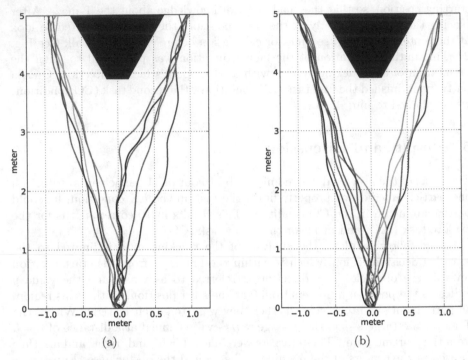

Fig. 3. All user paths from the study. Only the lower part of the T-maze is shown. (a) EX condition paths and (b) CO condition paths.

Based on the facing direction, a predictor would thus predict the target which is closer 0 degree. In Fig. 4(c) for instance, the predictor would choose the wrong target for $y \in [0.6, 1]$, while its prediction would be correct for $y > 1$.

Table 1 shows the relative hit rate r within the evaluation area.

Table 1. Relative hit rate of the facing direction predictor averaged over all participants within the evaluation area $y \in [0, 3]$

	EX	CO	both
mean	0.91	0.95	0.93
standard deviation	0.09	0.06	0.08

Discussion. The data shown in Fig. 4 is the raw data from the tracking system. It only contains little noise and thus the plots represent quite well a subject's head orientation. For this case, smoothing cannot further improve the prediction. In Fig. 4(c) at position $y = 0.7$ for example, the participant turned his head to look towards another target.

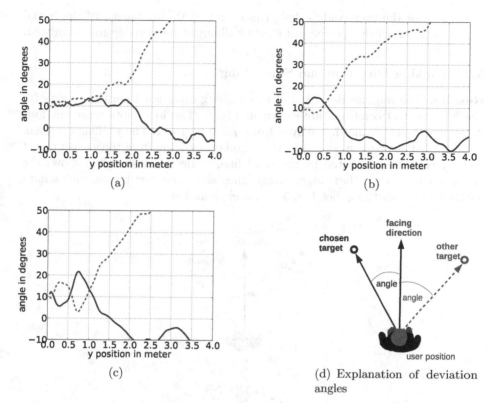

(a)

(b)

(c)

(d) Explanation of deviation angles

Fig. 4. Angular deviation of the facing direction from the two targets while a subject is moving from y=0 to y=4. (a), (b) were recorded during the EX condition and (c) was recorded during the CO condition. A solid blue line shows the deviation from the chosen target direction and the dashed red line the deviation from the other target, see (d). The angular deviation is positive for rotations from the targets towards the center of the obstacle.

Generally spoken, the facing direction should be used with care for a prediction. This is mainly because of two reasons. First, the head orientation does not necessarily correspond to a person's actual gaze, since a person might just turn his eyes instead of the whole head. Second, the facing direction is not always aligned with the walking path, but can be highly influenced by visual distractions in the environment. Although the performed user study was designed to have no visual distractions, any picture on the wall would have, however, made a subject looking at it while walking towards the target. Thus, the average facing direction would have been biased by the picture and thus would not point to the target.

For the user study mentioned in the above, it can be assumed that the high hit rate is mainly due to the experimental design. Nevertheless, [14] shows that most of the time the gaze direction is aligned with the walking path. This could also explain the high hit rate, but does not imply that the facing direction is a stable predictor in a general environment.

Because of the user study's design (see Sect. 4.4), an analysis of the initial facing direction when a person just starts walking, is not possible and is omitted.

5.2   Walking Direction and Smoothing

Results. The angular deviation of the walking direction from the targets for the EX and CO condition are shown in Fig. 6. The four plots represent four different subjects while they moved from $y = 0$ to $y = 4$. The walking direction is calculated as given in Sect. 3.2. The angular deviation from the chosen target (out of two) is represented by the solid line, while the dashed line shows the deviation from the other target. Gray lines show the raw measurement data without any smoothing. See Fig. 5 for an explanation.

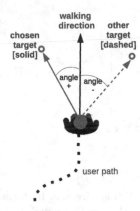

Fig. 5. Definition of the deviation angles for the walking direction analysis (see Fig. 6)

As for the facing direction above, the relative hit rate r is calculated within the evaluation area, see Table 2. Further, an additional robustness factor is introduced in order to demonstrate how smoothing could improve the robustness of the prediction.

As it could be seen from the above analysis, the predictor could switch between the two targets depending on smallest angle between the facing direction and one of the given targets. Any switch, however, is counterproductive to the robustness of a predictor and should be avoided. Thus, the relative robustness measures the average reduction in the number of prediction switches between the two predefined targets for a smoothed prediction in relation to the raw walking direction data. A relative robustness of 2 for the exponential smoother for example means that the exponentially smoothed predictor makes only half as many switches between left and right target as the raw walk direction predictor.

Discussion. In all plots, gait oscillations are clearly visible. These gait oscillations are the largest and most challenging disturbance when using walking direction data for prediction. Compared to the magnitude of gait oscillations,

Table 2. Relative hit rate of the walking direction predictor averaged over all participants within the evaluation area $y \in [0, 3]$. The standard deviation is denoted by sd. The relative robustness shows the improvement of the smoothing on the prediction relative to the raw walk direction prediction.

		EX	CO	both
raw walk direction	mean	0.81	0.87	0.84
	sd	0.13	0.10	0.12
	rel. robustness	1	1	1
exp. smoothed	mean	0.85	0.85	0.85
	sd	0.16	0.16	0.16
	rel. robustness	2.0	1.8	1.9
double exp. smoothed	mean	0.86	0.86	0.86
	sd	0.16	0.16	0.16
	rel. robustness	2.0	2.1	2.0

tracking noise is negligible. In order to overcome disturbances from gait oscillations, it is essential to apply smoothing. In Fig. 6, the colored lines represent smoothed values using either exponential or double exponential smoothing. The initial value of w_0 is chosen as suggested in Sect. 3.3 (f_0 points to the center of the obstacle). Compared to this, smoothing with a moving average performs worst due to the problems mentioned in the above. Hence, the results are not presented here.

Like for the facing direction, a predictor based on the walking direction also predicts that target which is closer to 0 degree in the plot. This means in other words that a wrong target is predicted if the dashed line is closer to 0 than its solid counterpart.

As shown in the above, the efficiency of the smoothers strongly depends on the correct setting of the smoothing factors α and β. For the given experiment, a smoothing factor of $\alpha = 0.004$ (for normal and double exponential smoothing) and a trend smoothing factor of $\beta = 0.004$ turned out to work best. These factors provide a stable prediction, while the smoothers still react in a reasonable time to changes in the intended direction of movement. Using (9) and the given update rate of 180 Hz, the percentage of change can be estimated. One second after a change in the walking direction, roughly 50% of that change will be included into the smoothed walking direction and roughly 75% after two seconds.

As it can be seen from Table 2, the relative hit rate is not significantly higher for a smoothed predictor in relation to an unsmoothed predictor. However, there is a significant improvement in the robustness of the prediction. Regarding robustness, the double exponentially smoothed predictor performs best.

Figure 6(a) and (b) both show data from subjects who did not decide right away for a target and first walked roughly straight forward. As it can be seen in Fig. 6(b) for instance, the double exponential smoother is slightly faster in detecting the decision and outruns the exponential smoother by $y \approx 2.2$. Figure 6(d) shows the extreme case, in which a participant changed his decision and turned around (see also Fig. 3). Similarly, the double exponential smoother is

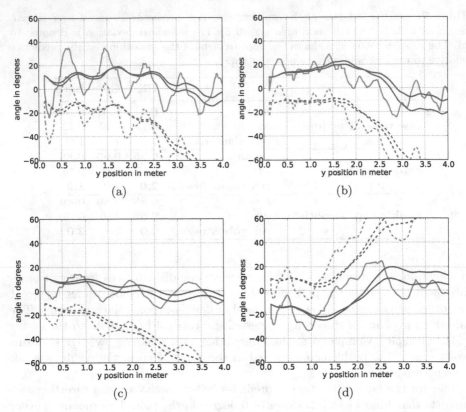

Fig. 6. Angular deviation of the walking direction from the two targets while a subject is moving from y=0 to y=4. (a) and (b) are from the EX condition, (c) and (d) from the CO condition. A solid line represents the deviation from the chosen target and a dashed line the deviation from the other target. The gray line is the raw data, red is the exponentially smoothed data and green is the double exponentially smoothed data.

faster in detecting this change. Figure 6(c) shows a typical plot of a subject who walked straight to the chosen target. In such cases, both smoothers provide reliable and robust predictions.

6   Conclusion

In this paper it is analyzed how head tracking data can be used to retrieve a person's intended direction of travel. A tracking system mounted on a person's head provides position and orientation data. As it is shown in this paper, this data suffices to make a robust and reliable short term path prediction that holds for a few seconds.

Using head position data, a displacement vector can be calculated to retrieve the head's movement direction. Intuitively, one would use this direction to extrapolate the person's intended direction of travel. However, as it is shown in the conducted user study, raw position data from the tracking data gives quite poor prediction results. In fact due to the mechanics of human gait, a person's head movement is not nicely aligned with the intended direction of travel.

Hence, in order to increase the reliability and the robustness of the prediction, a smoothing of the tracking data is required. Different smoothing methods are introduced that are suitable for path prediction. Especially double exponential smoothing turns out to work best and doubles the robustness of the prediction compared to using raw tracking data.

Nevertheless, using smoothing increases the latency of the path prediction. Hence, a suitable trade-off has to be found between robustness and latency. For this purpose, an equation is derived that allows choosing the proper smoothing factor depending on the requirements.

Head orientation data actually is a person's facing direction, which provides another approach for path prediction. However, it is problematic to use only the facing direction for prediction, since a person might move the eyes instead of the head. This could happen in particular if some targets or close to each other and thus making it obsolete to turn the head. Nevertheless, if a person is not moving or just starts to walk, the facing direction can be used as an initialization value for the walking direction smoother.

7 Future Work

To overcome the problem with the facing direction, eye trackers could be used together with a regular tracking system in order to correctly identify the user's gaze direction. Even though Hollands et al. [14] thoroughly studied how gaze behavior and walking direction are related to each other, it requires further research to answer the question how gaze behavior could be used for prediction.

The conducted user study has shown that the major problem for path prediction from head tracking data is "gait noise". So far, this problem has been solved with generic smoothing approaches while in fact this noise is partially systematic. It depends on the mechanics of human gait, the step length, person specific walking patterns, and so forth. Hence, these patterns instead could be learned from the data to better filter the data. E.g. a physical gait model together with a Kalman filter could provide far better smoothing with low latency than exponential smoothing. Similar approaches used for so-called walk-in-place interaction devices might be adapted for this purpose [25].

Additional sensors could also be used to get more data for better prediction. For instance, accelerometers might be used to detect steps and thus learn the step length from the user data. Knowing the step length for example would allow an automatic adaptation to a person in order to improve the prediction. Other approaches could be more suitable for pocket worn mobile phones. In such a scenario, the displacement of the pelvis while walking might give additional information for path prediction [26].

Acknowledgment. The authors would like to thank the Swiss National Science Foundation (project number 127298) for funding this work.

References

1. Souman, J.L., Giordano, P.R., Schwaiger, M., Frissen, I., Thümmel, T., Ulbrich, H., Luca, A.D., Bülthoff, H.H., Ernst, M.O.: Cyberwalk: Enabling unconstrained omnidirectional walking through virtual environments. TAP 2008: Transactions on Applied Perception 8(4), 25:1–25:22 (2008)
2. Harms, H., Amft, O., Winkler, R., Schumm, J., Kusserow, M., Troester, G.: Ethos: Miniature orientation sensor for wearable human motion analysis. IEEE Sensors, 1037–1042 (2010)
3. Leuenberger, K., Gassert, R.: Low-power sensor module for long-term activity monitoring. In: 2011 Annual International Conference of the IEEE Engineering in Medicine and Biology Society, EMBC, pp. 2237–2241 (2011)
4. Welch, G., Bishop, G.: Scaat: incremental tracking with incomplete information. In: Proceedings of the 24th Annual Conference on Computer Graphics and Interactive Techniques, SIGGRAPH 1997, pp. 333–344. ACM Press/Addison-Wesley Publishing Co. (1997)
5. Razzaque, S., Swapp, D., Slater, M., Whitton, M.C., Steed, A.: Redirected walking in place. In: Proceedings of the Workshop on Virtual Environments, EGVE 2002, pp. 123–130. Eurographics Association (2002)
6. Nitzsche, N., Hanebeck, U.D., Schmidt, G.: Motion compression for telepresent walking in large target environments. Presence: Teleoperators and Virtual Environments 13(1), 44–60 (2004)
7. Steinicke, F., Bruder, G., Kohli, L., Jerald, J., Hinrichs, K.: Taxonomy and implementation of redirection techniques for ubiquitous passive haptic feedback. In: Proceedings of the 2008 International Conference on Cyberworlds, CW 2008, pp. 217–223. IEEE (2008)
8. Gandhi, T., Trivedi, M.: Image based estimation of pedestrian orientation for improving path prediction. In: 2008 IEEE Intelligent Vehicles Symposium, pp. 506–511 (2008)
9. Peck, T., Fuchs, H., Whitton, M.: The design and evaluation of a large-scale real-walking locomotion interface. TVCG 2012: IEEE Transactions on Visualization and Computer Graphics 18(7), 1053–1067 (2012)
10. Razzaque, S., Kohn, Z., Whitton, M.C.: Redirected walking. In: Proceedings of Eurographics, pp. 289–294 (2001)
11. Su, J.: Motion compression for telepresence locomotion. Presence: Teleoperators and Virtual Environments 16(4), 385–398 (2007)
12. Interrante, V., Ries, B., Anderson, L.: Seven league boots: A new metaphor for augmented locomotion through moderately large scale immersive virtual environments. In: IEEE Symposium on 3D User Interfaces, 3DUI 2007, pp. 167–170. IEEE (2007)
13. Grasso, R., Prvost, P., Ivanenko, Y.P., Berthoz, A.: Eye-head coordination for the steering of locomotion in humans: an anticipatory synergy. Neuroscience Letters 253(2), 115–118 (1998)
14. Hollands, M., Patla, A., Vickers, J.: "look where you're going!": gaze behaviour associated with maintaining and changing the direction of locomotion. Experimental Brain Research 143, 221–230 (2002)
15. Koo, S., Kwon, D.S.: Recognizing human intentional actions from the relative movements between human and robot. In: The 18th IEEE International Symposium on Robot and Human Interactive Communication, pp. 939–944 (2009)

16. Hoogendoorn, S.P.: Pedestrian flow modeling by adaptive control. Transportation Research Record: Journal of the Transportation Research Board 1878(1), 95–103 (2004)
17. Foxlin, E.: Pedestrian tracking with shoe-mounted inertial sensors. CGA 2005: Computer Graphics and Applications 25(6), 38–46 (2005)
18. Fischer, C., Muthukrishnan, K., Hazas, M., Gellersen, H.: Ultrasound-aided pedestrian dead reckoning for indoor navigation. In: Proceedings of the First ACM International Workshop on Mobile Entity Localization and Tracking in GPS-Less Environments, MELT 2008, pp. 31–36. ACM (2008)
19. Kiruluta, A., Eizenman, M., Pasupathy, S.: Predictive head movement tracking using a kalman filter. IEEE Transactions on Systems, Man, and Cybernetics 27(2), 326–331 (1997)
20. LaViola, J.J.: Double exponential smoothing: an alternative to kalman filter-based predictive tracking. In: Proceedings of the Workshop on Virtual Environments 2003, EGVE 2003, pp. 199–206. ACM (2003)
21. van Rhijn, A., van Liere, R., Mulder, J.: An analysis of orientation prediction and filtering methods for vr/ar. In: Proceedings of the IEEE Virtual Reality, VR 2005, pp. 67–74 (March 2005)
22. Hirasaki, E., Moore, S.T., Raphan, T., Cohen, B.: Effects of walking velocity on vertical head and body movements during locomotion. Experimental Brain Research 127, 117–130 (1999)
23. Terrier, P., Schutz, Y.: How useful is satellite positioning system (gps) to track gait parameters? a review. Journal of NeuroEngineering and Rehabilitation 2(1), 28 (2005)
24. Foxlin, E., Naimark, L.: Vis-tracker: A wearable vision-inertial self-tracker. In: Proceedings of the IEEE Conference on Virtual Reality, VR 2003, p. 199. IEEE, Washington, DC (2003)
25. Wendt, J., Whitton, M., Brooks, F.: Gud wip: Gait-understanding-driven walking-in-place. In: Proceedings of the IEEE Conference on Virtual Reality, VR 2010, pp. 51–58 (March 2010)
26. Zijlstra, W., Hof, A.: Displacement of the pelvis during human walking: experimental data and model predictions. Gait and Posture 6(3), 249–262 (1997)

A Computational Model of Emotional Attention for Autonomous Agents

Silviano Díaz Barriga[1], Luis-Felipe Rodríguez[1], Félix Ramos[1], and Marco Ramos[2]

[1] Department of Computer Science, Cinvestav Guadalajara, México
{sdiaz,lrodrigue,framos}@gdl.cinvestav.mx
[2] Department of Computer Science,
Universidad Autónoma del Estado de México, Campus Toluca, México
mramos@univ-tlse1.fr

Abstract. A major challenge in artificial intelligence has been the development of autonomous agents (AAs) capable of displaying very believable behaviors. In order to achieve such objective, the underlying architectures of these intelligent systems have been designed to incorporate biologically inspired components. It is expected that through the interaction of this type of components, AAs are able to implement more intelligent and believable behavior. Although the literature reports several computational models of attention and emotions developed to be included in cognitive agent architectures, these have been implemented as two separated processes, disregarding essential interactions between these two human functions whose modeling and computational implementation may increase the believability of behaviors developed by AAs. In this paper, we propose a *biologically inspired computational model of emotional attention*. This model is designed to provide AAs with adequate mechanisms to attend and react to emotionally salient elements in the environment. The results of four types of simulations performed to evaluate the behavior of AAs implementing the proposed model are presented.

Keywords: Emotions, Attention, Computational Modeling, Autonomous Agents.

1 Introduction

The underlying mechanisms of human emotions and attention have been widely investigated in multiple disciplines [13, 22]. Evidence shows that the attention process allows humans to focus on the most relevant elements in the environment and disregard those irrelevant. Moreover, attention provides humans with a control mechanism for the allocation of limited processing resources in charge of interpreting incoming stimuli. On the other hand, emotion processes allow humans to evaluate their environment from an emotional perspective and prepare appropriate responses to deal with emotional stimuli. Importantly, emotions endow humans and other animals with proper mechanisms for their adaptation to

M.L. Gavrilova et al. (Eds.): Trans. on Comput. Sci. XVIII, LNCS 7848, pp. 192–211, 2013.
© Springer-Verlag Berlin Heidelberg 2013

very dynamic environments. The importance of these two brain processes to the development of rational behavior in humans and their interrelationships have been discussed elsewhere [13, 20, 27].

In the fields of artificial intelligence (AI), virtual reality (VR), and human-computer interaction (HCI) a primary goal has been the development of autonomous agents (AAs) capable of displaying very believable behavior. The architectures of these intelligent systems usually incorporate components that implement models of cognitive and affective functions underlying human behavior such as perception, decision making, planning, attention, and emotions. The main purpose of this methodology has been to imitate some aspects of human behavior in AAs and allow them to implement intelligent, social, and emotional responses. In this sense, computational models of emotions and attention have been proposed to be included in or as part of cognitive agent architectures. However, although considerable efforts have been made to incorporate attentional and emotional mechanisms in AAs, these have been mostly incorporated as two separate processes, disregarding multidisciplinary evidence that suggests that the mechanisms underlying human emotions and attention interact extensively [29]. In this context, despite numerous developments of AAs whose architecture includes emotion and attention mechanisms, there is still a need for models that take into account essential interactions between these two processes.

In this paper we propose a *biologically inspired computational model of emotional attention* for AAs. This model is designed to synthesize some essential aspects of the interrelationship between human attention and emotions. In particular, the proposed model is designed to provide autonomous agents with adequate mechanisms to attend and react to emotionally salient visual elements in the environment. This fundamental characteristic of human behavior is essential for the development of AAs for several reasons. As an illustration, in situations in which an agent is exposed to environments that contain threatening objects, it is necessary for the agent to embody mechanisms that allow it to properly attend and react to these types of objects (independently of its current task-relevant activities), which may even appear spontaneously or be placed outside the agent's focus of attention. In addition, given the evidence that human behavior is highly influenced by emotionally salient elements in the environment, specially fear-relevant stimuli, virtual entities in HCI and VR applications must correspond to such behavior by being capable of also attending and reacting to such emotionally salient elements, thus establishing more natural interactions.

This paper is structured as follows. In section 2 we review computational models developed to include synthetic emotions and attention mechanisms in AAs. After that, we explore theoretical and empirical evidence from psychology and neuroscience about the interactions between these two processes (which inspired the design of the proposed model). We present the high-level design of the proposed model and implementation details in section 4. In section 5 we describe the case study used to evaluate the proposed model, provide details of the simulations performed, and present some results. Finally, a discussion is provided in section 6 and concluding remarks in section 7.

2   Related Work

The literature reports a variety of computational models developed to provide AAs with mechanisms for attentional and emotional processing. However, these models have been mostly designed and implemented separately, without establishing an explicit relationship between them. In this section, we review computational models whose design takes into account some aspects of the interactions between attention and emotion processes.

Kismet is a social robot designed to socially interact with humans [4]. Its underlying architecture includes an attention system responsible for directing the robot's eyes toward stimuli that satiate its social and stimulation drives. In order to determine the most salient objects in the environment and thus determine the robot's focus of attention, three visual features are considered: *motion saliency, color saliency*, and *face pop-outs*. As shown in Figure 1, a saliency map is derived for each of these features, which are then combined with a habituation function using a weighted sum (this function helps to decrease the saliency of attended objects so that the robot's eyes can be directed to other locations). The specific weight given to each saliency map is adjusted based on the status of Kismet's drives. For example, if the stimulation drive needs to be satiated, the color saliency map is enhanced because color is characteristic of toys. Similarly, when such drive is over-stimulated, the color saliency is suppressed. The combination process generates a *global attention activation map*, which is finally used to direct the robot's attention and display consistent emotional facial expressions.

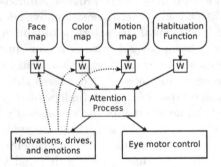

Fig. 1. The attention system of Kismet (adapted from [4])

Peters [21] proposes a model that considers some aspects of the relationship between emotion and attention in AAs. In this model, visual stimuli captured by the agent (a virtual infant) serve as the input to a perceptual pipeline in which these stimuli are progressively appraised in terms of their relevance. This relevance is determined by assessing basic features of stimuli and other attributes such as levels of valence and arousal. On the basis of this kind of characteristics, four *synthetic perceptual maps* are derived: the saliency perceptual map (considers basic features such as color and orientation), the uncertainty map (based on the uncertainty value of objects already stored in memory), and the threat and reward perceptual maps (derived from the level of arousal and valence of stimuli). These four maps are then weighted and combined to derive a global *relevance master map*, the output of the perceptual pipeline. This map determines the relevance of the contents in a scene captured by the agent and influences its internal attentive and emotional states as well as its expressive behavior.

Methodology for Analysis and Modeling of Individual Differences (MAMID) [11] associates two main concepts: a methodology for modeling the influences of stable traits (e.g., personality) and dynamic states (e.g., emotions) on cognitive processes, and an affective-cognitive architecture that implements such methodology. The main assumption of this methodology is that emotions can modulate cognitive processes by adjusting the architectural parameters that control the processing capabilities of each component in the MAMID architecture. In particular, elicited emotions and basic traits of AAs implementing the MAMID architecture are mapped into parametric values that influence the attention component. Thus, according to the values derived, elicited emotions reduce or increase the attention system capacity to filter incoming cues. For example, reduced attentional capacities are consequence of emotions such as anxiety or fear, causing the agent to attend to fewer cues.

We conclude this section with a brief discussion on the reviewed models. The model of attention of Kismet [4] seems to be designed to search for two types of objects in the environment and to direct the robot's attention to them depending on the robot's internal state. This model does not allow Kismet to attend and react to salient elements in the environment regardless of its current affective state and needs. In contrast, in the model proposed by Peters [21], AAs are able to attend to emotional objects in the environment. However, this model does not present simulation results that determine its adequacy to improve the believability of agent's behavior. Regarding the MAMID methodology and architecture [11], its attention component is not modulated by the emotional significance of environmental stimuli perceived by an AA (at least not directly). As a result, although highly emotional objects in the environment help determine the agent's current emotional state (which does influence the attention component), they are unable to quickly capture the agent's attention.

3   Theoretical Evidence

The proposed computational model of emotion and attention interaction is designed to model the mechanisms that allow humans to attend and react to emotionally relevant visual elements in the environment. In this section, we review multidisciplinary evidence that explains this crucial aspect of human behavior.

There is a wealth of evidence suggesting reciprocal interactions between the attention and emotion processes in humans. Results from multidisciplinary experiments demonstrate that humans have a predisposition to attend to emotionally relevant elements in the environment [19, 26, 29]. Öhman et al. [17] propose that humans have evolved in environments where the ability to efficiently detect important events such as those of survival relevance is essential. They further suggest that certain types of stimuli (e.g., threatening ones) automatically capture individuals' attention regardless of the locations of such stimuli in the environment and the number of distractors. Moreover, evidence shows that unexpected and highly emotional relevant events may interrupt individuals' current cognitive and behavioral activities and capture their attention and sensory processing resources. This aspect of selective attention is usually referred to as preattentive visual attention, which is fast, automatic, and parallel and considers low-level stimulus features [18].

Regarding the implications of attention in emotional processing, it has been suggested that attended stimuli influence the emotional experience and behavioral response of individuals [19, 23, 29]. Frijda [10] proposes that there are different states of action readiness in the individual (dispositions or indispositions to face a situation) that are elicited by objects appraised as emotionally relevant. These are action tendencies that take the form of approaching, protection, avoidance, attending, disinterest, apathy, and others. According to Frijda, these modes of action readiness activate or deactivate the mechanisms in the individual that are necessary to respond to emotional contingencies. Ekman [6] suggests that individuals' facial expressions have a direct correspondence to the emotional experiences elicited by emotional events. He further states that some emotional facial expressions are universal, such as those associated with fear, disgust, happiness, and surprise. Experiments by Fredrickson and Branigan [8] have also revealed important patterns of behavior induced by attended relevant stimuli. Particularly, these showed that positive emotions broaden individuals' thought-action repertoires whereas negative emotions narrow thought-action repertoires.

The neural substrates supporting the interactions between emotion and attention processes have been also investigated in several disciplines. Multidisciplinary studies indicate that visual information is processed in the brain throughout two main paths: ventral and dorsal [5, 13, 25]. In the ventral pathway, which is responsible for object recognition, there are several processes serving as bottom-up mechanisms for visual attention. These include the processing of basic object's features such as color and orientation and the grouping of these basic features into visual representations [28]. On the other hand, the amygdala is a brain structure that has been identified as the main center for the processing of emotional information and the organization of emotional reactions [14]. In order to appropriately perform these tasks, the amygdala has extensive connections with other brain structures that underlie cognitive and viseral functions. Importantly, this structure plays a key role in the influence of emotions on the attention process [26]. It has been suggested that the amygdala is involved in a circuit that preattentively registers the emotional significance of environmental stimuli [26]. Furthermore, experimental findings show that the amygdala receives inputs from early stages of the ventral visual pathway and fast subcortical routes such as the tecto-pulvinar pathway, and that projects back to virtually all processing stages along this visual system [9,29]. These connections provide an effective mechanism to enhance processing of emotional objects in the environment.

4   Model of Emotional Attention

In this section, we present a high-level description and provide implementation details of the proposed *computational model of emotional attention* (see Figure 2). This model is designed to provide AAs with mechanisms for attending and reacting to emotionally relevant elements in the environment. Its architectural and operational designs are inspired by recent evidence from fields studying the brain information processing such as neuroscience, neuropsychology, and neurophysiology. Its architectural components represent brain structures involved in the process of emotional attention in humans, their interrelationships are based on how these structures interact in the human brain, and the model's operating cycle imitates some of the phases implicated in the mentioned process. Table 1 briefly explains the role that each architectural component plays in the model.

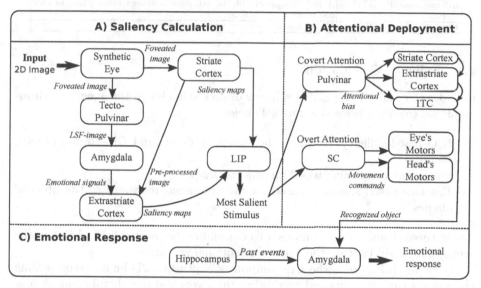

Fig. 2. The proposed computational model of emotional attention (some components are used more than once to facilitate data flow understanding)

The model proposed implements an operating cycle that consists of three phases: *saliency calculation, attentional deployment,* and *emotional experience and expression.* In the first phase (Figure 2, part A), the most salient environmental stimulus is determined based on its physical characteristics and emotional relevance. In the second phase (Figure 2, part B), this stimulus is attended to and interpreted. Finally, in the third phase (Figure 2, part C), an emotional response is generated according to the significance of the attended stimulus. In the remainder of this section, we explain the proposed model based on these three phases.

Table 1. Components of the proposed computational model of emotional attention

Component	Abbr.	Description
Synthetic Eye	Eye	Captures a 2D image representing the agent's environment.
Tecto - Pulvinar	TP	Transforms the perceived 2D image into a low-spatial frequency (LSF) image.
Amygdala	Amy	Determines the emotional significance of the stimuli in the captured 2D image and organizes emotional responses.
Striate Cortex	ST	Creates intensity, color, and orientation saliency maps from the 2D image.
Extrastriate Cortex	EST	Identifies the shapes of the stimuli in the 2D image.
Lateral Intraparietal Area	LIP	Computes ICO-based and shape-based saliencies for each object in the 2D image. Then combines these saliencies to determine a global feature-based saliency for each object.
Pulvinar	PUL	Distributes information about the most salient stimulus in the 2D image to the ST, EST, and ITC components so that the stimulus is attended covertly.
Superior Colliculus	SC	Provides motor commands to move the agent's eyes and head to an intended position for the foveation of visual stimuli.
Inferotemporal Cortex	ITC	A full recognition of the attended stimulus takes place in this component.
Hippocampus	HIP	Maintains memories of past experiences.

4.1   Saliency Calculation

In order to calculate the global saliency of each stimulus in the agent's environment, we calculate three separate saliencies:

1. ICO-based saliency: based on the *Intensity*, *Color*, and *Orientation* of each stimulus.
2. Shape-based saliency: based on objects' shapes.
3. Emotion-based saliency: based on the emotional relevance of the objects' shapes.

These three saliencies are combined to determine the most salient object in the scene, which will capture the agent's attentional resources.

As shown in Figure 2, the Eye component captures a 2D image (representing the agent's environment) and establishes the foveal and peripheral areas. A blur is applied to the peripheral area whereas the foveal one remains with a high resolution, as occurs in the actual process of the human eye [1]. The processed image is sent simultaneously to the Striate Cortex (ST), via the thalamic relay, and to the Tecto-Pulvinar (TP) components.

Based on evidence that indicates that neurons in the striate cortex of the human brain respond to simple visual attributes [16], in the ST component, intensity, color, and orientation saliency maps are calculated. First, the ST component creates spatial scales from the blurred image that was received from the Eye component by using dyadic Gaussian pyramids, which yields image-reduction factors ranging from scale zero (1:1) to scale eight (1:256). According to evidence, visual neurons are very sensitive to the stimuli contained in a small region of the visual space (the center), but less susceptible to those stimuli presented in a broader, weaker, antagonistic region concentric to the center (the surround). Based on such evidence, the intensity, color, and orientation saliency maps are computed using a set of linear center-surround operations as in [12]. In particular, in the proposed model center-surround is implemented as the difference between fine and coarse image scales: the center is a pixel at scale c and the surround is the corresponding pixel at scale $s = c + d$, with $d > 0$. The across-scale difference between two maps is obtained by interpolation to the finer scale and point-by-point subtraction.

Once the input image is scaled, the ST component computes the intensity, color and orientation conspicuity maps. The intensity map is concerned with intensity contrast, which in humans is detected by neurons that are sensitive either to dark centers on bright surrounds or to the converse [15]. These types of sensitivities are simultaneously computed in a set of six intensity maps $I(c, s)$ as in equation (1) in [12]. The ST component also constructs a set of maps for the color channels, which, in the human cortex, are represented through a color double-opponent system. In the center of their receptive fields, neurons are excited by one color and inhibited by another, while the converse is true in the surround [7]. Accordingly, the ST component creates six maps $RG(s, c)$ to simultaneously account for red/green and green/red double opponency and six maps $BY(c, s)$ for blue/yellow and yellow/blue double opponency. $RG(c, s)$ and $BY(c, s)$ maps are computed as in equations (2) and (3) in [12], respectively. Finally, the ST component computes orientation saliency maps $O(c, s)$ using Gabor pyramids and considering four orientations $\theta \in \{0°, 45°, 90°, 180°\}$, resulting in twenty four different maps. These orientation maps are calculated as in equation (4) in [12]. Gabor filters allows us to approximate the response of orientation-selective neurons in primary visual cortex.

After the ST component computes the feature maps, it proceeds to calculate the intensity, color and orientation maps from which the ICO-based saliency will be computed. Intensity conspicuity map I, color conspicuity map C and orientation conspicuity map O are obtained by a reduction of each feature map to scale four and point-by-point addition. These maps are computed in the same way as in equations (5), (6) and (7) in [12], respectively. The derived saliency maps are sent to the LIP and to the SC components. In addition, the ST component classifies the pixels in the 2D image in color classes and sends these data to the extrastriate cortex (EST) component.

Regarding the projection from the Eye to the TP component, in the TP the foveated image is transformed into a blurry low-spatial frequency (LSF) image and then sent to the Amygdala (Amy) component. According to Vuilleumier [29], the human amygdala is sensitive to such type of coarse visual data, which are provided through the tecto-pulvinar route. Moreover, this brain structure has been considered the main center for emotional processing [14]. Thus, in the Amy component, the LSF image is segmented in order to extract the objects in the agent's environment. These objects are then compared with objects stored in the Amy's internal memory, which maintains information about objects previously perceived by the agent and their associated emotional significance. Emotional values of the objects in such memory are represented in terms of pleasantness and activation [24]. For example, a dangerous object can be represented by highly unpleasant and high activation values. The comparison process is based primarily on the shape of objects and supposed to take place relatively fast (this process should be fast as its results need to be completed before full representations of perceived stimuli are done). However, these comparisons might result imprecise in certain scenarios, such as those in which objects with different emotional significances share similar shapes (e.g., a rope and a snake). According to the level of similarity between the shapes of objects in the agent's scene and the shapes of objects in the Amy's memory, a specific emotional significance value S_{e_k} is assigned to each k object in the agent's environment. This shape correspondence depends on a predefined threshold. If the similarity between two objects exceeds such threshold, then objects are assumed to have similar shapes. Furthermore, if the shape of an object in the agent's scene is similar to more than one object stored in the Amy's memory, then the one with the highest emotional value will determine the emotional significance of the object being compared. Once this process finishes, the Amy projects information about the objects and their emotional values to the EST component.

In the EST, the shapes of the objects in the 2D image are defined. Evidence suggests that neurons in the extrastriate cortex respond to the geometric shapes of stimuli [28]. In particular, the EST groups pixels with similar properties in the processed image received from the ST component. This procedure allows the identification of regions that are used to define the shapes of the objects in the 2D image, which are sent to the ITC component to continue the visual object recognition process. Finally, using the emotional signals received from the Amy, the EST assigns the corresponding emotional value to each basic shape f_k of every k extracted object and projects this information to the LIP.

In the brain, the lateral intraparietal area (LIP) contains a representation of the relative stimulus saliency across the entire visual field [3]. In our model, the LIP component calculates the overall saliency of each object in the 2D image and determines the most salient stimulus. We proceed to explain how it happens. First, the LIP computes the ICO-based saliency of each pixel in the 2D image based on the intensity, color, and orientation saliency maps received from the ST component. These three saliency maps are normalized by multiplying each location in these maps by $(M - \mu)^2$, where M is the global maximum of the feature (intensity, color, or orientation) map and μ is the average of its local maxima. This normalization operation results in normalized intensity, color and orientation saliency maps: $N(I), N(C)$, and $N(O)$, respectively. The ICO-based saliency for each pixel i of the input image is computed as an average of the three ICO saliency maps:

$$S_{ICO_i} = \frac{N(I)_i + N(C)_i + N(O)_i}{3} \tag{1}$$

Then, an ICO-based saliency value S_{ICO_k} is associated to each object k identified in the EST, which is the average of all ICO-based saliencies of the pixels that comprise such basic shape. This value is computed as folows:

$$S_{ICO_k} = \sum_{i=1}^{n_k}(S_{ICO_i})/n_k \tag{2}$$

where i represents the index of a pixel that is contained in the k object shape and n_k is the number of pixels that conform the k object shape. Once the LIP component computes these ICO-based saliencies, it proceeds to compute a shape-based saliency value S_{S_k} for each extracted object k taking into account the extent to which their shapes stand out from the shapes of neighboring objects (note that these shapes already have associated an emotional value). This value is computed as follows:

$$S_{S_k} = \sum_{j=1}^{N_k} D(f_k, V(f_k)_j) + \sum_{j=1}^{N_k} |S_{e_k} - V(S_{e_k})_j| \tag{3}$$

where $D(x, y)$ is a function that indicates how different are the x and y objects with respect to their shapes, $V(x)$ is a function that returns a neighbor of the x object, and N_k is the total number of neighbors of the k object. In this manner, the shape-based saliency is computed by considering the differences (physical and emotional) of one object with respect to the objects in its neighborhood.

After the LIP defines the ICO-based and shape-based saliencies for each object in the 2D image, it proceeds to calculate their feature-based saliency. This process consists basically of a weighted average of the two saliencies.

The LIP component computes the average of the ICO-based saliencies μ_{ICO} and the average of the shape-based saliencies μ_S of the objects in the input image. Then, it computes the weights for the ICO and shape-based saliencies w_{ICO_k} and w_{S_k}, respectively, of the k object. The LIP will give a greater weight to the ICO- or shape-based saliency value when the difference between this value and the corresponding average saliency value of the objects is greater than a predefined threshold. If $S_{ICO_k} - \mu_{ICO} > \delta_1$, then

$$w_{ICO_k} = \frac{S_{ICO_k} + \delta_1}{S_{ICO_k}} \tag{4}$$

in other case, $w_{ICO_k} = 1$. δ_1 is a predefined threshold. With respect to the shape-based saliency weight, if the $S_{S_k} - \mu_S > \delta_2$, then

$$w_{S_k} = \frac{S_{S_k} + \delta_2}{S_{S_k}} \tag{5}$$

in other case, $w_{S_k} = 1$. As δ_1, δ_2 is a predefined threshold. The LIP component calculates the feature-based saliency of the k object in the following way:

$$S_{F_k} = \frac{w_{ICO_k} S_{ICO_k} + w_{S_k} S_{S_k}}{2} \tag{6}$$

Once the LIP component has computed the feature-based saliency for every object that is present in the input image, it selects the object with the greatest feature-based saliency, $o_{winner} = max(S_{F_k})$, which will be attended either overtly or covertly.

From the above procedure, the most salient stimulus in the agent's environment is determined (the one with the greatest feature-based saliency value), which is selected by the agent for either covert or overt attentional deployment as explained in the following section.

4.2   Attentional Deployment

The environmental stimulus with the greatest feature-based saliency should be attended to by the agent, either overtly or covertly. If such stimulus is located at the foveal area, the LIP sends attentional modulations to ST, EST, and ITC components through the pulvinar (PUL) component. The pulvinar is an associative nucleus of the thalamus in the brain that offers a route for indirect transcortical communication [25]. The PUL component distributes information about the ICO, shape, and class of the most salient stimulus (o_{winner}) to the ST, EST, and ITC components, respectively, so that the visual processing of such stimulus is favored (covert attention). According to Kastner and Ungerleider [13], neural responses to the attended stimulus are enhanced in visual processing areas such as the striate and extrastriate cortices, thereby biasing information processing in favor of an attended stimulus.

In case the most relevant stimulus is located outside the foveal area (peripheral area), eye and head movements are required in order to attend to this stimulus properly. The LIP projects information about the stimulus to be attended to the SC component, which generates appropriate commands to move the agent's eyes and head. The SC is capable of directing the agent's eyes and head to the appropriate location as it maintains saliency maps of the 2D image perceived (received from the ST component). Once the necessary movements have been carried out and the most salient object is located at the agent's focus of attention, covert attention takes place.

The ITC is the last step in the process of recognition of the most salient stimulus (and the others around it). It interprets the object's characteristics and projects to the Amy to influence the subsequent agent's emotional response.

4.3   Emotional Response

In order to determine the emotional expression to be displayed by the agent once the most salient stimuli in the environment is attended to, the Amy component carries out an evaluation of the emotional significance of the stimuli received from the ITC. In humans, the Amygdala has been recognized as an important center for the organization of emotional responses [14]. This brain structure organizes these responses based on the evaluation of data projected from several structures (e.g., unimodal and multimodal sensory information) and the modulation of neural systems that underlie cognitive and visceral functions [22]. Unlike the evaluations performed by the Amy in the first phase (saliency calculation), which are fast and based on coarse data, in this phase, the Amy evaluates the emotional significance of fully recognized objects. This allows us to determine more precisely the emotional significance of the objects perceived by the agent.

In the proposed model, the Amy receives from the hippocampus (HIP) component information about the emotional significance of the attended (and fully recognized) object. Evidence indicates that the hippocampus is a human brain structure that maintains memories of past experiences, including memories of emotional events in which the object being attended to has been involved [22]. Although the main role of the human amygdala is to organize the inputs from several neural systems and organize an emotional response by modulating several neural systems in charge of controlling a variety of behaviors, in our model the Amy component is responsible for organizing and deciding the specific emotional response to be displayed by the agent. The Amy receives from the ITC information about the attended object and from the HIP information about its emotional significance. As in the Amy's memory, emotional values of objects in the HIP are represented in terms of pleasantness and activation. The Amy implements a two-dimensional space based on Russell's model [24] (see Figure 3) consisting of pleasantness (pleasure/displeasure) and activation (arousal/non-arousal) to decide the agent's emotional response. In this space, specific types of emotions such as happiness and fear are associated with well-defined regions. In this manner, when the emotional significance of the attended object is determined (and represented in terms of pleasantness and activation), it is appropriately situated within the two-dimensional space. The particular position of the object in the two space and its proximity to a particular region is what defines the emotional response to be implemented by the agent. In the proposed model, these emotional responses are implemented as emotional facial expressions. For example, an object associated with high pleasure and moderate activation may fall in the region of happy responses, whereas an object associated with high displeasure and high activation in the region of fear responses [24].

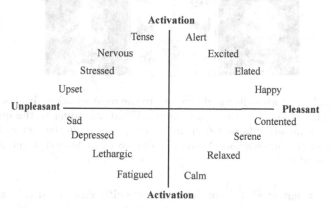

Fig. 3. Two-dimensional space used to represent emotional significances and derive emotional responses [24]

Nevertheless, the response displayed by the agent is not only determined by this last evaluation procedure. As explained above, in the first phase of the process being described the Amy component carries out a fast evaluation of the stimuli in the agent's environment based on coarse data (shapes extracted from a LSF image). This evaluation assigns an initial emotional significance to all objects in the scene, including that object that will be attended to by the agent in a posterior phase. Moreover, in a last phase the Amy re-appraises the object being attended to by the agent using information of fully recognized objects, which allows us to assign more accurate emotional values to such object. Based on the results of these two evaluations, the agent's response is determined. For example, if the first evaluation assigns a highly unpleasant value to the attended stimulus and the second evaluation assigns to such stimulus a highly pleasant value, relief expressions may be displayed instead of happiness.

5   Simulations and Results

In this section, we describe the case study used to evaluate the proposed computational model of emotional attention and present the results of the simulations conducted.

5.1   Case Study

We consider a case study in which a virtual agent is exposed to 2D images containing arrays of different types of stimuli (see Figure 4 and Figure 5). As mentioned before, the 2D image represents the agent's environment and the stimuli placed in the arrays represent the objects in such environment. In particular, these stimuli differ in the following aspects:

Fig. 4. A virtual agent attending and reacting to the most emotionally salient stimulus in the array. The left part of the figure shows Alfred attending to the object at the lower right side of the array (a snake) in the 2D image shown in the center of the figure. The right part of the figure shows Alfred reacting to the attended stimulus through a facial expression of fear.

- *Emotional valence*: each stimulus has a specific emotional relevance to the agent.
- *Physical characteristics*: each stimulus have specific ICO-based and shape-based saliencies.

The main purpose of this case study is to evaluate the agent's ability to attend and react to the most emotionally significant object in the 2D image. In addition, we analyze the influence that physical characteristics of objects

(ICO- and shape-based saliencies) have in such process. As explained before, evidence indicates that individuals tend to direct their attention to emotionally relevant stimuli when presented among a series of non-emotionally relevant stimuli, and that attended stimuli appraised as emotionally relevant influence individuals' subsequent behavior. In this sense, we particularly examine the following two aspects during the simulations:

1. The specific stimulus at which the agent directs its attentional resources.
2. The agent's emotional reaction once it fully interprets the attended object.

5.2 Simulations

We conducted a variety of simulations for the case study described above. In these simulations, a virtual agent was exposed to arrays of size 3x3 containing stimuli with different physical characteristics and emotional significances, as shown in Figure 5.

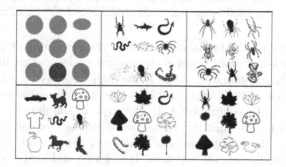

Fig. 5. Some of the arrays used in the simulations

We used Alfred [2], a Facial Animation System designed to create facial expressions for animated agents, to implement the virtual agent used in the simulations. Alfred enables virtual agents to control many individual facial muscles and head movements. Moreover, it allows the generation of a diversity of emotional facial expressions based on the Facial Action Coding System (FACS). Particularly, based on these Alfred's abilities, our virtual agent is capable of simulating gaze shifts when overt attention is required and of displaying emotional responses through facial expressions according to the attended stimulus.

We defined four different types of simulations based on the case of study in order to evaluate the proposed model in various scenarios. In general, these scenarios try to cover common situations in which there are more than one emotional object or multiple objects with highly salient properties which compete for the agent's attention. Furthermore, these four types of simulations allowed us to evaluate the two aspects mentioned above. Table 2 describes the main objective of each type of simulation performed and the specific characteristics of the objects in the arrays used.

Table 2. Simulations performed to evaluate the proposed model

Type	Objective	Objects' Attributes in the Arrays
A	Evaluate the extent to which objects' physical attributes determine the most salient stimulus in the arrays.	a) All stimuli are emotionally neutral. b) In all trials, the ICO-based saliency of one stimulus and the shape-based saliency of another are greater than the others in the array. c) In all trials, objects' ICO- and shape-based saliencies ranges from low to high.
B	Evaluate if the most emotionally relevant stimulus always captures the agent's attention when it is among stimuli that have different physical characteristics.	a) In all trials, the emotional relevance of one object is greater than those of the others in the array. b) In all trials, the most emotionally relevant object differs from the other objects in terms of physical attributes.
C	Evaluate the extent to which the similarity of objects' shape influence the agent's attentional deployment. Evaluate the agent's reaction once it recognizes the attended object.	a) Two stimuli have similar shapes, but one is emotionally neutral (e.g., a rope) and the other is emotionally relevant (e.g., a snake). b) In all trials, ICO- and shape-based saliencies of the two stimuli with similar shapes can be similar or higher than the other objects in the array.
D	Evaluate if the agent is capable of attending to emotionally relevant stimulus even when the array also contains a neutral stimulus whose shape seems emotionally relevant. Evaluate the agent's reaction once it recognizes the attended object.	a) One stimulus is emotionally neutral but its shape seems emotionally relevant (e.g., a rope). b) One stimulus is emotionally relevant but differs in shape from the emotionally neutral (e.g., a spider). c) In all trials, ICO- and shape-based saliencies of the two mentioned stimuli can be similar or higher than those of the other objects in the array.

We provide details the simulation results in the remaining of this section. In general, the results of the four types of simulations performed are depicted in Figure 6. Particularly, in simulations type A the main objective was to measure the impact of the physical attributes of objects in determining the most prominent stimulus in the agent's environment. In this type of simulation, the ICO-based saliency of one stimulus and the shape-based saliency of another are always greater than the others in the arrays. Moreover, the stimuli presented in the arrays are emotionally neutral and their ICO-based and shape-based saliencies are low, medium, or high. Important results of these simulations are summarized as follows:

1. When all stimuli are appraised by the agent as emotionally neutral, the physical characteristics of objects are determinant.
2. When the ICO-based saliency of one stimulus and the shape-based saliency of another are greater than the others in the array, the object with the greatest ICO-based saliency (shape-based saliency) in the array is usually attended to when the shape-based saliency (ICO-based saliency) of the other objects are medium or low.
3. When the object with the greatest ICO-based saliency differs from the rest of the objects in the arrays in the same degree the object with the greatest shape-based saliency does, both are attended to almost the same number of times. However, during the simulations we noted that the stimulus with the greatest ICO is slightly favoured.

In the simulations type B, the main objective was to evaluate if the most emotionally relevant stimulus is always attended to regardless of the physical characteristics of the objects in its surrounding. The arrays used in these simulations

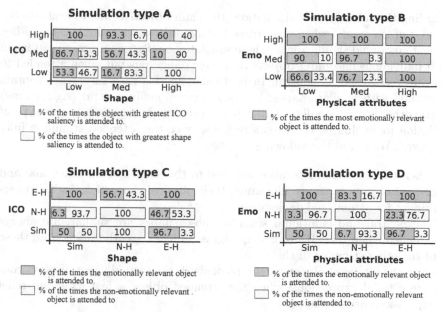

Fig. 6. Simulation results. In simulations type A, the y-axis (x-axis) indicates the difference between the object with the greatest ICO-based (shape-based) saliency and the others in the array in terms of ICO-based (shape-based) saliency. In simulations type B, the y-axis (x-axis) indicates the difference between the object with the greatest emotional significance and the others in the array in terms of emotional relevance (physical attributes). In simulations type C, the y-axis (x-axis) indicates that the ICO-based (shape-based) saliency of (1) the two stimuli with similar shapes is similar (Sim), (2) the neutral stimulus is the highest in the array (N-H), and (3) the emotionally relevant is the highest in the array (E-H). In simulations type D, the y-axis (x-axis) indicates that the emotional significance (physical attributes) of (1) the two stimuli being tested is (are) similar (Sim), (2) the neutral stimulus is (are) the highest in the array (N-H), and (3) the emotionally relevant is (are) the highest in the array (E-H). The x-axis indicates that the physical attributes of (1) the two stimuli being tested are similar (Sim), (2) the neutral stimulus are the most salient in the array (N-H), and (3) the emotionally relevant are the highest in the array (E-H).

contain one stimulus whose emotionally relevance is always greater than that of the remaining stimuli. We summarize some important results as follows:

1. When the emotional significance of the objects in the array is very similar, their physical attributes play a key role in the agent's attentional deployment. In this case, the stimulus with the highest emotional values is not always attended to.
2. When one stimulus in the array greatly differs in terms of emotional value from the others, it is mostly attended to regardless of the ICO- and shape-based saliencies of the other objects.

Regarding the third type of simulation, the main objective was to evaluate the behavior of the model when the arrays include objects with similar shapes but different emotional significances. These simulations reflect common situations in which individuals encounter objects that seem dangerous but when attended to these are recognized as neutral. In particular, in this case the arrays contain two stimuli with similar shapes, but one is emotionally neutral (e.g., a rope) and the other is emotionally relevant (e.g., a snake). In addition, in this type of simulation we evaluated the agents response once the attended stimuli is fully recognized. We found the following results:

1. When the emotional relevance assigned to the shapes of the emotional and neutral objects is almost the same, their physical characteristics are determinant for attentional deployment.
2. The neutral and emotional stimuli, whose shapes are similar, are always attended when their ICO- or shape-based saliency greatly differs from those of the other stimulus in the array.
3. Once the attended object is fully recognized, the virtual agent displays consistent facial expressions: when the attended object is fear-irrelevant relief expressions are displayed.

Finally, in simulations type D we evaluated if the agent is able to attend to the most emotionally relevant stimulus when the arrays contain neutral stimuli whose shape seems emotionally relevant. In this case, the shape of the emotionally relevant stimulus differs from the neutral one (e.g., a spider versus a rope). Moreover, as with simulations type C, in this type of simulation we evaluated the agents response once the attended stimuli is fully recognized. We summarize important conclusions of these simulations as follows:

1. When the emotional value assigned to the objects with emotionally relevant shapes is very similar, objects' physical characteristics may be determinant for attentional deployment.
2. When the emotional value assigned to one of the objects with emotionally relevant shapes is very high, it is mostly attended to, even when this object is not emotionally relevant to the agent.
3. Once the attended object is fully recognized, the virtual agent displays consistent facial expressions: when the attended object is fear-irrelevant relief expressions are displayed.

6   Discussion

The results of the simulations carried out demonstrate that the proposed model allows virtual agents to direct their attentional resources toward the most emotionally salient stimulus in the environment. In addition, when all stimuli in the environment are emotionally neutral, the agent directs its attention to the stimulus with the higher ICO- and shape-based saliency. Furthermore, when the emotional significance of two or more objects is the same, the evaluation of the object's intensity, color, orientation, and shape helps determine the object to be attended to. These changes of attention to the most salient stimulus occurred regardless of the location of such stimulus in the arrays. The agent's reaction induced by attended objects was also consistent to the emotional valence given to such objects.

The simulations performed above highlight the significance of the proposed model for AAs when facing a variety of situations in AI, HCI, and VR applications. In HCI applications, for example, virtual entities are expected to exhibit very believable and natural behaviors that resemble those of humans. Thus, as a key aspect of human behavior is the predisposition to attend and react to emotionally relevant stimuli in the environment, virtual entities must be able to correspond to such behavior by directing their attentional resources toward the emotionally relevant objects attended to by humans when they share a virtual scenario, as well as by developing consistent reactions. Similarly, the proposed model allows the simulation of virtual environments in which a series of emotionally significant stimuli can compete among themselves and with other non-emotional stimuli to capture the agent's attention. Furthermore, in situations where it is difficult to determine the most relevant emotional stimulus, the proposed model provides appropriate mechanisms to decide the most relevant stimulus based on other objects' characteristics. A particular scenario that clearly demonstrates the importance of a model of emotional attention are dangerous situations. An agent should be able to attend and react to threatening objects when these appear unexpectedly or are present outside its current focus of attention. Otherwise, its behavior would seem very unnatural. This further allows AAs to prepare fast responses such as those of flight-or-fight when required. These examples illustrate the extent to which the proposed model of emotional attention can improve the believability of the agents' behavior in common scenarios in AI, HCI, and VR applications.

There are many parameters that can be adjusted in the model. For example, the emotional significance value given to the objects stored in the Amy component used in the fast evaluations carried out in the first phase, the weights given to each of the three saliencies combined in the LIP component when determining the most salient stimulus, and the emotional value of the objects stored in the HIP also used by the Amy component to decide the agent's response. The regulation of these parameters enables the development of AAs that show different tendencies to attend to emotional and non-emotional stimuli. In addition, the biological basis of the model brings many benefits. For example, its architectural design, based on components that simulate brain structures, may facilitate the integration of new biologically inspired components or procedures to computationally synthesize other aspects of the interactions between the emotion and attention processes.

7 Conclusion

In this paper we presented a computational model of emotional attention. It was designed to provide autonomous agents with mechanisms to attend and react to emotionally salient elements in the environment. The main purpose of this model is to improve the believability of responses that AAs may implement when facing emotional scenarios and thus increase the range of applications in which they can be used. We conducted four types of simulations that consider different scenarios in order to evaluate the proposed model. The results demonstrate that the model allows virtual agents to show very believable behaviors in scenarios where emotional stimuli calls for the agent's attention. Moreover, the proposed model, which addresses one key aspect of the interactions between emotions and attention, demonstrates the need for more integrative computational models that recognize the importance of the interrelationships of the processes involved in agent architectures. It also suggest that biologically inspired computational models may help address serious challenges in the development of autonomous agents capable of displaying very believable, social, and natural behaviors.

References

1. Baluch, F., Itti, L.: Mechanisms of top-down attention. Trends in Neurosciences 34(4), 210–224 (2011)
2. Bee, N., Falk, B., André, E.: Simplified facial animation control utilizing novel input devices: a comparative study. In: Proceedings of the 14th International Conference on Intelligent User Interfaces, pp. 197–206. ACM, New York (2009)
3. Bisley, J.W., Mirpour, K., Arcizet, F., Ong, W.S.: The role of the lateral intraparietal area in orienting attention and its implications for visual search. European Journal of Neuroscience 33(11), 1982–1990 (2011)
4. Breazeal, C., Scassellati, B.: A context-dependent attention system for a social robot. In: Proceedings of the Sixteenth International Joint Conference on Artificial Intelligence, IJCAI 1999, pp. 1146–1151 (1999)
5. Bullier, J.: Integrated model of visual processing. Brain Research Reviews 36(2-3), 96–107 (2001)
6. Ekman, P.: Facial expressions. In: Dalgleish, T., Power, M.J. (eds.) Handbook of Cognition and Emotion, pp. 301–320. John Wiley and Sons (1999)
7. Engel, S., Zhang, X., Wandell, B.: Colour tuning in human visual cortex measured with functional magnetic resonance imaging. Nature 388(6637), 68–71 (1997)
8. Fredrickson, B.L., Branigan, C.: Positive emotions broaden the scope of attention and thought-action repertoires. Cognition & Emotion 19(3), 313–332 (2005)
9. Freese, J.L., Amaral, D.G.: Neuroanatomy of the primate amygdala. In: Whalen, P.J., Phelps, E.A. (eds.) The Human Amygdala, pp. 3–42. The Guilford Press (2009)
10. Frijda, N.: The Emotions. Cambridge University Press (1986)
11. Hudlicka, E.: Modeling the mechanisms of emotion effects on cognition. In: Proceedings of the AAAI Fall Symposium on Biologically Inspired Cognitive Architectures, pp. 82–86 (2008)
12. Itti, L., Koch, C., Niebur, E.: A model of saliency-based visual attention for rapid scene analysis. IEEE Transactions on Pattern Analysis and Machine Intelligence 20(11), 1254–1259 (1998)
13. Kastner, S., Ungerleider, L.G.: Mechanisms of visual attention in the human cortex. Annual Review of Neuroscience 23(1), 315–341 (2000)
14. LeDoux, J.E.: Emotion circuits in the brain. Annual Reviews 23, 155–184 (2000)

15. Leventhal, A.G.: The Neural Basis of Visual Function: Vision and Visual Dysfunction. CRC Press (1991)
16. Li, Z.: A saliency map in primary visual cortex. Trends in Cognitive Sciences 6(1), 9–16 (2002)
17. Ohman, A., Flykt, A., Esteves, F.: Emotion drives attention: Detecting the snake in the grass. Journal of Experimental Psychology 130(3), 466–478 (2001)
18. Öhman, A., Flykt, A., Lundqvist, D.: Unconscious emotion: Evolutionary perspectives, psychophysiological data, and neuropsychological mechanisms. In: Lane, R.D., Nadel, L. (eds.) Cognitive Neuroscience of Emotion, 1st edn. Oxford University Press (2000)
19. Pessoa, L.: On the relationship between emotion and cognition. Nature Reviews Neuroscience 9, 148–158 (2008)
20. Pessoa, L., Pereira, M.G., Oliveira, L.: Attention and emotion. Scholarpedia 5(2), 6314 (2010)
21. Peters, C.: Designing an emotional and attentive virtual infant. In: Paiva, A.C.R., Prada, R., Picard, R.W. (eds.) ACII 2007. LNCS, vol. 4738, pp. 386–397. Springer, Heidelberg (2007)
22. Phelps, E.A., Ling, S., Carrasco, M.: Emotion facilitates perception and potentiates the perceptual benefits of attention. Psychological Science 17(4), 292–299 (2006)
23. Phepls, E.A.: Emotion and cognition: Insights from studies of the human amygdala. Annual Review of Psychology 57, 27–53 (2006)
24. Russell, J.A.: Core affect and the psychological construction of emotion. Psychological Review 110(1), 145–172 (2003)
25. Shipp, S.: The brain circuitry of attention. Trends in Cognitive Sciences 8(5), 223–230 (2004)
26. Taylor, J.G., Fragopanagos, N.F.: The interaction of attention and emotion. Neural Networks 18(4), 353–369 (2005)
27. Taylor, J., Fragopanagos, N.: Modelling human attention and emotions. In: Proceedings of the 2004 IEEE International Joint Conference on Neural Networks, pp. 501–506 (2004)
28. VanRullen, R.: Visual saliency and spike timing in the ventral visual pathway. Journal of Physiology-Paris 97(2-3), 365–377 (2003)
29. Vuilleumier, P.: How brains beware: neural mechanisms of emotional attention. Trends in Cognitive Sciences 9(12), 585–594 (2005)

Haptic Rendering of Volume Data with Collision Detection Guarantee Using Path Finding

Roman Vlasov, Karl-Ingo Friese, and Franz-Erich Wolter

Institute of Man-Machine-Communication, Leibniz Universität Hannover, Germany
{rvlasov,kif,few}@gdv.uni-hannover.de

Abstract. In this paper we present a novel haptic rendering method for exploration of volumetric data. It addresses a recurring flaw in almost all related approaches, where the manipulated object, when moved too quickly, can go through or inside an obstacle. Additionally, either a specific topological structure for the collision objects is needed, or extra speed-up data structures should be prepared. These issues could make it difficult to use a method in practice. Our approach was designed to be free of such drawbacks. An improved version of the method presented here does not have the issues of the original method – oscillations of the interaction point and wrong friction force in some cases. It uses the ray casting technique for collision detection and a path finding approach for rigid collision response. The method operates directly on voxel data and does not use any precalculated structures, but uses an implicit surface representation being generated on the fly. This means that a virtual scene may be both dynamic or static. Additionally, the presented approach has a nearly constant time complexity independent of data resolution.

Keywords: haptics, haptic rendering, collision detection, collision response, collision resolution, ray casting, implicit surface, path finding.

1 Introduction

Nowadays 3D data processing and visualization, especially medical imaging, are widely used for analysis, diagnosis, illustration and other purposes, such as neurosurgery planning and reconstruction of volumetric data from Magnetic Resonance Imaging (MRI) and industrial CT (Computed Tomography).

When one works with 3D data, it is not very natural to navigate and manipulate it using a standard computer mouse and keyboard. A more intuitive way would be to use a device with more Degrees-of-Freedom (DoF). Several haptic devices fulfill this purpose, additionally providing an additional channel of interaction: feeling the objects – a user can both manipulate a virtual object and feel force feedback reactions. Since 3D data is widely used not only in medicine but in many different areas, such as CAD-applications, entertainment, museum display, sculpting, geology, military applications, various scientific applications and others, haptic devices could be also useful in these fields. Additionally, user studies were performed showing that a training with haptic devices gives better results than a training without them [1, 2].

M.L. Gavrilova et al. (Eds.): Trans. on Comput. Sci. XVIII, LNCS 7848, pp. 212–231, 2013.
© Springer-Verlag Berlin Heidelberg 2013

There exist many different surface- and voxel-based haptic rendering methods, and almost all of them give no collision detection guarantees and/or require a special topology and/or precalculations, which is not acceptable for such precise procedures as pre-operation planning in surgery. Additionally, in practice the real medical data we work with can have any structure if segmentation has been done automatically. In order not to have the aforementioned issues, we propose our haptic rendering approach. The approach is an improved version of the method presented in [3], addressing the following issues: sometimes there are oscillations of the interaction point (IP) around the locally closest surface point to the current position of the device manipulator, and the direction of the friction force could be incorrect in the case of multiple obstacles or a complex surface. Our improved method uses the ray casting technique for collision detection and a local path finding approach for rigid collision response. As in the original method, the improved approach has been implemented within the bounds of the YaDiV platform [4] – a virtual system for working with high-quality visualization of 3D volumetric data. For a moderate end-user PC, up to 750 points could be simulated at about 1 kHz for collision detection without collision response, and up to 145 points for the collision detection and collision response.

2   Definitions

2.1   Volumetric Data

Generally, 3D data could be in different representations (triangulated surface, hexahedrons, volumetric, ...). Here we focus on a volumetric one, since it is a direct output from the scanning devices. Other data types could be transformed to this one, if necessary.

Volume data, also called **volumetric data**, is a data set consisting of pairs $< coordinates, intensity\_value >$, where the intensity value is a scalar measured by a scanning device (e.g. the value of unabsorbed X-rays) [5]. One can take a look for a detailed description of volumetric data and related terms in [6].

Since scanned data has no color or tissue information, a **segmentation** step of the data could be further needed. That is, if explicit segmentation algorithms are used, a tag is applied to each voxel. This tag indicates whether the voxel belongs to a certain structure (e.g. to kidneys or bones) or not. We use a bit cube representation of segments for this (see [7]). The development of segmentation processes is a large field of research, and different approaches for different purposes have already been proposed (see e.g. [5] and [7] for an overview and suggested methods). Further we assume that the 3D volumetric data is already segmented, i.e. that a set of segments (a set of scene objects) is provided.

2.2   Haptics

The term **haptic** (originating from the Greek *haptesthai*, meaning "to touch") is an adjective used to describe something relating to or based on the sense of touch. The word "haptic" is in relation to the word "touching" as "visual" is to "seeing" and as "auditory" is to "hearing".

Below are the definitions being used in the rest of this work.

Definition 1. *A **haptic device** (or a **haptic display**) is capable of tracking its own position and/or orientation and stimulates the kinesthetic sense of the user via a programmable force feedback system.*

Definition 2. *A **probe** (or **end-effector**) (of a haptic display) is the part of the device for which the position/orientation is tracked (passive DoF) and to which a force feedback is applied (active DoF).*

Definition 3. *A **tool** (in a virtual world) is an object in a virtual world the user manipulates via the probe. A particular case is the **(haptic) interaction point** (if the object is a 3D point).*

Definition 4. *A **handle** (in a virtual world) is a grasped part of the tool.*

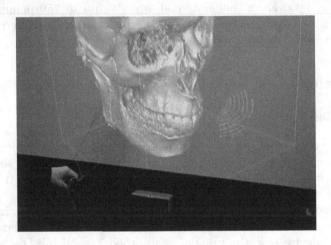

Fig. 1. Haptic rendering of the data set Head$_{big}$ using the INCA 6D device

3   Related Work

We would like to start with a description of a haptic rendering pipeline. Generally it has three stages as shown in Fig. 2. All stages are often tightly integrated in order to effectively use a solution of one task for solving others.

To communicate with the haptic device, there exist two ways:

- admittance control scheme: a user applies a force to the manipulator of the device, and the application program sends a command to the hardware to move the manipulator according to the simulation
- impedance control scheme: a user moves the manipulator, and the application program calculates forces and applies them to the manipulator. This scheme is shown in Fig. 2 and is usually used nowadays (see [8, 9]). It is also assumed in our work.

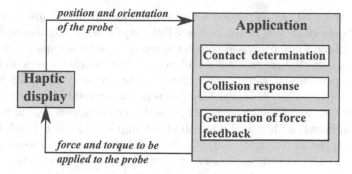

Fig. 2. Haptic rendering pipeline for the impedance control scheme

Colgate et al. showed in [10] that in order to have high quality haptic rendering it is important to compute feedback forces at a high update rate. According to Brooks et al. [11] it should be at least 0.5-1 kHz.

Remark 1. A force update rate of 1 kHz is generally not sufficient for stable haptic rendering. This means that other issues, such as too fast object movement or too strong forces, should be addressed in the system.

Further on, there exist two main techniques for dealing with the manipulation of the handle. The aim of both of them is to provide the user with stable haptic rendering. The techniques are:

- direct rendering: apply manipulations with the haptic probe directly to the handle
- virtual coupling (first proposed by Colgate et al. [10]): connect the haptic probe to the handle through a virtual spring-damper connection.

Each technique is suitable for a certain case. The direct rendering is good if all the stages of the haptic rendering pipeline can perform at 1 kHz (an update rate sufficient for a stable user interaction). The virtual coupling is good in the remaining cases, e.g. for multirate approaches, when force feedback is generated at 1 kHz, but physics simulation runs at, say, at 30 Hz.

There are different haptic rendering approaches, for which in the following we will give an overview by groups.

We start with **rigid-rigid methods**, i.e. for which the tool and all objects in the virtual world are rigid. Adachi et al. [12] and Mark et al. [13] were the first to propose an intermediate representation of the virtual environment. Zilles and Salisbury [14] proposed a god-object non-penetration approach for 3-DoF. Later the aforementioned approach was extended to 6-DoF by Ortega et al. [15]. An extension of the god-object idea in 3-DoF is a concept called "virtual proxy" [16]. At each frame, the position of the probe in the virtual environment is set as a goal for the tool. Then possible constraint surfaces are identified using the ray between the old position of the virtual proxy (the tool) and the goal position. After that a quadratic optimization problem is solved and a subgoal position is found. This process is repeated until the subgoal position could not be closer to the goal. An extended 6-DoF technique of virtual proxy was used in [17]. McNeely et al. [18] developed a 6-DoF haptic rendering method for the Boeing Company. They proposed to use a voxmap (spatial occupancy map) and object pointshells. Volumetric data and penalty pre-contact forces were used. Later this approach was significantly improved in the next works of McNeely and others [19] and [20]. A completely different haptic rendering approach was suggested by Otaduy, Lin et al. [21, 22]. Their method allows haptic rendering of interaction between "haptically textured" triangulated models (with fine surface details stored as a height field). Collision detection between low-resolution meshes is based on sensation-preserving contact levels of detail from [23, 24]. Another interesting approach was suggested by Johnson and Willemsen [25, 26]. They used spatialized normal cone hierarchies for fast collision detection between the tool and an environmental object. Weller and Zachmann [27] presented inner sphere trees – a structure which bounds an object from inside with a set of non-overlapping bounding volumes – and employed it for haptic rendering. Vidal et al. [28] made a simulation of ultrasound guided needle puncture and proposed a proxy-based surface/volume haptic rendering for that. Palmerius et al. [29] have shown in their work how subdivision of proxy movements can improve precision of volume haptic rendering. Kim and others [30] presented a method that uses implicit surface representations and requires some preprocessing and a certain topology. An approach devoted to haptic rendering of volume-embedded isosurfaces was suggested by Chan et al. [31]. Another haptic rendering method, which uses isosurfaces defined by interpolating on tetrahedral meshes, was recently proposed by Corenthy et al. [32].

Another group consists of **rigid-defo methods**, i.e. for which the tool is rigid and the environment is deformable. The following methods could be marked out. Debunne et al. [33] presented a method for animating dynamic deformations of a visco-elastic object with a guaranteed frame-rate, built into a 6-DoF haptic rendering framework. An object is represented via a tetrahedral mesh, and the proposed physical simulation approach belongs to the domain of physics-based continuous models. Basing on [19], Barbic et al. [34, 35] proposed their own approach, which supports contact between rigid and reduced deformable models, both with complex geometry. A distributed contact between objects is allowed, i.e. an interaction with potentially several simultaneous contact sites. A pointshell-based hierarchical representation was used for the deformable object and a signed-distance field for the rest of the scene. Kuroda et al. [36] presented a simulation framework, where the manipulating point pushes a deformable object, which is in contact with another one. A work of Basdogan et al. [37] is devoted to 6-DoF haptics in minimally invasive surgical simulation and training. One more method for a "physically realistic" virtual surgery was suggested by De et al. [38]. They used the Point-Associated Finite Field (PAFF) approach. The idea is to discretize the computational domain (e.g. an organ) using a scattered set of points ("nodes") with spherical influence zone and defined a nodal shape function for it. In [39] Otaduy and Gross represented environmental deformable objects by tetrahedral meshes, In [40], a layered representation of objects is employed: a low-resolution mesh for the collision detection and haptic interaction, a deformable tetrahedral mesh for deformation computations and a detailed surface mesh for the deformable skin simulation. Luciano et al. [41] devoted their work to a local elastic point-based deformation around a contact point in 3-DoF haptic rendering. Ikits et al. [42] presented a 3-DoF constraint-based technique for haptic volume exploration. Chang et al. [43] proposed a 6-DoF haptic rendering method using the mass-spring simulation model.

For the **defo-defo methods**, i.e. for methods for which tool and environment are both deformable, the following methods should be noted. In the later work of Barbic et al. [44] the distance field was made parametrically deformable. In [45] Garre and Otaduy proposed haptic rendering of complex deformations through handle space force linearization. Duriez et al. [46] proposed a method using Signorini's contact model for deformable objects in haptic simulations with a focus on contact response. It belongs to approaches with non-penetration constraints and is independent from a collision/proximity detection. In the later work [47] the authors incorporated friction into the simulation model. Maciel et al. [48] also presented a haptic rendering method for physics-based virtual surgery by using NVIDIA's PhysX physics library, which is GPU accelerated. The latter method supports 6-DoF. Peterlik et al. [49] suggested an asynchronous approach for haptic rendering of deformable objects. In [50, 51, 52] Boettcher et al. suggested a kinesthetic haptic rendering of virtual fabrics grasped by two fingers (the HAPTEX project [53, 54, 55]). The fingers are represented by spherical tools manipulated via two 3-DoF probes. The simulation of tactile perception of the fabrics was proposed by Allerkamp et al. [56, 57]. The VR system developed in the HAPTEX project was the first one and until today still appears to be the only one offering (simultaneously) an integration of combined haptic and tactile perception, cf. [50, 51, 52, 53, 54, 55, 56, 57]. The exact physical properties of fabrics were simulated in the system, see [58]. Later on, in [59] Boettcher et al. described a generalized multi-rate coupling scheme of physical simulations for haptic interaction with deformable objects.

As was stated in the introduction, the motivation for our approach was that almost all methods referenced above can not give collision detection and non-penetration guarantees, as well as require a pre-specified topological structure of objects. We would like to provide the user with a method, which does not have these drawbacks.

4   Our Method

4.1   Collision Detection

The collision detection in our haptic rendering pipeline employs the ray casting technique (see e.g. [60, 61, 62, 63, 64, 65]), which has its roots in computer graphics. A short description was given in our work [66], and in this subsection we present it in more detail.

The idea of ray casting in visualization is to numerically evaluate the volume rendering integral in a straightforward manner. According to [67], the rendering integral $I_\lambda(x, r)$, i.e. the amount of the light of wavelength λ coming from a ray direction r that is received at location x on the image plane, is:

$$I_\lambda(x,r) = \int\limits_0^L C_\lambda(s)\mu(s)e^{-\int\limits_0^s \mu(t)dt} \, ds, \qquad (1)$$

where L – the length of the ray r; μ – absorption (extinction) coefficient at the specified position on the ray r; C_λ – amount of the light of wavelength λ emitted at the specified position on the ray r.

From the algorithmic point of view, ray casting in visualization works as follows: for each pixel of the image a ray is cast into the scene. Along the cast ray the intensity values of the volumetric data are resampled at equidistant intervals, usually using trilinear interpolation. After the resampling an approximation of the volume rendering integral along the ray in either back-to-front or front-to-back order is computed. In this process the mapping of the $< coordinates, scalar\_value >$ pairs for the resampled points to colors and opacities according to a previously chosen transfer function is used.

In haptic rendering, for the collision detection of the interaction point (IP) following the position of the manipulator, we perform ray casting from its last position to the current one – Fig. 3(a). In more detail, we are going along the ray with 1-voxel steps – Fig. 3(b). If the value of any bit cube representing an obstacle at the sampled point is *true* – Fig. 3(c), – then a collision information and *true* is returned by the collision detection procedure – Fig. 3(d). *False* is returned otherwise. We use 1-voxel steps, because a minimum possible thickness of an object is also one voxel. By performing the ray casting we can always find the exact collision, if it happened between the haptic rendering updates, and react to it accordingly. To our best knowledge, there exists only one method (see [15]), which provides the same collision detection guarantees as ours, but it only works with triangulated objects and not with volumetric / voxel based data.

In case a higher precision for the collision detection is needed, ray casting at sub-voxel resolution or sampling once between each pair of consecutive intersections of the ray and a grid plane could be used. In our experiments, we found that 1-voxel step is sufficient for our data though.

In order to speed up computations further, a dynamic list of objects being determined as *collision candidates* is updated at each haptic frame. For that, we check if the ray from the last position of the IP to the current one collides with the Axis-Aligned-Bounding-Box (AABB) of each object. If so, then the object is a candidate. The detailed collision detection is performed for the collision candidates only. Furthermore, we put a reasonable upper limit on the maximal movement of the IP between two haptic frames. This allows to perform localized and therefore faster ray casting using the cached information from the previous frame and avoid possible haptic rendering instabilities (the last technique is also used in [35]).

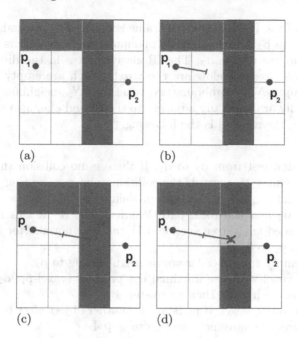

(a)   (b)

(c)   (d)

Fig. 3. The ray from the previous position p_1 to the current one p_2 is cast with 1-voxel steps until an obstacle is found or p_2 is reached

The time complexity of the method is

$$O\left(N_{obj}\frac{w_{max}}{step}\right), \tag{2}$$

where N_{obj} – number of objects in the scene; w_{max} – maximum path length per frame, in voxels; $step$ – the sampling step of ray casting (chosen as 1).
Indeed, in the worst case all objects in the scene could become the collision candidates and be checked all the way from the previous position of the IP to the current one.

4.2   Collision Response

The original version of our joint collision detection and response stage of the haptic rendering pipeline was proposed in our work [3]. Here we present its improved version, which uses the path-finding approach combined with the god object/proxy paradigm. It works directly with volumetric data and has no limitations. The idea of the original method from [3] was as follows.

Because of the collision detection and non-penetration guarantees the IP should not go inside any object or pass through it. Therefore we made it slide over the surface. The surface is calculated locally "on the fly". The IP can encounter multiple surfaces on its way. It is connected with the actual position of the device's manipulator via a virtual spring. The approach was made to test the capacities and speed of our collision detection method and as a base for further experiments.

The position of the IP from the last frame is denoted as p_1, and the position to be calculated – as p_2. For the device's manipulator, we denote its last position as d_1 and the current one as d_2. The IP always moves in the direction of d_2. *Empty-space border voxels* below are the voxels which are empty but have at least one non-empty N_{26}-neighbour (two voxels are N_{26}-neighbours if the first one is orthogonally or diagonally adjacent to the second one, also see [7]).

In more detail, the method is the following:

1. $p_2 := p_1$
2. Do the collision test from p_2 to d_2. If there is no collision then $p_2 := d_2$ and exit. Else move p_2 towards the collision point p_{col}, so that the distance between p_2 and p_{col} is less than the predefined $\epsilon < 1$
3. While $p_2 \neq d_2$ *and* the total path length of the IP at this haptic frame has not exceeded w_{max} (see section 4.1) *and* it is not shorter just to move directly from p_2 to d_2 do:
   (a) Locate empty-space border voxels neighbouring to p_2
   (b) Select a voxel with the maximal dot product (voxel-p_2, d_2-p_2) > 0. If there is no such voxel then go to step 4
   (c) Move p_2 to this voxel. If p_2 is inside another object after this movement then cancel the movement and go to step 4
   (d) go to step 3
4. If the path length of the IP at this haptic frame $\leq w_{max}$ *and* $p_2 \neq d_2$ *and* $p_2 \neq$ the value of p_2 at the beginning of step 2, then go to step 2. Else exit.

Remark 2. There are some additional checks and minor details, which we omitted in the above description for clarity. A complete listing of the algorithm can be found in [3].

An example of how the method works is shown in Fig. 4. After the initialization at step 1, Fig. 4(a), the collision test is performed at step 2, Fig. 4(b). There is a collision, so the "sliding along the surface" part of the algorithm – step 3 – is executed, Fig. 4(c). Then the conditions for the outer loop (steps 2-4) are checked at step 4. As long as they are fulfilled, step 2, Fig. 4(d), and step 3, Fig. 4(e), are executed again. At step 4 these conditions are met again, therefore the method starts the third iteration of the outer loop. But the IP cannot come closer to d_2 this time, so nothing is changed, and the algorithm stops at step 4.

We have found out that the use of the dot product of the vectors at step 3b in order to find the next voxel to move to sometimes leads to an issue, namely that the IP oscillates around the point being locally the closest surface point to d_2 (lets denote it as p_2'). This oscillation could happen because of the following. If there is always a next voxel on the surface, to where the IP can move in the direction of d_2-p_1 according to the conditions at step 3b, the IP may pass p_2' and go further. This could happen because the IP will move until its total path length at this haptic frame is less than w_{max} and because w_{max} may be not exceeded at p_2'. If d_2 remains unchanged at the next haptic frame then the IP will go the way back and will also pass p_2' backwards direction and go further because of the same reason. At the next haptic frame the IP will go in the same

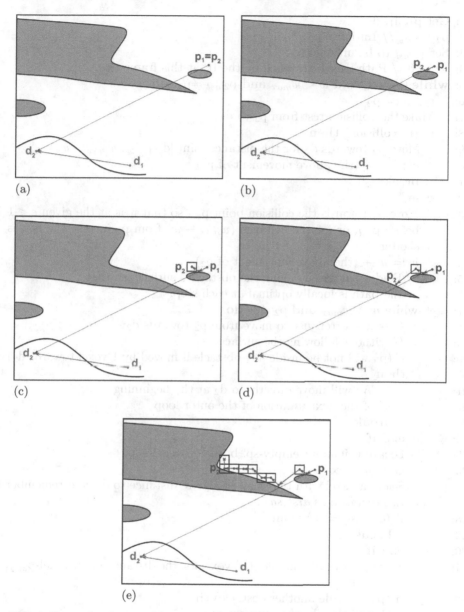

Fig. 4. Example of execution of the original "sliding along the surface" approach

direction as at the first haptic frame and will pass p_2' again. These oscillations may continue until the position of the probe is changed.

In order to eliminate this drawback, we suggest to replace the use of the dot product at step 3b with the search for the voxel with the smallest distance to d_2. In other words, we suggested to use a path finding algorithm looking for a locally optimal path to d_2 for the given metric and limitations. Our improved method still deals with different obstacles at the same time and looks as follows:

1: Get p_1, d_1, d_2
2: $p_2 := p_1$ // Initialize p_2
3: Set p_{2last} to be unequal to p_2
4: $w := 0$ // Path length travelled by the IP at this frame
5: **while** ($p_2 \neq d_2$ **and** $w < w_{max}$ **and** $p_{2last} \neq p_2$) **do**
6:    $p_{2last} := p_2$
7:    Make the collision test from p_2 to d_2
8:    **if** (no collision) **then**
9:        Move p_2 towards d_2 for the distance $\min(||d_2\text{-}p_2||_2, w_{max} - w)$
10:        $w := w +$ (the above movement of p_2)
11:        **break**
12:    **else**
13:        Move p_2 towards the collision point p_{col} so that it is at the given $\epsilon < 1$ before p_{col}, or for the distance $(w_{max} - w)$ from p_2 in case the last is shorter
14:        $w := w +$ (the above movement of p_2)
15:        // Find a path to d_2 along the obstacle's surface, so that
16:        // the path is locally optimal at each step:
17:        **while** $w < w_{max}$ **and** $p_2 \neq d_2$ **do**
18:            // Is it shorter just to move from p_2 towards d_2
19:            // without following the surface?
20:            **if** (p_2 will not be inside any obstacle if moved by 1 voxel towards d_2) **then**
21:                // We will move directly to d_2 at the beginning
22:                // of the next iteration of the outer loop
23:                **break**
24:            **end if**
25:            Locate neighbour empty-sp. border voxels for p_2
26:            $dist\_sq := \infty$
27:            Select a voxel with the smallest square distance to d_2, and remember this distance as $dist\_sq$
28:            **if** ($dist\_sq = \infty$) **then**
29:                **break**
30:            **end if**
31:            Move p_2 towards the selected voxel for the distance $\min(||voxel\text{-}p_2||_2, w_{max} - w)$
32:            **if** (p_2 is inside another obstacle) **then**
33:                Cancel the above movement of p_2
34:                **break**
35:            **end if**
36:            $w := w +$ (the above movement of p_2)
37:        **end while**
38:    **end if**
39: **end while**

Note 1. Here and further in this work we assume that the empty-space border voxels are not precalculated. If they are precalculated for each segment at the preprocessing step then it will give 25% speed-up.

Additionally, we would like to note, that we still use the ideas from the original approach combined with the one presented here in order to add mass to the IP. This work is in progress.

4.3   Force Feedback

We improved our force feedback generation comparing to the one in [3]. This was necessary because the direction of the friction force F_{fr} could be wrong in the case of multiple obstacles or a complex surface, since we used the direction of p_2-p_1. Additionally, in the formula for F_{fr} we used w_{bv}, *the path length* which the IP travelled through empty-space border voxels, instead of *the number* of those empty-space border voxels. This was done, since the IP could move less than one voxel in the inner loop of the algorithm above.

We do not use surface normals, because we do not employ an explicit surface representation. The total force transferred to a user via the haptic manipulator is $F = F_c + F_{fr}$, where F_c is a coupling force. If F exceeds a maximum for a given haptic device then we scale it as to fit to the device limitations. We define F_c as

$$F_c = -\frac{d_2 - p_2}{\|d_2 - p_2\|_2}(k\|d_2 - p_2\|_2) = k(p_2 - d_2),\tag{3}$$

where k is the coefficient of the spring.

For F_{fr} the updated expression could be written as

$$F_{fr} = -\mu\frac{v_{bv}}{\|v_{bv}\|_2}|F_c \cdot n|\frac{w_{bv}}{w},\tag{4}$$

where μ is the friction coefficient; $v_{bv} = \sum_i v_i$, and v_i are linear path segments being travelled by the IP through the empty-space border voxels at this haptic frame; n – a normal vector being perpendicular to v_{bv} and located on the plane spanned by v_{bv} and d_2-p_2; w_{bv} – the length of the path where (during this haptic frame) the IP travelled through the empty-space border voxels in the algorithm described above; w – the total of the path covered by the IP during this frame according to the algorithm described above.

For easier calculations $|F_c \cdot n|$ could be rewritten as $\|F_c\|_2 - \left|F_c \cdot \frac{v_{bv}}{\|v_{bv}\|_2}\right|$.

We suggest the new formula for F_{fr} as opposed to [3] because at the end of a haptic frame the IP is moved from p_1 to p_2, so it is logical to turn F_{fr} into the direction of the normalized vector given by the average obtained (via their sum) from all path segments, where the IP travelled along a surface. Additionally, we ensure F_{fr} to be proportional to the part of F_c which is perpendicular to v_{bv} in analogy to the normal force for a dry friction, Finally, we make it proportional to w_{bv}, i.e. the path length that the IP actually slid over a surface. We would like to note that making the forces related to physical properties of certain materials was not our goal on this stage of research.

5   Implementation

5.1   Prototype System

We developed our interactive VR system as a plug-in for the YaDiV Open-Source platform [4]. YaDiV is used for teaching and in various research projects, and was developed in Java. The last is the case for our system, too. Only the device dependent part was developed using C++, because there are no device APIs on Java being supported by the devices manufacturers. Our system is independent from a haptic display, so that a wide range of devices can be used, including Phantom Omni, High-end Phantom Premium 1.5 6-DOF and INCA 6D with a very large workspace of approx. 2x1x1.6m (Fig. 1). The size of the virtual workspace can be scaled and varies from case to case.

Since Java is executed on a Virtual Machine (VM), we experienced indeterministic delays from a few milliseconds to tens of milliseconds from time to time during the run of the haptic system. This a is serious drawback, since the haptic update rate should constantly be at least 1 kHz. We conducted experiments and found out that the delays appear even with the simplest Java application. The authors of [68], [69] wrote that a real-time VM can provide a deterministic execution time, i.e. to eliminate the aforementioned issue. We conducted experiments with two common real-time VMs: Sun JavaRTS and IBM Web Sphere Real Time. We followed all recommendations of the developers, like installation of Linux with a real-time core and fine tuning of the VM. As a result, we found out that there are still delays of 1-3 ms. We would like to point out that the observed results differ from the information stated in [68] and [69], which was officially presented by IBM and Sun respectively.

5.2   Synchronization Issues

The graphical representation of objects in YaDiV is re-rendered upon request. That is, when properties (color, position, ...) of a scene object are changed, the scene is redrawn. Together with haptic interaction, this rendering scheme leads to synchronization problems. If we would change graphics properties directly in the haptic thread, then every change in the properties would cause a new redraw event, creating unacceptable delays of tens of ms during the execution of the haptic thread.

In order to deal with the aforementioned issues, we proposed to use special objects in the haptic thread, which accumulate changes of the graphics properties, and apply them to the corresponding YaDiV entities in a dedicated synchronization thread. In other words, these accumulating objects wrap all object properties which could cause re-rendering. An access to them is made using synchronized Java-statements. In case a wrapped property was changed, a corresponding accumulating object is added to the list of objects which should be synchronized. The synchronization thread performs a synchronization with the corresponding entities of the graphics thread at about 30 Hz by going through this list.

6   Results

Using the improved method, we repeated the tests as stated in [3]. Since we improved our method, it was necessary to perform the tests again. We used the same real tomography data sets as in our last work, including Torso (520x512x512, Fig. 5), Head$_{big}$ (464x532x532, Fig. 1) and Head$_{small}$ (113x256x256, Fig. 6).

The point-object collisions mode with no collision response remained unchanged, therefore the haptic update rate did not change and is about 750 kHz during the *peak load* on our moderate high-end user PC (8 x Intel Xeon CPU W5580 @ 3.20GHz, 24 GB RAM, NVIDIA Quadro FX 5800). For our improved joint collision detection and response approach the value is about 140-150 kHz. Both values still exceed the minimum requirement for real-time haptics by orders of magnitude. The values were obtained for the virtual haptic device, which is simulated in Java. For real devices, the resulting update rate is a little lower – about 135 kHz. We have measured the timings of each step and found out that the update rate is lower because of the required Java-C++ communication (transferring of the device transformations and forces), since the haptic device dependent part was developed using C++ (see section 5). All values for the data sets for the joint collision detection and response approach are shown in table 1. *Triangles* denotes the number of triangles in the scene for the graphics rendering as a reference. The triangulation was extracted from the volumetric data using a modified marching cubes algorithm. *Update Rate* is given for real devices and during the peak load.

Additionally, we would like to mention that the users of our prototype system with the improved haptic component reported about a better and more natural haptic experience. The system was tested under Microsoft Windows and Linux. Under Linux it was also run using the stereo graphics mode. The users found the last one especially useful for an intuitive interaction with 3D data comparing to the normal graphics mode.

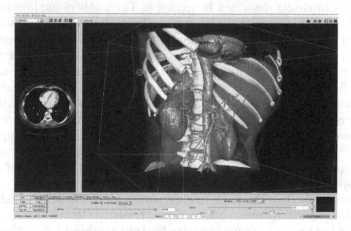

Fig. 5. Working with the Torso data set

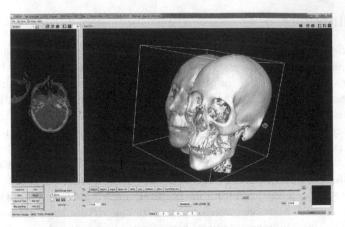

Fig. 6. The data set Head$_{small}$

Table 1. Resulting update rates

Data	Size	Triangles	Update Rate
Head$_{small}$	113x256x256	690K	146 kHz
Torso	520x512x512	2,222 Mi	134 kHz
Head$_{big}$	464x532x532	6,136 Mi	141 kHz

7   Summary and Future Work

In this work we presented an improved version of our haptic rendering approach originally proposed in [3]. The improved approach has all properties of the original method (including an implicit surface representation "on the fly") and does not have the drawbacks described in section 4. The method employs local path finding and ray casting concepts and gives collision detection guarantees that a manipulated object does not pass through "thin" obstacles and is never inside any of them while not requiring any special topological object structure. Additionally, we presented an improved force feedback generation scheme, which does not suffer issues of the original scheme given in [3]. The results show that our approach is a good alternative to existing techniques, while avoiding most common drawbacks. Furthermore, it contrasts most triangle-based approaches, where millions of triangles would be generated and complex speeding-up traversing structures are required for the collision detection with the same guarantees. The prototype was implemented as a plug-in of the YaDiV system and supports different haptic devices and operation systems.

Our work shows that the path finding paradigm could be successfully employed in other research areas, such as haptic rendering in our case.

As an ongoing research, we plan to introduce object-object interactions, where the controlled object is represented as a set of points, and implement the collision detection stage on GPUs, since ray casting could be efficiently parallelized (see e.g. [61], [65]). This will allow us to make computations faster and therefore represent the controlled object with more points and/or perform a more sophisticated collision response. For the latter case, we plan to use FEM-based approaches for simulation of elastic deformations, as e.g. in [47], [39], [44], but we will work directly with volumetric data. The practical use cases of our VR system could be assembling a fractured bone being an important step for pre-operation planning in facial surgery, putting landmarks for automatic segmentation and registration methods and correction of the results of automatic approaches. For that, it is planned to make an assessment of our VR system by physicians from Hanover Medical School (MHH).

Acknowledgements. This research is sponsored by a grant provided by Siemens/DAAD Postgraduate Programme (DAAD - German Academic Exchange Service). The authors would like to thank B.Berger, P.Blanke, A.Vais and R.Buchmann for helpful comments.

References

[1] Nakao, M., Kuroda, T., Komori, M., Oyama, H.: Evaluation and user study of haptic simulator for learning palpation in cardiovascular surgery. In: Proc. of Int. Conference of Artificial Reality and Tele-Existence (ICAT 2003), pp. 203–208 (2003)

[2] Sewell, C., Blevins, N.H., Peddamatham, S., Tan, H.Z., Morris, D., Salisbury, K.: The effect of virtual haptic training on real surgical drilling proficiency. In: 2nd Joint EuroHaptics Conf. and Symp. on Haptic Interfaces for Virtual Environment and Teleoperator Systems (WHC 2007), pp. 601–603 (2007)

[3] Vlasov, R., Friese, K.-I., Wolter, F.-E.: Haptic rendering of volume data with collision determination guarantee using ray casting and implicit surface representation. In: Proc. of Cyberworlds 2012 Int. Conference, pp. 91–99 (September 2012)

[4] Friese, K.-I., Blanke, P., Wolter, F.-E.: Yadiv – an open platform for 3d visualization and 3d segmentation of medical data. The Visual Computer 27, 129–139 (2011)

[5] Chen, M., Correa, C., Islam, S., Jones, M., Shen, P.Y., Silver, D., Walton, S.J., Willis, P.J.: Manipulating, deforming and animating sampled object representations. Computer Graphics Forum 26(4), 824–852 (2007)

[6] Kaufman, A., Cohen, D., Yagel, R.: Volume graphics. IEEE Computer 26(7), 51–64 (2007)

[7] Friese, K.-I.: Entwicklung einer Plattform zur 3D-Visualisierung und - Segmentierung medizinischer Daten. PhD thesis, Leibniz Universitat Hannover, Germany (2010)

[8] Glencross, M., Chalmers, A.G., Lin, M.C., Otaduy, M.A., Gutierrez, D.: Exploiting perception in high-fidelity virtual environments. ACM SIGGRAPH 2006 Courses (July 2006)

[9] Otaduy Tristan, M.A.: 6-dof haptic rendering using contact levels of detail and haptic textures. PhD thesis, University of North Carolina at Chapel Hill (2004)

[10] Colgate, J.E., Stanley, M.C., Brown, J.M.: Issues in the haptic display of tool use. In: Proc. of IEEE/RSJ International Conf. on Intelligent Robots and Systems, pp. 140–145 (1995)

[11] Brooks Jr., F.P., Ouh-Young, M., Batter, J.J., Kilpatrick, P.J.: Project grope - haptic displays for scientific visualization. ACM SIGGRAPH Computer Graphics 24(4), 177–185 (1990)

[12] Adachi, Y., Kumano, T., Ogino, K.: Intermediate representation for stiff virtual objects. In: Virtual Reality Annual International Symposium, pp. 203–210 (1995)

[13] Mark, W.R., Randolph, S.C., Finch, M., Van, J.M., Russell, V., Taylor II, M.: Adding force feedback to graphics systems: issues and solutions. In: Proc. of the 23rd Annual Conf. on Comp. Graphics and Interactive Techniques, pp. 447–452 (1996)

[14] Zilles, C.B., Salisbury, J.K.: A constraint-based god-object method for haptic display. In: Proc. of the Int. Conf. on Intelligent Robots and Systems, vol. 3, pp. 31–46 (1995)

[15] Ortega, M., Redon, S., Coquillart, S.: A six degree-of-freedom god-object method for haptic display of rigid bodies with surface properties. IEEE Transactions on Visualization and Computer Graphics 13(3), 458–469 (2007)

[16] Ruspini, D.C., Kolarov, K., Khatib, O.: The haptic display of complex graphical environments. In: Proc. of the 24th Ann. Conf. on Comp. Gr. and Interact. Techn., pp. 345–352 (1997)

[17] Gregory, A., Mascarenhas, A., Ehmann, S., Lin, M., Manocha, D.: Six degree-of-freedom haptic display of polygonal models. In: Proc. of the Conf. on Vis. 2000, pp. 139–146 (2000)

[18] McNeely, W.A., Puterbaugh, K.D., Troy, J.J.: Six degree-of-freedom haptic rendering using voxel sampling. In: Proceedings of the 26th Annual Conference on Computer Graphics and Interactive Techniques, pp. 401–408 (July 1999)

[19] Wan, M., McNeely, W.A.: Quasi-static approximation for 6 degrees-of-freedom haptic rendering. In: Proc. of the 14th IEEE Vis. Conf. (VIS 2003), pp. 257–262 (2003)

[20] McNeely, W.A., Puterbaugh, K.D., Troy, J.J.: Voxel-based 6-dof haptic rendering improvements. Journal of Haptics-e 3(7) (2006)

[21] Otaduy, M.A., Jain, N., Sud, A., Lin, M.C.: Haptic display of interaction between textured models. In: Proc. of the Conf. on Visualization 2004, pp. 297–304 (October 2004)

[22] Otaduy, M.A., Lin, M.C.: A perceptually-inspired force model for haptic texture rendering. In: Proc. of the 1st Symp. on App. Perception in Graphics and Vis., pp. 123–126 (2004)

[23] Otaduy, M.A., Lin, M.C.: Stable and responsive six-degree-of-freedom haptic manipulation using implicit integration. In: Proc. of the 1st Joint Eurohaptics Conf. and Symp. on Hapt. Interf. for Virt. Env. and Tel. Syst., pp. 247–256 (2005)

[24] Otaduy, M.A., Lin, M.C.: A modular haptic rendering algorithm for stable and transparent 6-dof manipulation. IEEE Trans. on Robotics 22(4), 751–762 (2006)

[25] Johnson, D.E., Willemsen, P.: Six degree-of-freedom haptic rendering of complex polygonal models. In: Proc. of the 11th Symp. on Haptic Interfaces for Virtual Environment and Teleoperator Systems (HAPTICS 2003), pp. 229–235 (2003)

[26] Johnson, D.E., Willemsen, P., Cohen, E.: Six degree-of-freedom haptic rendering using spatialized normal cone search. IEEE Transactions on Visualization and Computer Graphics 11(6), 661–670 (2005)

[27] Weller, R., Zachmann, G.: A unified approach for physically-based simulations and haptic rendering. In: Proceedings of the 2009 ACM SIGGRAPH Symposium on Video Games, pp. 151–160 (August 2009)

[28] Vidal, F., John, N., Healey, A., Gould, D.: Simulation of ultrasound guided needle puncture using patient specific data with 3d textures and volume haptics. Journal of Visualization and Computer Animation 19, 111–127 (2008)

[29] Lundin Palmerius, K., Baravdish, G.: Higher precision in volume haptics through subdivision of proxy movements. In: Ferre, M. (ed.) EuroHaptics 2008. LNCS, vol. 5024, pp. 694–699. Springer, Heidelberg (2008)

[30] Kim, L., Kyrikou, A., Desbrun, M., Sukhatme, G.: An implicit-based haptic rendering technique. In: Proc. of the IEEE/RSJ International Conf. on Intelligent Robots (2002)

[31] Chan, S., Conti, F., Blevins, N., Salisbury, K.: Constraint-based six degree-of-freedom haptic rendering of volume-embedded isosurfaces. In: W. Hapt. Conf. 2011, pp. 89–94 (2011)

[32] Corenthy, L., Martin, J.S., Otaduy, M., Garcia, M.: Volume haptic rendering with dynamically extracted isosurface. In: Proc. of Haptics Symp. 2012, pp. 133–139 (2012)

[33] Debunne, G., Desbrun, M., Cani, M.P., Barr, A.H.: Dynamic real-time deformations using space & time adaptive sampling. In: Proc. of the 28th Annual Conference on Computer Graphics and Interactive Techniques, pp. 31–36 (2001)

[34] Barbic, J., James, D.: Time-critical distributed contact for 6-dof haptic rendering of adaptively sampled reduced deformable models. In: Proc. of the 2007 ACM SIGGRAPH/Eurogr. Symp. on Comp. Animation, pp. 171–180 (2007)

[35] Barbic, J.: Real-time reduced large-deformation models and distributed contact for computer graphics and haptics. PhD thesis, Carnegie Mellon University, Pittsburgh (2007)

[36] Kuroda, Y., Nakao, M., Hacker, S., Kuroda, T., Oyama, H., Komori, M., Matsuda, T., Takahashi, T.: Haptic force feedback with an interaction model between multiple deformable objects for surgical simulations. In: Proceedings of Eurohaptics 2002, pp. 116–121 (July 2002)

[37] Basdogan, C., De, S., Kim, J., Muniyandi, M., Kim, H., Srinivasan, M.A.: Haptics in minimally invasive surgical simulation and training. IEEE Computer Graphics and Applications 24(2), 56–64 (2004)

[38] De, S., Lim, Y.J., Manivannan, M., Srinivasan, M.A.: Physically realistic virtual surgery using the point-associated finite field (paff) approach. Presence: Teleoperators and Virtual Environments 15(3), 294–308 (2006)

[39] Otaduy, M.A., Gross, M.: Transparent rendering of tool contact with compliant environments. In: Proc. of the 2nd Joint EuroHaptics Conf. and Symp. on Haptic Interfaces for Virt. Env. and Teleoperator Systems, pp. 225–230 (2007)

[40] Galoppo, N., Tekin, S., Otaduy, M.A., Gross, M., Lin, M.C.: Interactive haptic rendering of high-resolution deformable objects. In: Shumaker, R. (ed.) HCII 2007 and ICVR 2007. LNCS, vol. 4563, pp. 215–223. Springer, Heidelberg (2007)

[41] Luciano, C.J., Banerjee, P., Rizzi, S.H.R.: Gpu-based elastic-object deformation for enhancement of existing haptic applications. In: Proc. of the 3rd Annual IEEE Conf. on Automation Science and Engineering, pp. 146–151 (2007)

[42] Ikits, M., Brederson, J.D., Hansen, C.D., Johnson, C.R.: A constraint-based technique for haptic volume exploration. In: Proceedings of the 14th IEEE Visualization 2003 (VIS 2003), pp. 263–269 (October 2003)

[43] Chang, Y.H., Chen, Y.T., Chang, C.W., Lin, C.L.: Development scheme of haptic-based system for interactive deformable simulation. Computer-Aided Design 42(5), 414–424 (2010)

[44] Barbic, J., James, D.L.: Six-dof haptic rendering of contact between geometrically complex reduced deformable models. IEEE Trans. on Haptics 1(1), 39–52 (2008)

[45] Garre, C., Otaduy, M.A.: Haptic rendering of complex deformations through handle-space force linearization. In: Proc. of the World Haptics Conf., pp. 422–427 (2009)

[46] Duriez, C., Andriot, C., Kheddar, A.: Signorini's contact model for deformable objects in haptic simulations. In: IEEE/RSJ International Conference on Intelligent Robots and Systems (IROS), pp. 32–37 (2004)

[47] Duriez, C., Dubois, F., Kheddar, A., Andriot, C.: Realistic haptic rendering of interacting deformable objects in virtual environments. IEEE Transactions on Visualization and Computer Graphics 12(1), 36–47 (2006)

[48] Maciel, A., Halic, T., Lu, Z., Nedel, L.P., De, S.: Using the physx engine for physics-based virtual surgery with force feedback. Int. Journal of Medical Robotics and Computer Assisted Surgery 5(3), 341–353 (2009)

[49] Peterlik, I., Duriez, C., Cotin, S.: Asynchronous haptic simulation of contacting deformable objects with variable stiffness. In: 2011 IEEE/RSJ Int. Conf. on Intelligent Robots and Systems, pp. 2608–2613 (2011)

[50] Boettcher, G.: Haptic Interaction with Deformable Objects. Springer (2011)

[51] Boettcher, G., Allerkamp, D., Wolter, F.-E.: Virtual reality systems modelling haptic two-finger contact with deformable physical surfaces. In: Proc. of HAPTEX 2007, pp. 292–299 (October 2007)

[52] Boettcher, G., Allerkamp, D., Gloeckner, D., Wolter, F.-E.: Haptic two-finger contact with textiles. Visual Computer 24(10), 911–922 (2008)

[53] Salsedo, F., Fontana, M., Tarri, F., Ruffaldi, E., Bergamasco, M., Magnenat-Thalmann, N., Volino, P., Bonanni, U., Brady, A., Summers, I., Qu, J., Allerkamp, D., Boettcher, G., Wolter, F.-E., Makinen, M., Meinander, H.: Architectural design of the haptex system. In: Proc. of the HAPTEX 2005 Workshop on Haptic and Tactile Perception of Deformable Objects (peer-reviewed), pp. 1–7 (December 2005)

[54] Magnenat-Thalmann, N., Volino, P., Bonanni, U., Summers, I.R., Bergamasco, M., Salsedo, F., Wolter, F.-E.: From physics-based simulation to the touching of textiles: The haptex project. Int. Journal of Virtual Reality 6(3), 35–44 (2007)

[55] Fontana, M., Marcheschi, S., Tarri, F., Salsedo, F., Bergamasco, M., Allerkamp, D., Boettcher, G., Wolter, F.-E., Brady, A.C., Qu, J., Summers, I.R.: Integrating force and tactile rendering into a single vr system. In: Proc. of HAPTEX 2007, pp. 277–284 (October 2007)

[56] Allerkamp, D., Boettcher, G., Wolter, F.-E., Brady, A.C., Qu, J., Summers, I.R.: A vibrotactile approach to tactile rendering. Vis. Computer 23(2), 97–108 (2007)

[57] Allerkamp, D.: Tactile Perception of Textiles in a Virtual-Reality System, vol. 10. Springer, Heidelberg (2011)

[58] Volino, P., Davy, P., Bonanni, U., Magnenat-Thalmann, N., Boettcher, G., Allerkamp, D., Wolter, F.-E.: From measured physical parameters to the haptic feeling of fabric. In: Proc. of the HAPTEX 2005 Workshop on Haptic and Tactile Perception of Deformable Objects (peer-reviewed), pp. 17–29 (December 2005)

[59] Boettcher, G., Allerkamp, D., Wolter, F.-E.: Multi-rate coupling of physical simulations for haptic interaction with deformable objects. Visual Computer 26(6-8), 903–914 (2010)

[60] Hadwiger, M., Ljung, P., Salama, C.R., Ropinski, T.: Advanced illumination techniques for gpu-based volume raycasting. In: ACM SIGGRAPH 2009 Courses (2009)

[61] Kruger, J., Westermann, R.: Acceleration techniques for gpu-based volume rendering. In: Proc. of the 14th IEEE Visualization 2003 (VIS 2003), pp. 287–292 (October 2003)

[62] Levoy, M.: Efficient ray tracing of volume data. ACM Transactions on Graphics 9(3), 245–261 (1990)

[63] Mensmann, J., Ropinski, T., Hinrichs, K.: Accelerating volume raycasting using occlusion frustums. In: IEEE/EG Int. Symp. on Vol. and Point-Based Graphics, pp. 147–154 (2008)

[64] Engel, K., Hadwiger, M., Kniss, J.M., Lefohn, A.E., Salama, C.R., Weiskopf, D.: Real-time volume graphics. ACM SIGGRAPH 2004 Course Notes (2004)

[65] Ropinski, T., Kasten, J., Hinrichs, K.H.: Efficient shadows for gpu-based volume raycasting. In: Proc. of the 16th Int. Conf. in Central Europe on Computer Graphics, Visualization and Computer Vision (WSCG 2008), pp. 17–24 (2008)

[66] Vlasov, R., Friese, K.-I., Wolter, F.-E.: Ray casting for collision detection in haptic rendering of volume data. In: I3D 2012 Proceedings of the ACM SIGGRAPH Symposium on Interactive 3D Graphics and Games, p. 215 (March 2012)

[67] Bruckner, S.: Efficient volume visualization of large medical datasets. Master's thesis, Vienna University of Technology, Austria (May 2004)

[68] Stoodley, M., Fulton, M., Dawson, M., Sciampacone, R., Kacur, J.: Real-time Java, Part 1: Using Java code to program real-time systems (April 2007)

[69] Oracle: Sun java real-time system 2.2 update 1 technical documentation (April 2010),
http://download.oracle.com/javase/realtime/rts_productdoc_2.2u1.html

Towards Early Diagnosis of Dementia Using a Virtual Environment

Syadiah Nor Wan Shamsuddin[1], Hassan Ugail[2], Valerie Lesk[3], and Elizabeth Walters[3]

[1] Faculty of Informatics, Universiti Sultan Zainal Abidin, Malaysia
syadiah@unisza.edu.my
[2] Centre for Visual Computing, University of Bradford, Bradford BD7 1DP, UK
h.ugail@bradford.ac.uk
[3] Division of Psychology, University of Bradford, Bradford, BD7 1DP, UK
v.lesk@bradford.ac.uk, E.R.Walters@student.bradford.ac.uk

Abstract. Dementia is one of the biggest fears in the process of ageing and the most common cause is Alzheimer's Disease(AD). Topographic disorientation is an early manifestation of AD and threatens activities of their daily lives. Finding solutions are essential in the early diagnosis of dementia if medical treatment and healthcare services to be deployed in time. Recent studies have shown that people with mild cognitive impairment (MCI) may convert to Alzheimer's disease (AD) over time although not all MCI cases progress to dementia. The diagnosis of MCI is important to allow prompt treatment and disease management before the neurons degenerate to a stage beyond repair. Hence, the ability to obtain a method of identifying MCI is of great importance. This work presents a virtual environment which can be utilized as a quick, easy and friendly tool for early diagnosis of dementia. This tool was developed with an aim to investigate cognitive functioning in a group of healthy elderly and those with MCI. It focuses on the task of following a route, since Topographical Disorientation (TD) is common in AD. The results shows that this novel simulation was able to predict with about 90% overall accuracy using weighting function proposed to discriminate between MCI and healthy elderly.

Keywords: Virtual environment, Dementia, Early diagnosis, Cognitive function.

1 Introduction

Dementia is one of the biggest fears in the process of ageing. Dementia is a terminal disease where patients are expected to live three to nine years after diagnosis. People who have dementia will gradually lose the ability to take care of themselves. The most common cause of dementia is Alzheimer's disease (AD) which substantially defined by the presence of verbal memory deficits. It is not unusual for Alzheimer's disease patients to get lost in unfamiliar places in the early stages of the disease and, in the later stages; they may become lost or disoriented in familiar places such as their home or neighborhood. This is a common manifestation of dementia of the Alzheimer's disease type that can occur in the early stages of the disease, particularly in less familiar settings. The ability to find one's way involves knowing the procedural

M.L. Gavrilova et al. (Eds.): Trans. on Comput. Sci. XVIII, LNCS 7848, pp. 232–247, 2013.
© Springer-Verlag Berlin Heidelberg 2013

components of the route to the destination which may require topographical knowledge about the surroundings.

As highlighted above, Alzheimer's disease (AD) is a neurological disorder that causes dysfunction in memory and cognition. Reference [1] defines AD as a deficit in the formation of new memories, difficulty remembering events and names, apathy and depression. AD is the most common form of dementia, which is associated with a decline in mental illness [2]. Currently, AD affects one in five people over the age of 80 [1]. AD not only affects the person himself, but also their family, friends and carers. These patients will need their families and carers to support their daily living.

The transitional zone between normal ageing and dementia is defined as mild cognitive impairment [3]. Consequently, investigation of MCI and early AD has increased substantially, even though there is currently no cure for AD [4]. Recently, some studies have reported that MCI will progressively develop to AD [5,6], but other studies have shown that many MCI patients will remain stable and recover [7,8]. Since not everyone with MCI goes on to develop AD, it is a challenge to be able to detect early AD or MCI. Existing methods for the early detection of MCI require clinical assessment of medical history, neuropsychological tests, laboratory examination and clinical judgment [1]. In spite of this, early diagnosis is still difficult to make, MMSE, one of the neuropsychological tests that has been widely used, is not sensitive to MCI [9,10].

An effective treatment or cure for dementia remains elusive, making prevention and delaying the age of onset important in order to meet the public health challenge of an exponential increase in dementia. In a recent strand of research, investigators identified a way of finding strategies among people with dementia in particular settings including residential homes. In a real environment of research involving way-finding tasks, researchers will accompany patients with dementia to certain destinations. Then, the researchers' observation needs to be noted or recorded. There may be a video camera filming everything the patients do. Issues arising from this approach involve health, safety and time consumption.

Virtual Environments (VE) allows a more or less complete functionality without requiring all the functions to be located in the same physical space to an integrated workspace [36]. VE as defined by reference [37] is interactive, virtual image displays enhanced by special processing and by non-visual display modalities. VE can also be defined as computer simulation environment with sense of presence that can be experienced [38]. A VE can be successful in providing a high level of sensory richness in immersing the user within a realistic 3D world [39].With Virtual reality (VR) technology, a VE lets the user freely explore the 3D space.VE known to experimental research conditions that are easy to identify, control, and replica [40].

VR can be applied in many applications including gaming, entertainment, training, education and health. This technology offer specific attributes that are well-suited to the needs of many medical applications which include exposure, distraction, motivation and interaction [41].VR is rapidly becoming a popular application in healthcare. Its promising technology offers opportunities to create new products in everyday situations. This software is thought to be more effective of everyday life situations than paper and pencil treatment procedures or other limited software [42]. Werner et. al.

developed Virtual Supermarket to examine the feasibility and the validity of the virtual action planning supermarket for the diagnosis of patients with mild cognitive impairment(MCI) [43]. Tippet et. al. designed and developed virtual city to examine the ability of MCI participants to navigate effectively through the VE [44].

This paper focused on the development of a virtual environment which can be utilized as a quick, easy and friendly tool for early diagnosis of dementia. This tool was developed with an aim to investigate cognitive functioning in a group of healthy elderly and those with MCI. The next section discusses the issues in AD and MCI followed by studies on virtual environment and spatial navigation. In this paper the discussion is focused on discriminating MCI patients with healthy elderly using virtual environment. The design criteria and development of Virtual Reality for Early Detection of Alzheimer's Disease (VREAD) are discussed in Section 3. The discussion on the prediction and the proposed weightage function to improve the discrimination of AD is discussed in Section 4 and Section 5 and ends with the conclusions.

2   Virtual Environment and Alzheimer's Disease

The issue in MCI and AD today is to identify the disease before neurons degenerate to a stage beyond repair. Therefore, early detection of MCI is really important: it may ensure early treatment and intervention. In addition, it can have a significant impact in improving quality of life. Indeed, the early detection of cognitive decline is critical for preventing the progression to AD.

2.1   Topographical Disorientation

Topographical disorientation (TD) is the inability to orient and navigate in the environment [11]. TD is usually the expression of defects in a variety of cognitive processes, including memory, attention, spatial skills or visual perceptual skills [12]. This is a common manifestation in AD that can occur in the early stages of the disease, particularly in less familiar settings [13]. The ability to find one's way involves knowing the procedural components of the route to the destination, which may require topographical knowledge about the surroundings [12]. It is not unusual for Alzheimer's disease patients to get lost in unfamiliar places in the early stages of the disease and, in the later stages; they may become lost or disoriented in familiar places, such as their home or neighbourhood [14]. As visuospatial deficits are manifested in early-stage AD, it is important to test spatial memory to investigate cognition in the elderly.

2.2   Virtual Environment and Spatial Navigation

In recent years, computer technology has evolved and the use of virtual environments has increased to simulate real-world tasks [15]. VR has been recognized as a technology that provides an effective and motivating way to help in many different areas. VR is a technology with many applications, from the arts to health care. In the latter area it has been used in fields such as phobias with regard to spiders [16], fear of flying [17], acrophobia [18], fear of public speaking [19] and motor rehabilitation [20]. VR provides valuable daily life scenarios with familiar elements for patients, thus extending the range of cognitive rehabilitation applications [21]. With VR technology, a virtual environment lets the user freely explore a 3D space.

The development of VR technology has brought major progress to the study of spatial navigation in a virtual environment [22]. The virtual environment provides an interesting opportunity for the evaluation of topographical disorientation by providing a representation of an interactive environment. Recent studies by [23, 24, 15, 25] has shown opportunities of using virtual environment for early detection of early AD and MCI. Despite the efforts of these researchers to explore the use of the virtual environment in the early detection of MCI, there is scope to improve on them.

Motivated by the promise offered by VR technology and the importance of early detection of MCI, the virtual simulation was developed. VREAD was developed with the specific objective of discriminating between healthy elderly and MCI and has been able to overcome the limitations of previous work in the field. The overarching aim is to use this test as a method for the early diagnosis of Alzheimer's disease.

3   The Virtual Environment

Elderly people who grew up without the benefit of computers may feel that computers are not meant for their use or are not relevant to them. It is of great importance that a design for the elderly should follow specific criteria to take their physical age impairment into account [26].

3.1   Design Criteria

Numerous studies have highlighted the design criteria for elderly users. Reference [27] identifies several game design opportunities for the creation of digital games for elderly users. Another study, by [28], lists gaming design criteria for the elderly from their comprehensive reading. Reference [29] proposed game attributes to meet users' requirements on the basis of psychological theories, such as cognitive, constructivist, behaviorist and neuroscience perspectives, for serious game design. Taking this into consideration and for the full potential of technology to be useful to these people, their needs and requirements must be considered in the design of the virtual environment.

The VR environment we have developed is based on the proposed design criteria as follows [30].

- Levels of difficulty.
- Different maps.
- Linking of psychological theories.
- Minimal use of landmarks.
- Data collection.

- Collision detection.
- Training module.
- Simple and structured interface.
- Inclusion of scenarios

3.2   System Overview

The virtual environment we have developed is a quick, easy and friendly tool that aims to investigate cognitive functioning in a group of healthy elderly participants and those with MCI. It focuses on the task of following a route, since TD is common in AD. The virtual simulation was developed on the basis of design criteria that were outlined earlier.

The ADDIE model was adopted as the flow guideline for the development process. The ADDIE model is a five phase model which stands for Analysis, Design, Development, Implementation and Evaluation. Although many different generic models could be adapted to meet specific user needs, ADDIE is a commonly used method that can be effective in almost every circumstance [31].

3.3   Hardware and Software

The development of this virtual environment required a high specification of hardware. In this development, the hardware consisted of a Pentium-based computer with NVIDIA graphic card of 512MB memory, 4MB RAM and an Intel Core Duo processor. Standard input and output devices, such as keyboard, mouse and computer monitor were used for this experiment.

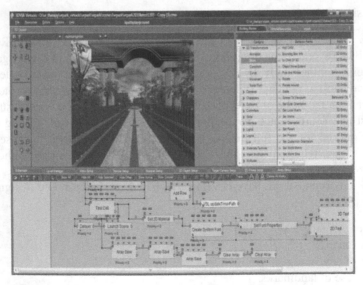

Fig. 1. A screenshot of programming and integration in Virtools

Software requirements for the development of this simulation were Maya Autodesk, Virtools 5.0, Visual Basic and 3DVIA Players. Modelling was performed using Maya to create models and scenes. Subsequently, the scenes were exported to Virtools, a 3D authoring tool which handled all the programming, including interactivity, setting and configuration (see Fig. 1).

Virtools is a complete development and deployment platform with an innovative approach to interactive 3D content creation. It integrates rich interaction block and custom scripting. To run the VR simulation 3DVIA Players needed to be installed. For analysis and representation of the results, an information system was developed using Visual Basic.

3.4   Virtual Environment

The proposed virtual environment which we refer to VREAD consists of three modules: VR Practice, VR Park and VR Games (see Fig. 2 and Fig. 3). VR Park and VR Games both have five levels from easy to complex (see Figure 3).

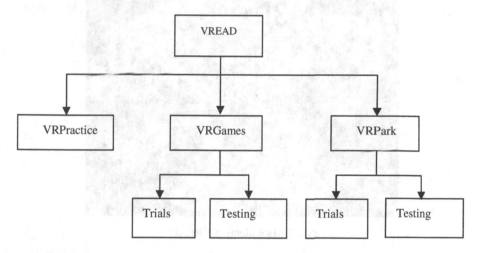

Fig. 2. Overview of VREAD

VR Practice

The VR Practice is the training module. In this module, users have the opportunity to practise cursor keys using keyboards. This module has been developed to meet the needs of the target users who are aged over 45 and who may need some time to practice with cursor keys so they can use the application easily.

VR Park

The scenario settings for this module are in a park. There are five specific target destinations including playground, art gallery, garden, rest area and picnic area. Users experience walking through a park in the city where there are tall buildings to be seen, trees all around and various other things.

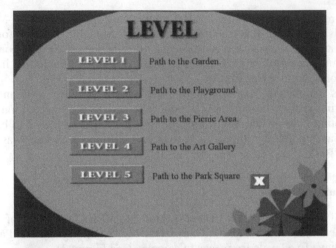

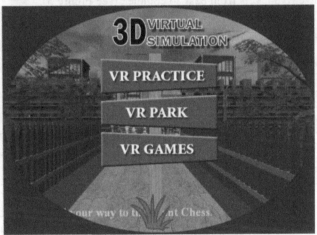

Fig. 3. Main Menu of VREAD

VR Games Land

In this module, the location is surrounded by tall buildings and houses. Inside the park, there are five different and specific types of giant games available, such as giant chess, giant board games, lawn bowls and mini golf.

Fig. 3 represents a procedure done in VREAD. First, users' information are recorded in the system. A unique user ID is given to each user. Then, in the VR simulation, users are able to see one of the two environments. The users are allowed to repeat the exercise of reaching the target destination three times by following the red ribbon attached to the path. Next, the user is tested on their ability to recollect given path. All data are collected and recorded during this phase. Lastly, all data were exported to the system to be analysed.

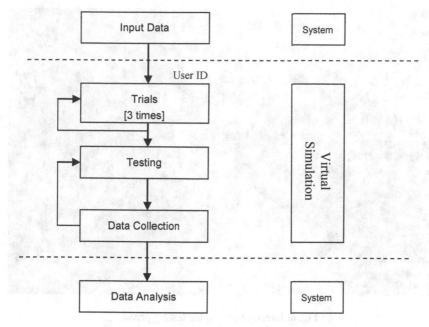

Fig. 4. Procedures of experiment in VREAD

Fig. 5. Interface with red ribbon attached to the path

Fig. 6. Interface during the testing phase

Data Collection

Data are collected during the testing phase. There are five attributes needed to diagnose early detection of dementia: correct path, incorrect path, correct sequences, incorrect sequences, timing and scores.

Path
During testing, users are allowed to move freely to the target destination. All the movement are captured and recorded for data analysis.

Path Sequence and Path Squares
Users are required to reach the target destination in the correct path sequence. The data from path-tracking will show correct and incorrect sequences and path squares.

Timing
During testing, the amount of time taken to complete the journey from the starting point to the target destination was recorded.

Score
Scores are then calculated based on path sequences and path squares. The scores show the percentage of performance done by users.

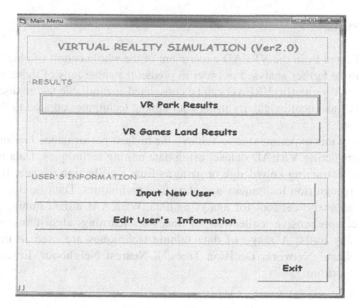

Fig. 7. Main Menu of Information System

Information System

An information system has also been developed to keep the users information and data collected. The text file produced by VREAD is then be transferred to the system to be recorded and analysed. Figure 6 and 7 shows interfaces of the system.

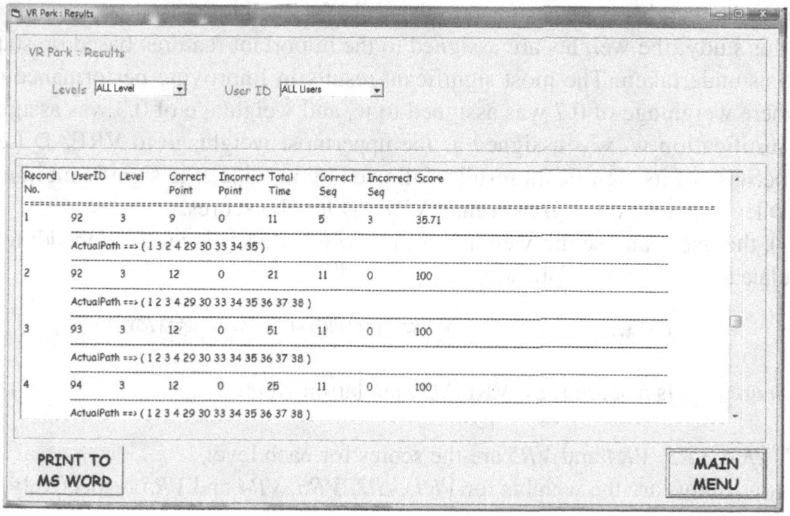

Fig. 8. Interface results of the system

4   Results

Results collected from the VREAD experiment of the whole cohort of elderly people together can be further analysed in order to predict the subgroups of those with MCI and those healthy elderly. VREAD can be considered as a reliable test to discriminate between MCI and healthy elderly using data mining techniques applied to the results for prediction.

The aim of this experiment is to achieve the highest performance measure of accuracy in predicting VREAD dataset using data mining techniques. Data mining is a process of extracting knowledge or patterns from a collection of data. It is based on pattern recognition techniques and statistical techniques. Data mining software is used as an analytical tool for analysing data. WEKA is a data mining tool that offers a comprehensive collection of machine learning algorithms and data pre-processing tools. A range of data mining techniques are used in this study, including Neural Network, Decision Trees, K-Nearest Neighbour, Ensemble and Bayesian algorithm.

4.1   Data Collection

Firstly, data was collected automatically from VREAD. These data have six main attributes including: correct path, incorrect path, correct sequences, incorrect sequences, overall score and time. The sample group consisted of 31 participants: 10 males and 21 females.

The results can be simplified by giving a weight to each score obtained for each level. The objective in giving the score is to give more weight to certain variables. In this study, the weights were assigned to the score for each level.

For this study, the weights are assigned to the important features based on statistical analysis undertaken. The most significant results in improving performance measures, where weightage of 0.7 was assigned to w_4 and weightage of 0.3 was assigned to w_5. A justification w_4 was assigned as the uppermost weightage to VREAD Level 4 scores because of its significant results, followed by w_5, since the significant impact of VREAD level 4 scores was greater than VREAD level 5 scores.

In (1), the user can use the weights of the score for each level by embedding them to calculate a new score as follows:

$$Score_{Weight} = (w_1 * VR1) + (w_2 * VR2) + (w_3 * VR3) + (w_4 * VR4) + (w_5 * VR5)$$

where $Score_{Weight}$ is a score for a VREAD simulation where,

$VR1, VR2, VR3, VR4$ and $VR5$ are the scores for each level,
w_1, w_2, w_3, w_4 and w_5 are the weights for $VR1, VR2, VR3, VR4$ and $VR5$ respectively.

Table 1. Summary of results obtained from the WEKA package using the weightage proposed

Classifiers	Accuracy	True Positive Rate	True Negative Rate
Naïve Bayes	**0.90**	**0.75**	**0.96**
J48	0.88	0.50	1.00
IBk	0.81	0.50	0.91
Bagging	0.77	0.38	0.91
Multilayer Perceptron	0.88	0.63	0.96

There are three performance measures presented, which include Accuracy, TPR (True Positive Rate). TNR (True Negative Rate), along with feature selection and classifiers. These three performance measures were chosen because these criteria are the most important measures in verifying the performance of classifiers' algorithms for MCI prediction. Accuracy is the total of correct observation for each class. In this study, TPR is the rate of correct classifications for the MCI class. In contrast, TNR is the correct observation for class No and for this study, is the correct classification for the Non-MCI patients.

Table 1 summarized the results achieved using the WEKA package when trained using 10-fold cross-validation. Accuracy is the most important feature because the aim of this study is to discriminate between MCI and healthy elderly people. Therefore, higher accuracy indicates that the classifier could predict MCI correctly.

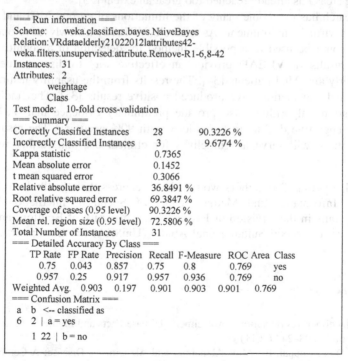

```
=== Run information ===
Scheme:      weka.classifiers.bayes.NaiveBayes
Relation:VRdataelderly21022012lattributes42-
weka.filters.unsupervised.attribute.Remove-R1-6,8-42
Instances:   31
Attributes:  2
            weightage
            Class
Test mode:   10-fold cross-validation
=== Summary ===
Correctly Classified Instances       28           90.3226 %
Incorrectly Classified Instances      3            9.6774 %
Kappa statistic                      0.7365
Mean absolute error                  0.1452
t mean squared error                 0.3066
Relative absolute error              36.8491 %
Root relative squared error          69.3847 %
Coverage of cases (0.95 level)       90.3226 %
Mean rel. region size (0.95 level)   72.5806 %
Total Number of Instances            31
=== Detailed Accuracy By Class ===
      TP Rate  FP Rate  Precision  Recall  F-Measure  ROC Area  Class
      0.75     0.043    0.857      0.75    0.8        0.769     yes
      0.957    0.25     0.917      0.957   0.936      0.769     no
Weighted Avg.  0.903   0.197   0.901   0.903   0.901   0.769
=== Confusion Matrix ===
 a   b   <-- classified as
 6   2 |  a = yes
   1  22 |  b = no
```

Fig. 9. Extracted output results using the Naïve Bayes Algorithm

In Fig. 9, the detailed results for the Naïve Bayes algorithm are presented. The extracted outputs from the Naïve Bayes results, consisting of 'detailed accuracy by class' and 'confusion matrix' can be found in Fig 9. The overall accuracy for the Naïve Bayes algorithm was 0.90, while the TPR was 0.75 and the TNR was 0.96. From the confusion matrix, 6 out of 8 MCI were correctly classified, and 22 out of 23 non-MCI were correctly classified.

The result of this study shows that Naïve Bayes Classifiers obtained the highest results, with an accuracy of 0.90, followed by TPR with 0.75 and TNR with 0.96 accuracy (see Table 1).

The ability to obtain a method of identifying MCI is therefore of great importance. It is also essential that techniques are established to discriminate between those with an MCI that will progress to a dementia and those who will not.

5   Conclusions

Early diagnosis is necessary before the neurons degenerate to a stage beyond repair. One importance of early diagnosis is to allow people with MCI to plan ahead and make important decisions about their future. Early diagnosis allows prompt treatment before patients suffer potential cognitive problems [32]. Another difficulty is that diagnosis often occurs at a late stage, when structural damage to the hippocampus and surrounding areas has already reached too great an extent [33].

This research has overcome many of the limitations of current MCI and early AD tests using a virtual environment. As a result, VREAD, a newly developed virtual simulation, could be used as a possible method for detection of a cognitive impairment. The results of VREAD provide an effective way to discriminate between healthy elderly and MCI patients [34]. The results from the usability testing on user acceptance and satisfaction have produced positive results [35]. The findings using machine learning algorithms also provide preliminary evidence that VREAD was sensitive to cognitive decline in the elderly with 90% accuracy. The results of this systematic study will serve as guidelines for clinical use and further research in the area.

Acknowledgements. The authors would like to express their gratitude to School of Computing, Informatics and Media, School of Social & International Studies, Rebecca Durrans in the Division of Psychology, University of Bradford and Faculty of Informatics, Universiti Sultan Zainal Abidin (UniSZA) for the support and facilities provided.

References

[1] The Alzheimer's Association. "Alzheimer's Disease Facts and Figures". Alzheimer's and Dementia 7, 208–244 (2011)
[2] Small, D.H., Cappai, R.: Alois Alzheimer and Alzheimer's Disease: A Centennial Perspective. Journal of Neurochemistry 99, 708–710 (2006)

[3] Morris, J.C.: Mild Cognitive Impairment Is Early-Stage Alzheimer Disease: Time to Revise Diagnostic Criteria. Archives of Neurology 63, 15–16 (2006)

[4] Korczyn, A.D.: Why Have We Failed to Cure Alzheimer's Disease? Journal of Alzheimer's Disease 29, 275–282 (2012)

[5] Blackwell, A., Sahakian, B., Vesey, R., Semple, J., Robbins, T., Hodges, J.: Detecting Dementia: Novel Neuropsychological Markers of Preclinical Alzheimer's Disease. Dementia and Geriatric Cognitive Disorders 17, 42–48 (2004)

[6] Petersen, R.C.: Mild Cognitive Impairment. Journal of Medicine 364, 2227–2234 (2011)

[7] Larrieu, S., Letenneur, L., Orgogozo, J., Fabrigoule, C., Amieva, H., Le Carret, N., Barberger–Gateau, P., Dartigues, J.: Incidence and Outcome of Mild Cognitive Impairment in a Population-Based Prospective Cohort. Neurology 59, 1594–1599 (2002)

[8] Ganguli, M., Dodge, H., Shen, C., Dekosky, S.T.: Mild Cognitive Impairment, Amnestic Type. Neurology 63, 115–121 (2004)

[9] De Jager, C., Milwain, E., Budge, M.: Early Detection of Isolated Memory Deficits in the Elderly: The Need for More Sensitive Neuropsychological Tests. Psychological Medicine 32, 483–491 (2002)

[10] Schultheis, M.T., Rizzo, A.A.: The Application of Virtual Reality Technology in Rehabilitation. Rehabilitation Psychology 46, 296–311 (2001)

[11] Iaria, G., Bogod, N., Fox, C.J., Barton, J.J.S.: Developmental Topographical Disorientation: Case One. Neuropsychologia 47, 30–40 (2009)

[12] Aguirre, G.K., D'esposito, M.: Topographical Disorientation: A Synthesis and Taxonomy. Brain 122, 1613–1628 (1999)

[13] Passini, R., Rainville, C., Marchand, N., Joanette, Y.: Wayfinding in Dementia of the Alzheimer Type: Planning Abilities. Journal of Clinical and Experimental Neuropsychology 17, 820–832 (1995)

[14] Cherrier, M., Mendez, M., Perryman, K.: Route Learning Performance in Alzheimer Disease Patients. Cognitive and Behavioral Neurology 14, 159–168 (2001)

[15] Tippett, W.J., Lee, J.H., Zakzanis, K.K., Black, S.E., Mraz, R., Graham, S.J.: Visually Navigating a Virtual World with Real-World Impairments: A Study of Visually and Spatially Guided Performance in Individuals with Mild Cognitive Impairments. Journal of Clinical and Experimental Neuropsychology 31, 447–454 (2009)

[16] Garcia-Palacios, A., Hoffman, H., Carlin, A., Furness, T., Botella, C.: Virtual Reality in the Treatment of Spider Phobia: A Controlled Study. Behaviour Research and Therapy 40, 983–993 (2002)

[17] Banos, R.M., Botella, C., Perpiñá, C., Alcañiz, M., Lozano, J.A., Osma, J., Gallardo, M.: Virtual Reality Treatment of Flying Phobia. IEEE Transactions on Information Technology in Biomedicine 6, 206–212 (2002)

[18] Coelho, C.M., Waters, A.M., Hine, T.J., Wallis, G.: The Use of Virtual Reality in Acrophobia Research and Treatment. Journal of Anxiety Disorders 23, 563–574 (2009)

[19] Slater, M., Pertaub, D.P., Barker, C., Clark, D.M.: An Experimental Study on Fear of Public Speaking Using a Virtual Environment. CyberPsychology & Behavior 9, 627–633 (2006)

[20] Holden, M.K.: "Virtual Environments for Motor Rehabilitation: Review2. CyberPsychology & Behavior 8, 187–211 (2005)

[21] Marques, A., Queirós, C., Rocha, N.: Virtual Reality and Neuropsychology: A Cognitive Rehabilitation Approach for People with Psychiatric Disabilities. In: Proc. International Conference on Disability Virtual Reality and Associated Technologies, ICDVRAT, pp. 39–46 (September 2008), http://www.icdvrat.rdg.ac.uk/2008/papers/ICDVRAT2008_S01_N03_Marques_Queiros_Rocha.pdf

[22] Moffat, S.D., Zonderman, A.B., Resnick, S.M.: Age Differences in Spatial Memory in a Virtual Environment Navigation Task. Neurobiology of Aging 22, 787–796 (2001)

[23] Cushman, L.A., Stein, K., Duffy, C.J.: Detecting Navigational Deficits in Cognitive Aging and Alzheimer Disease Using Virtual Reality. Neurology 71, 888–895 (2008)

[24] Werner, P., Rabinowitz, S., Klinger, E., Korczyn, A.D., Josman, N.: Use of the Virtual Action Planning Supermarket for the Diagnosis of Mild Cognitive Impairment. Dementia and Geriatric Cognitive Disorders 27, 301–309 (2009)

[25] Pengas, G., Patterson, K., Arnold, R.J., Bird, C.M., Burgess, N., Nestor, P.J.: Lost and Found: Bespoke Memory Testing for Alzheimer's Disease and Semantic Dementia. Journal of Alzheimer's Disease 21, 1347–1365 (2010)

[26] Mahmud, N., Vogt, J., Luyten, K., Slegers, K., Van Den Bergh, J., Coninx, K.: Dazed and Confused Considered Normal: An Approach to Create Interactive Systems for People with Dementia. Human-Centred Software Engineering, 119–134 (2010)

[27] Ijsselsteijn, W., Nap, H.H., De Kort, Y., Poels, K.: Digital Game Design for Elderly Users. In: Proc. Conference on Future Play 2, pp. 17–22. ACM (November 2007), http://www.nus.edu.sg/nec/InnoAge/documents/Digital%20Game%20Design%20for%20Elderly.pdf

[28] Flores, E., Tobon, G., Cavallaro, E., Cavallaro, F.I., Perry, J.C., Keller, T.: Improving Patient Motivation in Game Development for Motor Deficit Rehabilitation. In: Proc. International Conference in Advances on Computer Entertainment Technology, pp. 381–384. ACM (2008)

[29] Yusoff, A., Crowder, R., Gilbert, L., Wills, G.: A conceptual framework for serious games. In: Proc. IEEE International Conference on Advanced Learning Technologies, pp. 15–17 (July 2009)

[30] Wan Shamsuddin, S.N., Lesk, V., Ugail, H.: Virtual Environment Design Guidelines for Elderly People in Early Detection of Dementia. In: Proc. International Conference of Computer and Information Science, pp. 751–755 (November 2011)

[31] Huang, S.-T., Cho, Y.-P., Lin, Y.-J.: ADDIE instructional design and cognitive apprenticeship for project-based software engineering education in MIS. In: Proc. Software Engineering Conference (APSEC 2005), pp. 15–17 (December 2005)

[32] Weimer, D.L., Sager, M.A.: Early Identification and Treatment of Alzheimer's Disease: Social and Fiscal Outcomes. Alzheimer's and Dementia 5, 215–226 (2009)

[33] Pantel, J., Schönknecht, P., Essig, M., Schröder, J.: Distribution of Cerebral Atrophy Assessed by Magnetic Resonance Imaging Reflects Patterns of Neuropsychological Deficits in Alzheimer's Dementia. Neuroscience Letters 361, 17–20 (2004)

[34] Lesk, V., Wan Shamsuddin, S., Walters, E., Ugail, H.: Using a Virtual Environment to Assess Cognition in the Elderly (unpublished)

[35] Wan Shamsuddin, S.N., Walters, E., Ugail, H., Lesk, V.: Evaluation of Users Acceptance in Virtual Environment for Early Diagnosis of Dementia. In: Proc. World Conference on Information Technology (WCIT), Antalya Turkey (November 2011)

[36] Moline, J.: Virtual reality for health care: a survey. In: Riva, G. (ed.) Virtual Reality in Neuro-Psycho-Physiology, pp. 3–34. IOS Press, Amsterdam (1998)

[37] Ellis, S.R.: What are virtual environments? IEEE Computer Graphics and Applications 14(1), 17–22 (1994)

[38] Sherman, W.R., Craig, A.B.: Understanding virtual reality: Interface, application and design. Morgan Kaufmann, San Francisco (2003)

[39] Bowman, D.A., North, C., Chen, J., Polys, N.F., Pyla, P.S., Yilmaz, U.: Information-rich virtual environments: theory, tools, and research agenda. In: VRST 2003 Proceedings of the ACM Symposium on Virtual Reality Software and Technology, Japan, pp. 81–90 (2003)

[40] Riecke, B.E., Van Veen, H.A.H.C., Bulthoff, H.H.: Visual Homing is possible without Landmarks - A Path Integration Study in Virtual Reality. Presence: Teleoperators and Virtual Environments 11(5), 443–473 (2002)

[41] Rizzo, A.A., Wiederhold, M., Buckwalter, J.G.: Basic issues in the use of virtual environments for mental health applications. In: Riva, G., Wiederhold, B.K., Molinari, E. (eds.) Virtual Environments in Clinical Psychology and Neuroscience: Methods and Techniques in Advanced Patient-Therapist Interaction, pp. 123–145. IOS Press, Amsterdam (1998)

[42] Costa, R.M., Carvalho, L.A.V., Aragon, D.F.: AVIRC: A Virtual city for cognitive rehabilitation. In: International Conference on Disabilities, Virtual Reality, and Associated Technologies, Italy, pp. 299–304 (2000)

[43] Werner, P., Rabinowitz, S., Klinger, E., Korczyn, A.S., Josman, N.: The use of the virtual action planning supermarket for the diagnosis of mild cognitive impairment. Dementia and Geriatric Cognitive Disorders 27, 301–309 (2009)

[44] Tippett, W.J., Lee, J.H., Zakzanis, K.K., Black, S.E., Mraz, R., Graham, S.J.: Visually navigating a virtual world with real-world impairments: A study of visually and spatially guided performance in individuals with mild cognitive impairments. Journal of Clinical and Experimental Neuropsychology 31(4), 447–454 (2008)

Providing Visual Support for Selecting Reactive Elements in Intelligent Environments

Martin Majewski, Andreas Braun, Alexander Marinc, and Arjan Kuijper

Fraunhofer Institute for Computer Graphics Research - IGD Darmstadt, Germany
{martin.majewski,andreas.braun,alexander.marinc,
arjan.kuijper}@igd.fraunhofer.de

Abstract. When realizing gestural interaction in a typical living environment there often is an offset between user-perceived and machine-perceived direction of pointing, which can hinder reliable selection of elements in the surroundings. This work presents a support system that provides visual feedback to a freely gesturing user; thus enabling reliable selection of and interaction with reactive elements in intelligent environments. We have created a prototype that is showcasing this feedback method based on gesture recognition using the Microsoft Kinect and visual support provision using a custom built laser-robot. Finally an evaluation has been performed, in order to prove the efficiency of such a system, acquire usability feedback and determine potential learning effects for gesture-based interaction.

Keywords: Gesture based interaction, Human-computer interaction, Feedback, Ambient intelligence.

1   Introduction

The following work is an extended version of our contribution to the Cyberworlds 2012 conference, titled "Visual support system for selecting reactive elements in intelligent environments" [1]

Ubiquitous Computing, Pervasive Computing, Ambient Intelligence and Smart Environments are interchangeable terms for a unique vision - a future of computing that shifts away from classical desktop applications and instead relies on devices so small and unobtrusive they can be placed throughout our immediate environment and thus enabling a new paradigm of human-computer-interaction. The systems will be able to infer our intentions from our actions without having to rely on classical input devices such as mouse and keyboard [2]. This interaction is natural and multi-modal - that is we interact with devices similar to interacting with other human beings using speech, gesture and facial expressions [3]. A specific application of gestural interaction is the pointing-for-selection process (PFS) that allows selecting of elements by pointing at them and performing a specific selection gesture. While humans are particularly sophisticated regarding analyzing gestural selection of other humans this task is very complex for computers, considering different types of gesturing and the

M.L. Gavrilova et al. (Eds.): Trans. on Comput. Sci. XVIII, LNCS 7848, pp. 248–263, 2013.

geometric offset caused by the displacement between eyes and arm. In the following work we will give an introduction to specific challenges of the pointing process and provide a visual feedback solution that improves gesture analysis by computer systems and therefore enables the application of the PFS in intelligent environments without requiring a static visual output. A prototype of this system has been built and evaluated for its efficiency in improving the selection process and occurring learning effects.

2   Background and Related Works

In the last few decades there have been numerous projects that investigated the potential applications, limitations and ramifications of intelligent environments. The term Intelligent Environment dates back to the term Ubiquitous Computing formed by Mark Weiser in his essay "The Computer for the 21st century" [2] where he introduced his vision of applying intelligent components in every single aspect of our physical world and thus replacing the single, spatially bound personal computer. In 1991 when he published his essay, an ordinary desktop PC was stationary, low on computation speed and the internet was in its early stages. But the vision of Mark Weiser goes far beyond these limitations. He postulated that in the future the paradigm of Ubiquitous Computing will turn into a variety of miniaturized, highly embedded, high-performance devices that communicate with each other, acting in the background, supporting the users in their daily activities. This "background work" should be so pervasive that the assistance of and interaction with the components vanishes from the users' consciousness - as distinguished from the "one, grey desktop-pc".

The terms Intelligent Environments, Ambient Intelligence and Pervasive Computing are often used as synonyms for Ubiquitous Computing In their projects AIR&D [4] and Oxygen [5] Philips research and various partners have investigated the extensive use of home automation systems and user context to control typical living spaces. The University of Essex has done similar research with a particular focus on student dormitories [6].

Gestural interaction using the whole body has been a research interest for many years. The first interaction with a virtual 3D environment can be traced back to the year 1961 when Morton Heilig submits his patent of the "Sensorama Simulator" to the United States Patent Office. It provided 3D visual, haptic, audio and motion feedbacks [7]. Another pioneering work was done by Ivan Sutherland with his PhD thesis work Sketchpad [8], a light-pen driven manipulation of objects, including grabbing, moving and scaling. With the implementation of the graphical programming language AMBIT/G [9], at the MIT's Lincoln Labs in 1968, gesture recognition was employed. The current state-of-the-art is mostly driven by virtual reality and entertainment applications [10, 11] that want to provide more immersive experiences. A driving factor for this work is the availability of the Microsoft Kinect that provides real-time pose information of several human bodies [12]. This is accomplished by PrimeSense 3D sensing technology [13], comprised of a near-field infrared laser projector and a monochrome CMOS Sensor. Additionally the system has a multi-array microphone included.

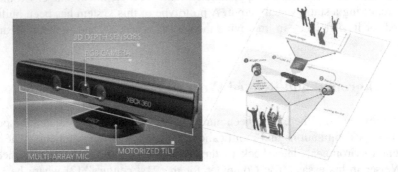

Fig. 1. Microsoft Kinect depth camera system (left) and principle of PrimeSense 3D sensing technology

A project similar to the work presented and source of inspiration has been realized in the 2000s by Wilson et al [14, 15]. The XWand is a dedicated input device based on inertial measurement units and infrared LEDs that allows determining position and orientation of the device in order to gather information about the device that is currently being pointed at and provides means for interaction. In later work this was augmented with the WorldCursor, a laser-pointing device that highlights the location currently selected by the XWand in the environment, in order to improve the selection process. Different working modes such as relative pointing and absolute pointing have been investigated and various application scenarios outlined.

Fig. 2. XWand input device (left) and WorldCursor (right)

Our system improves upon this work by providing device-free gesture interaction, using a more sophisticated method of modeling devices in intelligent environments and providing an evaluation that proves the benefits of such a system and the existence of the PFS offset that will be described in detail in the following section.

3   Pointing-for-Selection Process

The process of pointing at and selecting a device via gestures can be abstracted to the more generic TOTE-model by Miller et al [16] that postulates a user achieving a certain goal by iteratively comparing the actual status with the desired target status and modifying the actual until a target criteria is met. The model is shown in **Fig. 3**.

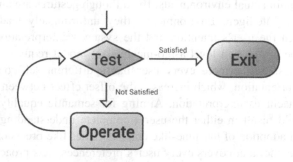

Fig. 3. The TOTE-Model by Miller, Galanter and Pirbram

Concerning gestural input with a feedback mechanism this means that the user is adjusting the pointing position until the feedback indicates that the desired target criteria have been met thus performing a successful selection.

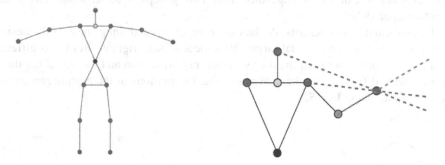

Fig. 4. Joint model on the left and different methods to project rays on the right

The actual biomechanical process of pointing is complex and can vary from person to person. A simplified skeletal joint structure is used that allows modeling of different pointing methods. The chosen joint model coincides with the skeletal data acquired by the Microsoft Kinect and is sufficient to model pointing processes that disregard fingers. Nonetheless, it is possible to create different rays from this model, e.g. the extensions of the eye-hand-vector, shoulder-hand-vector or elbow-hand-vector. Both joint model and rays described are shown in **Fig. 4**. A ray here is defined as the parametric equation of a line g with any point $\vec{r}$ defined through the origin vector $\vec{o}$, direction vector $\vec{d}$ and a multiplier λ in the following equation.

$$g: \vec{r} = \vec{o} + \lambda \vec{d}; \lambda \in \mathbb{R}; \vec{o}, \vec{d} \in \mathbb{R}^3$$

4   Visual Assistance of Pointing-for-Selection Processes

The following section will describe the challenges that occur in typical PFS processes and propose a system that allows to overcome these disadvantages by providing a visual feedback system, allowing both user and machine to properly evaluate the gestures. It may also provide a learning effect, enabling users to perform better in PFS applications within actual environments. Even though gestures are an intuitive way of interacting with Intelligent Environments, they unfortunately lead to unavoidable conflict between the user's intention and the system's interpretation. This disparity results from the abstraction level a bio-mechanical model requires to be reasonably simulated ranges. Furthermore every user has a different self-conception of their body's spatial orientation, which increases the offset effect between the user's intention and the machines interpretation. Aiming for semantic equality is not trivial or desired. It would result in either the user's complete understanding of the technical abstraction and adoption of machine-like characteristics like precision and endurance, or a technical model that covers every user's preferences, acts proactive to recognize the user's intentions and handles incorrect input without making the user feel patronized.

4.1   Challenges in Pointing Gesture Recognition

The challenges can be distinguished into two groups - target-actual errors and input-reaction delay.

Target-actual errors describe deviations in exactness and uniqueness of the desired target as opposed to the actual target. Exactness offset originate from two different sources - the offset between the user's mental ray projection and the actual ray direction as derived from biomechanical posture and limitations of the gesture recognition system, as shown in **Fig. 5**.

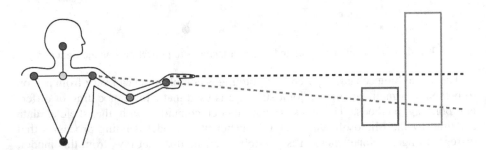

Fig. 5. Offset between mental ray projection (originating from finger) and actual ray projection (originating from shoulder)

The use of the index finger as pointer and the ray's constructing source is a common choice by humans but is not supported by using our simplified skeleton model. This alternative ray construction can lead to significant confusion between the user's mental ray representation and system's ray construction, resulting from the appearing offset seen in **Fig. 5**.

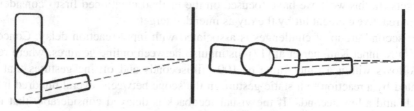

Fig. 6. Parallax between eye viewpoint and shoulder viewpoint

Another factor is the parallax between eye viewpoint and arm viewpoint that is affecting the perceived direction of the pointing. **Fig. 6** shows this effect from top perspective. If the ray is constructed based on the shoulder or elbow joints there is a considerable difference between the two viewpoints, resulting in differently calculated angels. The closer the target object is, the higher the offset. In certain situations, this parallax can be reduced as highlighted on the right side. In some cases even elimination is possible, if eye viewpoint results in the same ray as shoulder-elbow viewpoint.

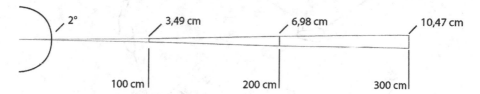

Fig. 7. Influence of detection errors based on distance

Fig. 7 highlights the influence of detection errors on the detected pointing target based on distance from the user. A minor error of 2° may result in an offset of several centimeters in a distance of a few meters, an example solution to the following equation.

$$offset = distance \cdot 2 \cdot \tan\left(\frac{angle}{2}\right)$$

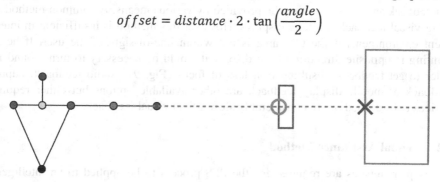

Fig. 8. The user's intention is to point at the largest object. The system chooses the nearest object.

The second target-actual errors are uniqueness errors, whereas the user wants to se-lect an ambiguous target. This means that in the line of the ray there are various reac-tive elements that could potentially be selected. This error type is displayed in **Fig. 8**. There are various methods available to determine the intended target, such as always picking first on ray, selecting the largest target on the ray or associating a priority to all targets. In this work we have focused on the method mentioned first - considering the first reactive element hit by the ray as intended target.

The second group of challenges is associated with input-reaction delay. Concern-ing gesture input Kammer et al [17] distinguish between online gestures, where reac-tion follows within a time frame of 100 milliseconds and offline gestures that are indicated by a reaction to a static gesture in the scope between several hundred milli-seconds and a few seconds. If the visual feedback is delayed considerably that may lead to backtracking - the user trying to compensate for the delay by moving back in direction even though the system would have followed shortly after, which may lead to confusion for the users. If offline gestures are associated with a time frame too long the user might stop the interaction without triggering a reaction.

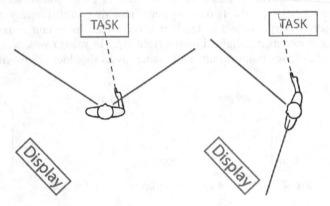

Fig. 9. Task is in the user's field of view, while the display is not (left). Display is in the user's field of view, while the task is not (right).

Feedback and assistance may be provided by various means. A common method is using visual feedback on static displays. However this method is insufficient in intel-ligent environments if the task area is not within line-of-sight of the user. If he is pointing in opposite direction of the display it would be necessary to turn around in order to get feedback, resulting in a loss of focus (**Fig. 9**). Audio feedback, haptic feedback or mobile display feedback are other available options but either require devices to be carried or are considerably slower than visual feedback.

4.2   Visual Assistance Method

A few prerequisites are required for the PFS process to be applied to an intelligent environment. First and most prominently a virtual representation of the environment is required that models all boundaries and reactive elements. The elements should be modeled in a way that they are applicable for ray intersection algorithms. Particularly well-suited are bounding boxes such as axis-aligned bounding boxes (AABB) or oriented bounding boxes (OBB) that form an outer shell of the actual object and can be calculated and intersected easily.

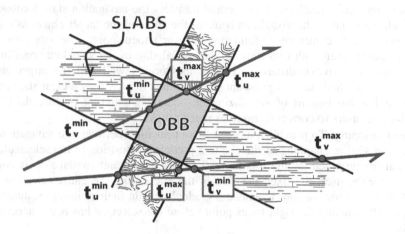

Fig. 10. The slab method for ray intersection detection [15]

The intersection with an object and therefor focal point of the gesture can be calculated using the slab method that considers the bounding box as the space inside of three pairs of parallel planes [18]. The ray is clipped from all planes and an intersection considered if a portion of the ray remains, as shown in **Fig. 10**. Nevertheless, simplification of a complex object often leads to results that violate one of the following aspects. A bounding box has to fulfill two spatial and one procedural requirement to be sufficient as a simplified representation:

1. It has to be large enough to cover the whole parent object to counteract Type-1 errors (also known as false-positive errors)
2. It has to be as small as possible not to intrude into another object's space, line of sight, causing Type-2 errors (also known as positive-false errors)
3. It has to be timely and spatially cost-efficient

Examining which bounding box fits best is not trivial. Not fulfilling one of the three aspects does not mean that this specific bounding box is not sufficient in any case. The second prerequisite is the presence of a gesture recognition device that allows gathering posture information in the skeletal model as described in Section 3. A camera based tracking system fits the needs for marker free interaction and unobtrusiveness, although optical occlusion may lead to a lack of availability.

As previously mentioned the first object intersected is considered as intended target, thus intersections with all available objects are performed to determine a minimum λ value. At the determined focal point visual feedback is given by means of projection from a device that is available in the device. This feedback is supporting both navigation and feedback on successful selection. Typically temporal gestures - that is gestures triggered by remaining on a selected target for a certain time - are suited for selection purposes. The feedback system can support this interaction method by various cues:

- Exact focus point tracking: This method transfers the navigation state feedback to the selection state. The visual cue behaves the same at the target object as e.g. on the room's wall, continuously following the user's focus point. The only noticeable transition between both PFS states is the spatial skip of the visual cue resulting in the immediate spatial difference of e.g. the room's wall and the target object. While this method shows significant shortcomings in providing a clear state transition, it has the benefit of signalizing an occurring pointing posture drift. This enables the users to correct themselves much quicker.
- Object snapping: To provide a more definite transition between the navigation and selection state, a snapping of the cue to a predefined position of the selectable target can be provided. While this immediate and significant spatial skip is conspicuous for the user, the fixed position of the cue during the entire selection state makes it hard for the user to notice a gradual drift in their pointing posture. This can result in losing the right focus point before the selection has been successfully made.
- Combinations of representations: Taking the positive and negative aspects of both previously introduced methods into account the third method should help to eliminate the drawbacks. Preferring the first method, a change of the cue's color can signal a state transition without disturbing the continuous feedback provision. Enabling the cue to blink in a reasonable frequency instead of using different colors makes the hardware implementation simpler, as no further light emitters have to be provided. Preferring the second method multiple encapsulated target areas can provide buffer zones in which the snap position can change relatively to the user's posture drift. The combination of the first two methods including the previously mentioned ideas is probably the best solution, as it provides spatial continuity and state change awareness. If the user is pointing precisely at the right focus point or a defined target area respectively, an immediate snap will make the user aware of their correct posture. A drift of the focus point out of the target area could be signalled with a transition to a continuously following visual cue in a different color but without the penalty of resetting pointing duration. Thus, the users can correct themselves and minimize the amount of trial and error sequences. These ideas are far from being exhaustively covered.

A system that implements all aspects previously mentioned is able to provide visual assistance for gestural interaction in intelligent environments.

5   System Prototype and the E.A.G.L.E. Device

We have created a prototype of the visual support system based on the Microsoft Kinect device for gesture recognition, a regular PC system to perform all required computations and a custom-designed laser robot - the E.A.G.L.E. Eye - that is able to project a laser dot freely into an environment. The whole setup is displayed in **Fig. 11**.

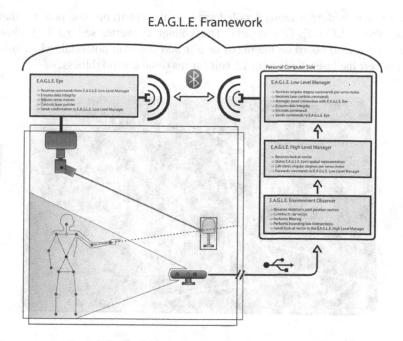

Fig. 11. E.A.G.L.E. visual assistance platform

The E.A.G.L.E. Eye is based on an Arduino microcontroller board that is operating a laser mounted on two servo motors that allow free and precise positioning of a laser dot in the room. These servos have a step width of about 0.2 to 0.3 angular degree, thus this is a restriction of the overall accuracy of the visual cue's movement and positioning.

The device is communicating with a PC wirelessly using Bluetooth but is also capable to communicate via a wired USB connection. The full setup is shown in **Fig. 12**.

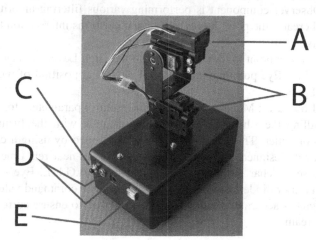

Fig. 12. View on the E.A.G.L.E. Eye: A - laser unit, B - servo motors, C - reset switch, D - power supply, E - USB port

Fig. 13 is providing a more detailed view of the electronic components that are powering the E.A.G.L.E. Eye system. The voltage converter setup (C) allows to operate the Arduino board on the maximal allowed five volt potential, while simultaneously power the laser diode with 12 volt for maximal cue brightness.

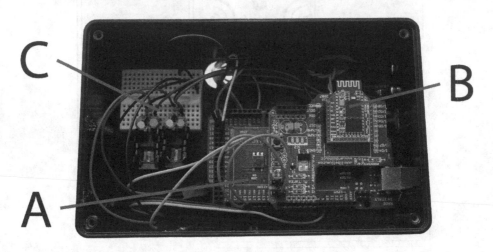

Fig. 13. View on the Arduino circuit: A - Arduino Mega 2560, B - BTBee Bluetooth shield, C - voltage converter with equalisation

Underlying is the virtual representation of the environment that is modeling all reactive elements, the position of the gesture tracking device and the position of the E.A.G.L.E. Eye. The Kinect is interfaced using the OpenNI framework and NITE middleware that are providing a skeleton tracking algorithm resulting in the joint model mentioned previously that is registered into the virtual representation. The Environment Observer component is performing various filtering algorithms on this joint model and creates the pointing ray vector and performs intersection tests with all available objects.

The resulting focus point is then forwarded to the High Level Manager that calculates the E.A.G.L.E. Eye pointing vector based on spatial position of the device and calculated focal point.

Finally, the Low Level Manager is determining control parameters for the laser robot and is handling the Bluetooth-based communication with the firmware on the Arduino microcontroller. This communication is performed by using a custom made command protocol, designed to provide a failure-save and near real time controlling. It consists of a seven char long frame, encoding the E.A.G.L.E. Eye's components (servo one / two, laser diode, macro id – e.g. blinking), the command value (laser on / off, angular degree – accurate to a tenth) and a checksum to ensure correctness of the received byte stream.

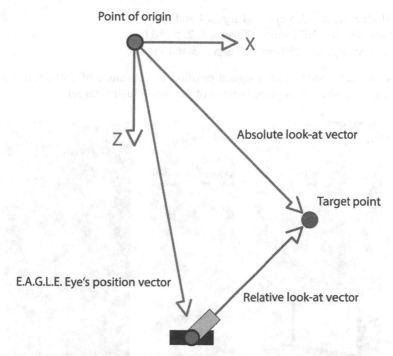

Fig. 14. An absolute look-at vector in comparison to a relative look-at vector

6   Evaluation

We have performed a quantitative and qualitative evaluation of our prototype system that had three distinct goals:

- Verifying the existence of an offset between perceived and actual pointing accuracy
- Investigate the precision gain of a visual feedback system such as the E.A.G.L.E. framework
- Determine if there is a learning effect for non-feedback gestural interaction after having used a visual feedback system for a certain time

Accordingly it was decided to perform a combination of cross-evaluation, which allows testing of the latter two aspects and a questionnaire that amongst other things asked for perceived precision.

The evaluation was performed with 20 subjects between 22 and 65 years and a median age of 27 years. The average experience with gesture input was rated as 5.75 on a scale of 1 (no experience) to 10 (very experienced). They were required to aim and select a sequence of eight different targets of different size that were placed in a room (see **Fig. 15**). These targets were made up of numbered paper sheets placed in the room and are configured as follows:

- Small-size targets: 225 cm^2 – (Targets 4 and 8)
- Mid-size targets: 1632 cm^2 – (Targets 1, 2, 5 and 6)
- Large-size targets: 3060 cm^2 – (Targets 3 and 7)

The test subjects stood at an assigned position at a distance of 180 cm in front of a Kinect camera, which was placed on top of the first mid-size target.

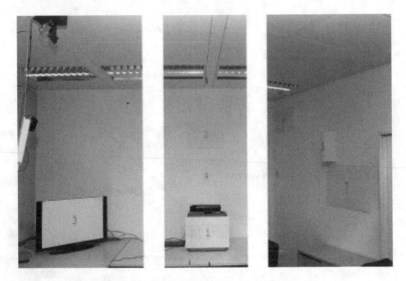

Fig. 15. Test course setup used for this thesis' evaluation

A successful selection was assumed by a target being aimed at continuously for two seconds. To make this assumption visible to the test subject the laser cue doubles its blinking speed after the two second time span. Because of the absence of the visual cue during the non-feedback run, the test subject had to count the time span manually while performing the aiming action. The real results were tracked with within a log-file that was not visible for the test subject during the test run.

Overall, each group could select up to 80 targets. Group one (G1) was first testing assisted, group two (G2) first unassisted.

Fig. 16 is showing the results of evaluation and questionnaire. The visual assistance system allowed both groups to successfully select all targets - without assistance the success rate is reduced severely to 8.75%. The perceived accuracy is in unassisted cases overestimated strongly, with subjects expecting to have selected 71.25% of all targets. The achieved accuracy gain is represented by the increase of successfully selected targets from the unassisted trial to the assisted trial of about 1042.86% on average. For end user applications the documented gap would lead to a significant decrease of the user experience, providing confusion and frustration. The likelihood of the occurrence of confusion and frustration is amplified by the results of the users' accuracy indication. An unguided gestural PFS process fails and is impracticable in terms of usability and the user's action awareness. The underestimation of successful

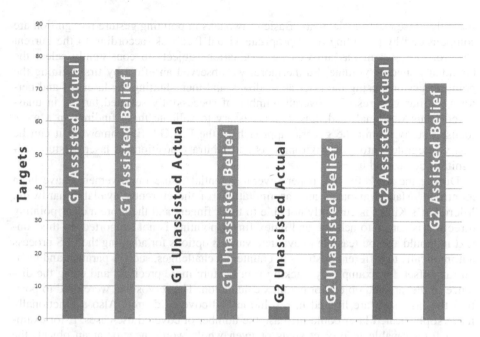

Fig. 16. Selection accuracy for assisted and unassisted PFS evaluation - actual and belief

selection in assisted runs is difficult to explain since there was a visual cue (faster blinking) in this case. We assume that this is the lack of experience with such systems that is causing this effect.

Concerning the questionnaire the users reported to feel assisted by the system and scored this feeling with 9.5 points out of 10 points. The intuitiveness of the constructed ray has been scored with 8.2 points from 10 points. This shows that although being not the best approximation of natural pointing the users could arrange themselves with it. The focusing and selecting by holding the arm still in one direction is scored with 8.45 points out of 10 points. This result shows that this kind of gestural posture is not unsuited for selection, but not the preference of every user. Some users reported they had expected a more active gesture like a swipe movement.

Ahead of the evaluation the appearance of a training effect was expected. This training effect is supposed to be existing as group one's users were able to successfully select 0.6 targets per user above group two's users. This makes an increase of successfully selected target of 150.00%. This assumption of the existence of a training effect has to be examined with further evaluations that are more focused on this aspect by e.g. providing longer training sessions.

7   Conclusion and Future Work

Above we have presented and successfully evaluated an intuitive solution to support the gesture-based control of intelligent environments. The visual feedback given by the laser of the E.A.G.L.E. Framework allows an exact selection of small and spatially close reactive elements. Basic drawbacks in pointing gesture recognition are compensated by providing an appropriate visual feedback, according to the current gesture. Our system has allowed the evaluation subjects to consistently select the intended bounding volume. Furthermore, we observed an effect by first training the pointing gestures using the laser as feedback and then shutting the laser off and perform similar gestures. The overall number of successfully selected targets in unassisted trials was small and thus it is necessary to validate these findings in a more focused study. Using the generic approach of the E.A.G.L.E. Framework it can be easily integrated into new environments and arbitrary positions of laser, gesture recognition device and users.

During the work for this paper several potential future improvements have been identified. Main drawbacks are the limitations of the currently available hardware. Microsoft's Kinect is currently not able to track fingers and therefore a clear pointing direction is harder to achieve and index finger pointing is not supported. In this context it should also be feasible to evaluate various options for adapting the PFS process automatically to different postures to counteract challenges, such as parallax and mental ray offset, for example by tracking user posture more precisely and using the distance to the targeted object for parallax calculation. The servos that were used to position the laser-spot are limited in resolution and covered degree. Also a functionally more sophisticated laser could increase the number of covered use-cases. If for example a laser capable to project signs or even whole words near or at an object, the whole surrounding can become more interactive. Choices and Feedback can be directly displayed at the device that a user is going to control. This would allow completely avoiding other external output devices like monitors or acoustic feedback.

The second group of open issues is related to software limitations. The current status of the user is a main issue to pay respect in future iterations. A central aspect is here to make sure that the laser does not point into the eyes of the user or other persons present. Furthermore, there are many possibilities to improve the overall process to include the E.A.G.L.E. into a new environment. Since the dimensions of the surrounding need to be known in detail to allow exact computations and avoid discrepancies between the virtual and physical space, methods more sophisticated than tape measurements are preferable. Otherwise a practical use of such a system in a common living area will be hard to archive, given that the effort for initial setup and necessary adaptations during time is considerable. Thus we need methods to support a common user to build up a feasible virtual representation of its individual surroundings. One idea here is to use recent developments in capturing reality using depth cameras and combine those with methods of manual and automatic object recognition.

However, we have shown that the E.A.G.L.E. system is already able to significantly improve the exactness of device selection by using pointing gestures. Further steps will help to improve the user experience and make control of the system even easier.

References

1. Majewski, M., Braun, A., Marinc, A., Kuijper, A.: Visual Support System for Selecting Reactive Elements in Intelligent Environments. In: International Conference on Cyberworlds, pp. 251–255 (2012)
2. Weiser, M.: The Computer for the 21st Century. Scientific American 265, 94–104 (1991)

3. Valli, A.: The design of natural interaction. Multimedia Tools and Applications 38, 295–305 (2008)
4. Aarts, E.: Ambient intelligence drives open innovation. Interactions 12, 66 (2005)
5. Massachusetts Institute of Technology: Oxygen project,
   http://oxygen.lcs.mit.edu/
6. Wright, S., Steventon, A.: Intelligent spaces — the vision, the opportunities and the barriers. BT Technology Journal 22, 15–26 (2004)
7. Heilig, M.L.: Sensorama simulator (1962),
   http://www.freepatentsonline.com/3050870.html
8. Sutherland, I.E.: Sketchpad: A man-machine graphical communication system. In: Afips Conference Proceedings, vol. 2, pp. 329–346 (1963)
9. Rovner, P.D., Henderson, D.A.: On the implementation of AMBIT/G: a graphical programming language, pp. 9–20 (1969)
10. Kessler, G.D., Hodges, L.F., Walker, N.: Evaluation of the CyberGlove as a whole-hand input device. ACM Transactions on Computer-Human Interaction 2, 263–283 (1995)
11. Lee, J.C.: Interaction Techniques Using The Wii Remote Nintendo Wii. Applied Sciences (2008)
12. Shotton, J., Fitzgibbon, A., Cook, M., Sharp, T., Finocchio, M., Moore, R., Kipman, A., Blake, A.: Real-time human pose recognition in parts from single depth images. In: CVPR 2011, pp. 1297–1304 (2011)
13. PrimeSense: PrimeSensor, http://www.primesense.com/
14. Wilson, A., Shafer, S.: XWand: UI for intelligent spaces. In: Proceedings of the ACM Conference on Human Factors in Computing Systems, pp. 545–552. ACM (2003)
15. Wilson, A., Pham, H.: Pointing in intelligent environments with the worldcursor. In: INTERACT International Conference on Human Computer Interaction (2003)
16. Miller, G.A., Galanter, E., Pribram, K.H.: Plans and the structure of behavior. Holt (1960)
17. Kammer, D., Keck, M., Freitag, G., Wacker, M.: Taxonomy and Overview of Multi-touch Frameworks: Architecture, Scope and Features. Architecture, 1–5 (2010)
18. Akenine-Möller, T., Haines, E., Hoffman, N.: Real-Time Rendering. AK Peters (2008)

Author Index